The Inexhaustible GOD

The Inexhaustible GOD

Biblical Faith
and the Challenge of Process Theism

Royce Gordon Gruenler

Baker Book House
Grand Rapids, Michigan 49506

Copyright 1983 by
Baker Book House Company

ISBN: 0-8010-3794-8

Library of Congress Card Catalog Number: 83-71010

Printed in the United States of America

Contents

A Critique of Neville, Ogden, Cobb, and Ford

7   Process Theism As a Hermeneutic
     for Biblical Interpretation
     A Critique   141

8   Process Theism As a Biblical Hermeneutic
     A Critique of Ford's *Lure of God*   163

     Epilogue   199

     Author Index   203

     Subject Index   205

     Scripture Index   209

Preface

Hardly a week goes by nowadays when there fails to come across my desk some notice from publisher or reviewer announcing the appearance of a new study that reflects the perspective of process theism. This point of view is becoming so widespread among theologians and biblical scholars that it seems to be growing in geometrical proportions.

The school has ancient origins. Heraclitus and Protagoras, repudiating their opponents' view that what is really real is the eternal and the changeless, long ago exalted time and space and man as the measure of all things. In our own day, Alfred North Whitehead and Charles Hartshorne have attempted to fuse these two poles together, but in point of fact they have come out on Heraclitus' side. In an age of vast change they have made relativity and timespace a given, even for God. For them the evolving and processing universe is as necessary for God as it is for us—more so, in fact, for God requires some world or other everlastingly if his experience is to have any actual content. Whatever God experiences is in terms of a finite and processing universe. Even his love and righteousness are only abstract possibilities without our processing world in terms of which alone they become personally real to him. In process thought there is no social Trinity of Father, Son, and Holy Spirit apart from our world, as Christian orthodoxy has taught from earliest times; rather, God has no real existence or social experience apart from us and the extensive continuum of finite entities in the universe that are independent of him.

Such a view of God is in focus with the contemporary scene. Process theism allows the modern thinker, as it did Protagoras of old, to be in charge of things. Although it tries to offer a solution to the problem of evil by limiting the power of God, its real motive, I am convinced, is to protect human freedom against the threat of a sovereign God. Accordingly, the real enemy of the modern process theist is not any one of the world religions or philosophies that competes with classical Christianity (for they are all, he holds, culturally relative and symbolic), but traditional biblical Christianity itself—orthodox, fundamental, evangelical faith as it was proclaimed by prophets, evangelists, and apostles; recorded in an infallibly inspired canon of Holy Scripture; and having to do with a God who is the sovereign creator, sustainer, and redeemer of the universe. It is this classical biblical faith, believed by Christians down to our own day, that is directly under attack.

The problem with orthodox Christianity, says the process theist, is its insistence on a God who has sovereignly brought the universe of time and space into being and who upholds it by his word of power. No, that God is too static, too uninvolved in our worldly evolution and history, too sovereign, too despotic, too threatening to our human freedom and independence to be allowed a voice in the modern world. Better to have a world that is open-ended and uncertain, and a deity that is limited, than to have a world controlled by a sovereign God who works all things according to the measure of his inscrutable will. Better to have a theology of redemption that allows us some power to contribute to God than to acknowledge our radical fallenness and to be thrown entirely upon the mercy of the crucified and risen Christ. Better to settle for a Bible that is fallible and subject to the control of human criticism than to assume a posture of obedience to the God who reveals himself in trustworthy Scripture.

These comments do not caricature modern process theists but describe the issues they are prosecuting with deadly seriousness. Having been a member of the school for a number of years, I know. We need to be aware in the theological world that, in spite of ecumenical dialogue across many lines of former separation, a spiritual battle is going on between classical biblical faith and contemporary theological relativism represented by the presuppositions of process theism. Ultimately the question has to do with who God is and what salvation and the meaning of life are all about.

Let me give some recent examples of what I consider a crisis in biblical interpretation and theology today. In *The Liberation of Life: From the Cell to the Community*, by Charles Birch and John B. Cobb, Jr. (New York: Cambridge University Press, 1982), the presuppositions of Whitehead are developed in such a way as to encourage a leap of faith in "Life," the basic cosmic principle that underlies all process. The authors argue that an ethic of service that will "trust Life" is more appropriate to the biblical God than is classical Christianity with its view of God beyond timespace. One does not have to read very far in the book to realize that classical theology (which has always been concerned to balance God's transcendence over and immanence within the world) is parodied, and any resemblance between impersonal "Life" and the infinite personal God of the Bible is exegetically irresponsible. What we have in this book is an ecological pantheism posing under Christian terminology. The ecological and covenantal questions the book raises need to be addressed in our day and can be addressed by evangelical scholars in ways that are faithful to Scripture; but the book itself fashions a new idolatry in terms of Whitehead's process theology.

Edward Farley, a former evangelical and now an ardent and feisty foe of traditional Christianity, attacks his former convictions in *Ecclesial Reflection: An Anatomy of Theological Method* (Philadelphia: Fortress, 1982). Farley's avowed foe is divine and biblical authority; his brief is for the process of human freedom and consciousness. The House of Authority, or biblical faith, with its trust in salvation history superintended by the sovereign God and revealed in inspired Scripture, is repudiated and deconstructed. In its place Farley substitutes the temporal process of reflective inquiry by the "ecclesial community." This is a "postauthority theology" that reinterprets the "symbols, stories and myths" of the biblical tradition for our own day. While Farley works more from a peculiar application of Edmund Husserl's phenomenology than from either Whitehead or Hartshorne, it is clear that his underlying presupposition is sympathetic to process theism and gives pride of place to human freedom and autonomy in the process of ecclesial reflection, out of which arises a humanly articulated and controlled set of "ecclesial universals." Farley, like Cobb and Birch, really believes that he is effectively reconstructing the Christian kerygma for the contemporary world and taking seriously the ambiguities of history and human freedom against the obsolescence of classical biblical faith, the House of Authority.

A recent book that comes closer to a satisfactory restatement of God's revealed nature in Scripture is *The Triune Identity* by Robert Jenson (Philadelphia: Fortress, 1982). In this study Jenson correctly sees that in the Bible God reveals himself as social; he is relational in his divine structure. However, what Jenson does not emphasize is that the biblical doctrine of creation compels us to insist that God's personhood as a communal reality is to be understood first as what he is within himself independent of the created world of timespace. Jenson, with other modern theologians and biblical interpreters, tends to see God's sociality and freedom too exclusively in terms of process theology (in this case combined with Barthian dogmatics), as open event within timespace, where classical biblical theology would remind us that God's creation and redemption of a social world are possible because he is social as divine

Triunity before he even brings the world into being. God does not depend upon the world process for his social experience; the world is not necessary to God. The idea that it is is latent in all postauthority theologies that assume God to be beholden to the process of time.

In biblical studies process theism is subtly present in the mainstream of research. One would not say that there are a great number of card-carrying process theists in our field. But the approach is pervasive in spite of the fact that biblical scholars like to think of themselves as above that sort of thing and quite neutral and inductive in their pursuit as historians of the facts. Nevertheless the critical eye discerns how widespread process assumptions are as tacit components of the historico-critical method within the guild. It is broadly assumed as regards the inspiration of Scripture that the biblical writer or community of faith felt led by divine "lure" to develop ideal concepts through myths, narrative, and symbols in the context of relative historical circumstances. Accordingly, the scholar interpreting the text will attempt to trace the trajectory of process to see how the mythology developed.

A study that recently came across my desk discusses "Old Testament Interpretation from a Process Perspective" (*Semeia* 22, An Experimental Journal for Biblical Criticism, published by the Society of Biblical Literature, 1982). In this set of technical essays the central presupposition of process theism—that God needs the world and that his power is not sovereign but only persuasive—is seen to affect profoundly the exegesis of the biblical text. *Semeia* 22 clearly demonstrates the interconnection between exegetical method and hermeneutical presuppositions, as Cobb and Lewis S. Ford (from the angle of philosophical theology) interact with biblical scholars like J. Gerald Janzen, James Luther Mays, and Kent Harold Richards. The process of the critical method is taken as the given, with the critical mind functioning as the final arbiter of the meaning, truth, or untruth of biblical texts. The basic assumption of the authors is that the God of the Scriptures is a deity who functions within the process of history as the "lure" toward "intensity of harmonious feeling." The critical analysis of any given biblical text will disclose the hybrid mix of divine truth and human error and misinterpretation in the process of faith's evolution. The debate among the contributors, although in-house, opens up serious problems in process hermeneutics and its applicability to biblical exegesis. It also underscores how pervasive among Old Testament scholars is a tacit commitment to pluralism and process in exegetical method.

I could say the same for New Testament scholars in general. There may not be large numbers of loyal process metaphysicians among them (few have the interest, inclination, or training to think critically of presuppositions), but a process view is tacitly and widely assumed in the field. One has only to read Werner Kelber's startling essay "Redaction Criticism: On the Nature and Exposition of the Gospels" (*Perspectives on Religious Studies* 6 [1979]: 4-16) to appreciate how present-day radical redaction criticism attempts to describe the Gospels' process of evolution in terms of a dazzling variety of theologies, differences, and even contradictions. The process of creativity in the early church was such, Kelber feels, that the one Jesus in the four Gospels is unrecoverable, since none of the evangelists practiced faith in "blind obedience to past and tradition," that is, had little concern for historical veracity in our sense of the term. The Gospels are to be identified more in terms of their diversity than their unity because of the pluralistic process of early Christian experience. A similar process model has been adopted by James D. G. Dunn, whose *Christology in the Making: A New Testament Inquiry into the Origins of the Doctrine of the Incarnation* (Philadelphia: Westminster, 1980) attempts to trace patterns of christological evolution and divergent theologies and doctrines in the documents of the New Testament. (For a critique of process and pluralistic models employed by radical New Testament critics in gospel research, see my *New Approaches to Jesus and the Gospels: A Phenomenological and Exegetical Study of Synoptic Christology* [Grand Rapids: Baker, 1982].)

All this is to say that my present study has application beyond the field of philosophical theology. All areas of theological interpretation today are becoming increasingly influenced by the spirit of the age, the Zeitgeist of process and pluralism. It threatens to sweep everything before it, including the bright young tribunes of evangelical thought who are becoming noticeably more attracted to process categories and radical critical theories in biblical exegesis and who seem captivated by the promises of ecumenical dialogue within the mainstream of scholarly and churchly life. Perhaps I shouldn't appear to be superior simply because all this seems to be déjà vu; I went through my stage of rebellion early on in my career and emerged from it, by God's grace, only ten years ago. The reader will forgive me for offering a hard-hitting critique of my former convictions. There is no longer time to go on playing daring language games or to walk through the Scriptures with hobnailed boots; for I have learned to take off my shoes and to walk gently and reverently through God's Word, to listen to his own revelation of his sovereign power and grace rather than to fashion him according to my images and rights. A thorough understanding of the doctrines of the process school and its profound weaknesses from a logical and biblical point of view should perform a healthy service, not only for those whose faith needs reassurance but also for those whose easy acceptance of process relativism invites a thoroughgoing challenge. I send the book out with the hope that both audiences will be reached and challenged.

I wish to thank Herman Baker, Allan Fisher, and Dan Van't Kerkhoff of Baker Book House for their willingness to publish a book of this scope and for their dedication to evangelical scholarship, even in the more esoteric area of philosophical theology. I am grateful for the four readers of the original manuscript who provided substantial support for its publication and who offered valuable suggestions for its improvement: David Beck, Bruce Demarest, Norman Geisler, and Clark Pinnock. In addition, my own colleagues at Gordon-Conwell Theological Seminary, Roger Nicole, David Wells, and Jack Davis, have afforded stimulating dialogue and encouragement in pressing on with the project. I deem it a great satisfaction and honor to join hands with these friends who subscribe to the plenary inspiration of Scripture and who sense the urgency of the hour with its exponential drift away from the authority of God's self-disclosure in Scripture.

At the same time as we make our mark as apologists for biblical faith in the forum of debate with nonevangelical theologies, it is important that all of us who represent the historic biblical faith reaffirm our fundamental agreements, which are far larger than our differences. This fact has been confirmed by the friendships established and deepened as the project has unfolded. I am grateful for the fellowship and unity in the body of Christ that I have experienced during the past year with those who represent the rich tradition of orthodox Christianity and who have encouraged interdisciplinary dialogue between my major field of New Testament studies and philosophical theology. I hope the present study will help theologians and biblical scholars alike to be alert to presuppositions that govern research and to be especially discerning where process assumptions are tacitly or focally operating. At the same time I want to suggest that evangelical scholars need to formulate an agenda and address those points at which process theism seems most attractive. Biblical faith is now challenged to draw from its own rich and superior scriptural resources a new articulation of God's inexhaustible dynamism as the First Family and of his power and grace as the Triune God who leaves his stamp of sociality upon the whole ecological creation. That is my next project: to restate the exegetical evidence in sacred Scripture for the Family of God, who fashions, sustains, and redeems the derivative families of his creation.

Again, as in my former book with Baker Book House, I wish to express my thanks to Linda Triemstra, project editor, for her careful and competent work in seeing the book into print.

Royce Gordon Gruenler
Gordon-Conwell Theological Seminary

Introduction

I can still remember my first excitement in reading Schubert M. Ogden's explosive *Christ Without Myth* in the early sixties and the promising challenges that seemed to be opened by his synthesis of Rudolf Bultmann's radical demythologizing and Charles Hartshorne's process philosophizing. It all seemed like a breath of fresh air to a young teacher, trained in evangelical and neoorthodox schools, who was looking for some new excitement as well as practical aids for teaching in a liberal academic setting. It was largely through our discussion of this book that my long-time colleague Eugene Peters, well known in process circles, decided to join our faculty, and it was largely through his expert knowledge of Alfred North Whitehead and Hartshorne that I subsequently undertook a patient and appreciative study of their views on God and the world and came to incorporate them in my own thinking.

What fascinated me most of all was their brilliant (I thought) solution to the old problems of the one and the many and being and becoming, which classical Christian theology had handled in its own way but seemingly to God's advantage as absolutely sovereign and to man's disadvantage as ultimately determined. Here was a bold new strike, a daring claim by sheer empirical evidence and rational argument that God must partake of two poles at once: he must be primordial, absolute, and changeless on one polarity (else all would be flux and relativity), yet engaged in the flux and relativity of timespace (else he would be irrelevant). God was accordingly to be seen as dipolar or bipolar, both primordial and consequent, both absolute and relative.

Now of course biblical and classical Christianity has been saying that for centuries—God as ontological triunity is eternally perfect, complete, and changeless, while incarnationally in Christ is subject to the vicissitudes of time and space. But, says Hartshorne, it is logically contradictory to claim on the one hand that God can be absolutely perfect in all respects and yet experience time, for to have all possibilities as perfectly realized actualities eternally would be to erase time, with its flow from what is possible to what by choice is made actual. And it would be to erase the freedom of the creature to choose and become, since he or she would be exhaustively known by God from all eternity.

No, argued Whitehead and Hartshorne, we can no longer tolerate this old Jewish-Christian-Islamic notion of God as the oriental despot who is absolute in all respects. Let us conceive of God differently, as absolute in some respects and not in others, and as relative in some respects and not in others. Let us assume that God is changeless in his mode of being or character and in his primordial aims, but dependent on the universe (or some universe or other during his everlasting procession) for the content of his experience. Let us say (said Hartshorne) that God is AR: Absolute (A) in his mode of being and Relative (R) in his actual existence. Or, alternatively, that God is ET: Eternal (E) in the abstract sense and Temporal (T) in the concrete. Or more exhaustively, that God is ECTKW: Eternal (E) in his mode, Conscious (C) in his experience of the world, Temporal (T) in his inseparability from procession; Knowing the world (K) and including the World (W) in his experience.

This seemed to me an attractive improvement on the immobility and seeming frozenness of classical theism with its absolutely perfect and timeless deity. If one could not logically derive the relativity of God from his absoluteness (so argued Hartshorne), one could derive God's abstract character from his concrete temporality. Accordingly, while dipolar theism was proffered as a superior solution, it was necessary to give pride of place to R and T, since A and E respectively could be derived from them, but not the other way round (so went the argument).

For a decade I applied this process model to my biblical and theological studies, confident of its greater adequacy and superiority over the biblical classical model. Of course it was necessary to make some adjustments. Biblical prophecy could no longer be taken at face value. While God might foresee and foretell with large brush strokes, fine detail could not be known even by him and must therefore be regarded as prophecy after the fact. Since salvation was no longer a radical matter of redemption from sin in the biblical sense, necessitating a divine-human Savior and the once-for-allness of the cross, Jesus became for me the consummate re-presentation of what God is to all persons everywhere as he seeks to lure them to maximum aesthetic feeling in the great creative synthesis and advance of the human race. Persons were seen to be "saved" by cooperating with the divine lure to creativity, thus not only acquiring personal satisfaction for themselves but also contributing to God's needs for fellowship in his own procession and self-surpassing. All religious and aesthetic impulses were seen as complementary paths to satisfaction for God and the world of persons. The narrowness of Christianity with its one Savior and infallible Scripture was modified to accommodate a number of points of view, and seen to be culturally relative as only one of God's many re-presentations of his love for the world. A canon within a canon perforce emerged in my critical assessment of Scripture. I selected largely love passages as authentic and discarded difficult material on justice and judgment. That period in my thinking found expression in a book-length manuscript I am now glad I never published. It bore the title "Love and Hate in the Bible" and attempted to show that the Old and New Testaments contain usable material on the theme of love that is compatible with process metaphysics, but also much on holy war, righteous judgment, sovereign election, the wrath of God, blood atonement, and weeping and gnashing of teeth that is culturally relative and expendable.

The subtle and often not so subtle effect of my shifting my focus of authority from Scripture to the philosophical canons of process theism was that I myself became the autonomous judge of what was acceptable in Holy Writ and what was to be discarded. For a fiduciary trust in the authority of the whole canon of Scripture I substituted the canon of "when in doubt, discard." For all the basic beliefs of biblical classical theology I found modern substitutes. For the ontological Trinity, a modal or demythologized trinity (as Hartshorne once suggested, all of us contribute to the "trinity" or plurality of God); for the preexistence and deity of Christ, a "divine" human figure who preeminently re-presented the love of God that is a possibility in fact for every person; for the vicarious atonement of Christ and the shedding of his blood for the remission of the sins of the world, a tragic event over which God had no control and before which Jesus himself may have emotionally collapsed (so said Ogden); for the supernatural resurrection of Jesus from the dead, an existentialist rising of the heart and will in faith; for the gifts and fruit of the Holy Spirit in the church, the broader belief that God offers these to everyone and does all he can to lure each individual to maximum creativity regardless of his or her cultural beliefs; for the biblical hope of perfected life after death, a denial of conscious existence after death but an objective immortality of our earthly life in the everlasting memory of God; for the eschatological hope of a final judgment of evil and the perfection of creation by the sovereign God, an optimistic/pessimistic belief in an everlasting evolutionary creative advance—"till the crack of doom," as Whitehead once expressed it. And finally, closest to home and most comforting, a denial of radical human sinfulness and a belief in the essential goodness and "salvation" of all if only they could be persuaded to follow God's lure to aesthetic enjoyment and creativity.

The reconstruction of classical theology was thus complete and followed upon the destruction of biblical faith. Every major doctrine of evangelical Christianity was redefined in terms of the philosophical norms of process metaphysics, ostensibly to meet the demands of logical and existential adequacy, especially in terms of a modern scientific world. Accordingly, I thought I was radically improving on Christianity as it had been believed for nineteen hundred years. Whitehead and Hartshorne claimed such, and I was impressed by the challenge and rigor of their thought. Not only was the exploration and adaptation of process literature exciting, but also the whole approach made life considerably easier for a former evangelical on a secular campus where I no longer felt any compulsion to witness for Christ but could simply argue philosophically for a modest liberal universalism. So it went for a decade.

The real shock came when conversation with a like-minded colleague revealed a serious logical flaw at the very core of process metaphysics. It began to come clear that process theism is not really compatible with modern relativity theory after all because it still insists on some important absolutes. God is absolute and unchangeable in his mode or character of being, and one of these qualities is his ability, said Hartshorne, to embrace all of the grand and immense procession of emergent reality at once, simultaneously. But that doctrine contradicts two empirical data, one of which is incontestable. The incontestable fact is that if God moves necessarily in time he is limited to some rate of velocity that is finite (say, the speed of light, if not the faster rate of some hypothetical tachyon). This means, unfortunately for process theism, that it is impossible for such a finite deity to have a simultaneous God's-eye view of the whole universe at once, since it would take him millions of light years or more to receive requisite data from distant points and places.

The other problem is peculiar to relativity theory. The doctrine is that no finite being (including God) could possibly embrace the whole universe simultaneously because there simply is no finite position that is not relative; hence no possibility of simultaneity exists from any possible finite vantage point. Time does not advance along a well-defined front but processes in all sorts of relative patterns which cannot be correlated into any one finite system. That is what relativity means. There is simply no privileged position, finitely speaking.

When that point came clear it was as though the scales had dropped off my eyes. I now began to see as I had never seen before why it is so important to insist (with biblical faith and classical theology) that God is ontologically beyond time and space, for only as such can he then embrace timespace and each of us within it with his sovereign righteousness and love. If one insists on locating God's actual existence as necessarily in time, God becomes irrelevant, for he is then limited to some finite velocity and is necessarily locked out of any comprehensive experience of the whole universe. Since process theism claims to be rational and to satisfy the canons of logic better than the biblical classical view of God, it is not reassuring to discover a fatal logical flaw at the heart of the system. I am now more convinced than ever that every system of thought begins with some prior agenda to which it is committed by faith, as "faith seeking understanding," and then utilizes logic to develop the implications of its presuppositions.

As I began to examine the process view with a more critical eye, other serious flaws began to appear. Eric Rust and Dallas High suggested I look more closely at the concept of persons in Whitehead and Hartshorne, and when I did I discovered that there really is no sense in which God in process theism is vitally conscious and personal in his eternal state of being, but is only in that polarity to be conceived of as abstract possibility. In his actual concrete existence, according to process metaphysics, God is forever processing and changing, since he is everlastingly self-surpassing himself and adding new data derived from the world and the universe. But God has no consciousness and no content of actual experience apart from what we supply him. In what sense, then, I began to ask, is he a person, conscious, willing, and acting, in his noncontingent state of A (Absolute)? The answer became clear: neither in Whitehead's system nor in Hartshorne's has God any conscious personality over and above the world. His factual intent and consciousness are only in terms of this world. Hence he is "relatively" (R) dependent on us—absolutely, actually, since in Whitehead's system God as primordial and logically prior to the world is pure abstract possibility without personal or conscious experience, while in Hartshorne's system God is greater than the sum of the parts of the universe only in an abstract sense. Since we comprise his "brain cells," so to speak (Hartshorne's image), it is mystifying to comprehend in what substantial sense God is person apart from the world and can function as its chief lure for creative advance.

Since there is a problem in the system with God as substantial person apart from the atomic parts of the universe, we might imagine that there would be a similar problem with the process view of the human person. And so there is, I discovered. For if, as Whitehead insists, the basic level at which creativity begins is the level of individual atomicity—that is, atomic occasions of feeling emerging and forming more complex occasions— then we have to ask where the notion of identity comes into the picture. If, for example, I come into being as the result of the complex democracy of myriads of atomic and cellular occasions which are constantly emerging and perishing, and if I myself am constantly changing as the dominant "monad" of this complex democracy, what accounts for the perseverance of my personal pronoun *I?* Process metaphysics denies that there is any substantial self underlying the process of ever-emerging occasions and, like Buddhism, affirms that the only reality is processing relativity.

This, I came to see, is hardly an advance on Judeo-Christian views regarding the substantial and responsible self, much less an advance on the pre-Socratic flux of Heraclitus and the radical relativism of Protagoras. It simply will not do to appeal to something purely abstract to account for God's identity, as Whitehead does with his primordial nature of God, or as Hartshorne does with his argument that God's A is simply the abstract and enduring characteristics in R (as a is the identity abstracted from our r). What we want to know is, what accounts for that identity being there at all, if the self is not in some sense substantial? Who am "I" if I am constantly changing into another "I"? Who is God, and what independent ability to lure his creation does he possess, if he has no consciousness or ability to will apart from the atomic creatures who make him actually existent or "consequent," as Whitehead described God's factual and conscious nature?

I have searched in vain to find an answer to this unsettling absence of an enduring "I" in process theism, either in regard to God's "I" or our own. The system seems to fail at the same crucial point as Buddhism, for in both world views the self is assumed to be dependent on the coorigination of skeins or atomic occasions of experience which have no enduring identity in any substantial sense. The only difference is that Buddhism has a logical advantage in the sense that it views the recognition of the nonenduring self as a deep enlightenment, for the impermanence of the self means that it will not always have to suffer the anguish of desire, but is destined for Nirvana, the extinguishing of the flame of process with its painful craving. Western process theism, on the other hand, is based on desire and sees the process of creativity itself as the beginning, middle, and end of reality—forever. Yet nothing actual endures, not even God. Identity and continuity are defined in purely abstract terms.

Perhaps the seriousness of the problem as it began to unfold before me can be better illustrated by describing what the stakes really are in the language game of process theism. At heart, I am convinced, the system sets out not so much to defend God against the charge of evil (God could still destroy this little globe if he chose to), but is designed to assure us that we are free from the despotic control of a sovereign God, such as confronts us in the Judeo-Christian Scriptures. In order to be really free to choose without external compulsion from a sovereign God, other persons, or other finite entities, the process system requires that the individual emerging occasion (let us say you the reader) must be completely alone on the very edge of creativity where your willing self chooses one of a number of possibilities and makes it actual. In that moment you are, so says the system, all alone, like one of Gottfried Wilhelm Leibniz's windowless monads. That is, on the front line of the emerging moment of creativity no one, not even God, looks sideways at your immediacy, nor do you look sideways at his immediacy. Each of us, from God down to the subatomic particle, is quite alone in the moment of choice (of course in the case of descendingly lower occasions of feeling the choice is correspondingly of lower intensity).

Now to total up the cost of this experience-oriented view of freedom. It means, first, that no one, not even God, experiences anything about anybody or anything else that is immediate. We have each other only as past and perished, although the proximity of the just-perished frames as they speed by gives the illusion of other persons in their immediacy. Such is not the case, for even God has us only as perished data, since the system requires that in order to protect personal freedom, God too is locked out of our immediacy.

This means, then, that not only does God not have the future as other than possibility, but also that he does not have any present except his own. He has the world only as perished and past. Think for a moment what that entails. It means that all of our immediacy as we process is forever lost. No one else, not even God, can ever know it. Hence, the process substitute of objective immortality for Christian resurrection entails not only the loss of any further subjective life on our part beyond death (it rejects the gift of eternal life), but also the loss forever of whatever subjective immediacy we experienced in this life. In other words, God is not perfect in his knowledge of the future, he is not perfect in his knowledge of the present, and he is not perfect in his knowledge of the past. He is a truly finite and defective God.

But we need to take the critical analysis of the process view of persons one step further. If the conscious personal self is the *end* result of a previous self in the series I call "myself," then my new emergent self comes only at the end of the democratic occasion of all the myriad feeling occasions of my body that contribute to it. I have, or am, my new "I" only for a fractional moment before it too perishes and becomes a datum for the next emerging "I." In other words, there is a serious problem of selfhood and identity for the finite person as well, since the "ego" (which is nothing substantial) is continually transcending itself. Hence the "self" lives into the unrealized possibilities of the future and has only a momentary immediacy in the present before it perishes as a dead datum into the past. A continuous series of substantially unrelated "I's" constitute the "person," with no enduring substantial self to remember the past or anticipate the future.

This view ends in enormous irony. What starts out as a brilliant venture in logic and a search for adequacy concludes in illogic and existential inadequacy. If biblical classical Christianity is going to be discarded for something else, the something else had better be worth the cost. Process theism attempts to best the biblical doctrine of God's sovereignty in order to protect human freedom; but in the process it renders the concept of God empty and even empties the finite self of any enduring personhood that would make "freedom of choice" a meaningful term. The irony of the situation is that the freedom of the very self of the future (for which the process theist is concerned) is a different self from his present-and-about-to-perish self. Since process theism has no explanation of the enduring self, and indeed denies the identical selfhood of the person from moment to moment, it is academic whether "I" have freedom of choice as "I" move into the future of possibility, since my present "I" will momentarily perish and be superseded by another "I" that has no substantial continuity with all "my" previous "I's." So serious is the absence of personal identity and continuity that Hartshorne can actually argue that "I" cease to exist in periods of unconscious sleep, and only "pop" back into selfhood (although as another "self") when I awake. Not only does this take us to the edge of absurdity and render the question of free will moot, but also it brings into question the biblical doctrine that a person is responsible for his or her action, a doctrine that clearly assumes that one who speaks or acts in a certain way is responsible for that behavior *as the same person.*

What I saw happening before my very eyes, therefore, was the logical self-destruction of the process attempt to define God and persons from a nonbiblical point of view. If God's sovereignty over timespace is denied, and if he is placed within time as necessary to his experience, he becomes bound by time and space and irrelevant because impotent, even though the ostensible reason for placing him ontologically or necessarily in time was to conceive of him as a God who cares. He is hardly a deity who cares for much, since he cannot care for everything and everyone, and he is able to care for others only as they are either some other selves they will presently become or the past selves they have already become. He cannot care for others as they actually are in the moment of their emergent immediacy because that is the free and private domain of the present self. In other words, in the process system *God does not have the world as present,* but only as future possibility or as past. But if God does not have the world as present then he, like us (although on a vaster scale), has only the perished data of the world to work on. In fact, those perished data of the past are supposed to be the effects that give rise to God himself as conscious cause. The mind boggles at such logic; the system bristles with difficulties.

It is far better, I began to realize, to stay with the self-revelation of God in the Judeo-Christian Scriptures and take the hard facts with the soft. That God is absolutely sovereign over the universe and timespace as its creator and sustainer is reiterated in the Scriptures. That God has created human beings to make responsible decisions is also a clear teaching of Scripture. The language is logically odd from a human point of view, but Scripture is full of logically odd events, proclamations, and persons (such as Abraham and his promise of offspring; Moses and the exodus; the Son of God born in Bethlehem, crucified on Calvary Hill, raised from the tomb, and coming again). Biblical merismus (a part here, a part there) is a major pattern of divine revelation. What the creature must do is not contest the rules, rail against God's language game, or complain about his or her rights, but worship the sovereign Lord, accept his grace by faith, and be obedient to him. My analysis of process theism's attempt to improve upon biblical classical Christianity has brought to light that the logically odd revelations of Scripture are replaced by the logically absurd when human speculation tries to explain the universe and its unavoidable polarities.

Can process theism teach the biblical theologian anything at all? I think the major challenge for evangelical theology is to make clear that neither biblical faith nor classical Christian theology really views God as statically frozen in his absoluteness. That criticism of process theism attacks a straw man, or a straw concept of God. Perhaps Thomistic theology might appear culpable because of its attachment to Aristotelian thought, but even there it is questionable whether the charge holds. The classical view of God as *actus purus*, Pure Act, really attempts to say that God's activity as self-contained and self-sufficient Trinity is absolutely pure: He is pure activity. Perhaps we need to say it in new ways and in other terms. I no longer have any difficulty conceiving of God as ultimate sociality, utterly inexhaustible in his love as archetypal Family of Father, Son, and Holy Spirit, One in Many, and Many in One. As the primordial Family in triunity, quite independent of created time and space and inexhaustible in terms of his dynamic love, God is the Archetype who has left his creative signature on all he has created in the ectypal or derivative universe. Everything created reflects one-in-manyness, manyness-in-oneness, being in becoming and becoming in being. God in his own supratemporal and supraspatial eternity is dynamic and inexhaustible love and communion between the Father, the eternally begotten Son, and the Holy Spirit who issues from both. We must not think for a moment that God as he is in his own triunity is lacking in dynamic activity; but we must not circumscribe that archetypal dynamism in terms of finite time and space. We are not necessary to God. Analogous to the mystery of atomic occasions that stretch our imagination by appearing in the same and different places at once, now as waves and again as particles, God's unity and plurality, his complementary changelessness and dynamic inexhaustibility simply stretch our imaginations to the breaking point. We understand the mystery of his inner relationships best through his own appearance in human form as Jesus of Nazareth, who makes such astonishing statements as "Truly, truly, I say to you, before Abraham was, I am" (John 8:58); and prays, "Father, I desire that they also, whom thou hast given me, may be with me where I am, to behold my glory which thou hast given me in thy love for me before the foundation of the world" (John 17:24); and assures his followers, "I will pray the Father, and he will give you another Counselor, to be with you for ever, even the Spirit of truth" (John 14:16f.).

All the witnesses of Scripture, and consummately Jesus Christ incarnate, point to Someone inexplicably perfect and dynamic who is sovereign over us yet who is with us as Redeemer and Lord and who is closer to us than we are to ourselves. Creative freedom is not some right independent of him, but a gift of his grace that we might worship him and become servants of one another in his name. This truth will never be realized as long as we contest the rules of the game. God sovereignly establishes the language game, and we tinker with it at our peril.

In the following chapters we will critically assess the validity of process theism from the twin perspectives of logical adequacy and fidelity to biblical revelation. Each of the questions I have raised in a brief and introductory manner will be examined extensively and rigorously in order to test the claim that process theism affords a more adequate world view for our time than biblical and classical theology. The first question we will address raises the question of the extent of God's power in a world with which he purportedly shares power. Is process theism really a theodicy? Does it absolve God of the charge that he is responsible for evil if he is conceived of in biblical terms? Or is it subtly an anthropodicy, a defence of the autonomy of the human mind? Let us see.

Suggested Reading

Cobb, John B., Jr. *A Christian Natural Theology Based on the Thought of Alfred North Whitehead.* Philadelphia: Westminster, 1965.
A standard introduction to the application of process thought to Christian theology by one of the school's most important interpreters.

Cobb, John B., Jr., and David R. Griffin. *Process Theology: An Introductory Exposition.* Philadelphia: Westminster, 1976.
One of the best introductions to the school, and a good place to begin reading.

Griffin, David R., and Thomas J. J. Altizer, eds. *John Cobb's Theology in Process.* Philadelphia: Westminster, 1977.
Evidence that process theologians keep moving to the left.

Hartshorne, Charles. *The Divine Relativity: A Social Conception of God.* New ed. New Haven: Yale University Press, 1964.
Hartshorne's clearest exposition of panentheism, and required, although not easy, reading.

———. *The Logic of Perfection and Other Essays in Neoclassical Metaphysics.* La Salle, IL: Open Court, 1973.
Only the experts will tackle the opening essays on Hartshorne's arguments for the existence of God. But the remaining essays are fascinating insights into the mind of this major proponent of process theism.

Schilpp, Paul Arthur, ed. *The Philosophy of Alfred North Whitehead.* The Library of Living Philosophers. New York: Tudor, 1956.
A helpful introduction to the difficult concepts in Whitehead's system.

Whitehead, Alfred North. *Modes of Thought.* New York: Capricorn Books, 1958.
One of the most stimulating and easy-to-read studies in brief compass.

———. *Process and Reality: An Essay in Cosmology.* New York: Harper and Row, 1957.
Whitehead's major work and very demanding, but well worth reading as a long-term project. This is the principal text of present-day Whiteheadians.

PART ONE

Problems of Power, Persons, and Time in Process Theism

A Critique of Whitehead, Hartshorne, and Cobb

1

Theodicy, Anthropodicy, and Power in Process Theism

A Critique

Certain evidence compels me to argue that while process thought is certainly correct in emphasizing God's engagement in the world, it is wrong in limiting his experience to cosmic time and space. As to the first, I heartily agree that God is engaged redemptively in this world of ours and does participate in time, space, and matter, preeminently in Jesus of Nazareth, in what Alfred North Whitehead calls "the Galilean origin of Christianity."[1] The redemptive process of God is realized in his love for the world:

> What is done in the world is transformed into a reality in heaven, and the reality in heaven passes back into the world. By reason of this reciprocal relation, the love in the world passes into the love in heaven and floods back again into the world. In this sense, God is the great companion—the fellow-sufferer who understands.[2]

And, as Charles Hartshorne writes, God's divine grace is ever with us in our human decisions: "He always does help us."[3]

1. *Process and Reality: An Essay in Cosmology* (New York: Harper and Row, 1957), p. 52.
2. Ibid., p. 532.
3. *The Divine Relativity: A Social Conception of God,* new ed. (New Haven: Yale University Press, 1964), p. 146.

These sentiments seem fundamentally biblical, as the Old and New Testaments attest. God has created the world and participates in spacetime to persuade his creatures through love to enter into creative covenant with him and with one another. But this has always been the witness of New Testament Christianity which has historically set store by the manifest love of God in Christ and the energizing power of the Holy Spirit. Whitehead and Hartshorne however have moved away from scriptural authority to the authority of speculative human reason, although their stores still seem to me to be in escrow in the biblical city as borrowed capital. So far there is a common source.

The principal error of process thought, it seems to me, is its assumption that God's engagement in finite time, space, and matter is an eternal and necessary contingency. This is the fundamental issue at stake. With biblical, historic Christianity I would say that God's participation in timespace is his own free and autonomous decision in regard to human choice for the tenure of this his own created world. This is the crucial issue in the debate; for if, as Whitehead and Hartshorne want to say, God's actual existence necessitates his having some universe or other forever, then God's actuality is everlastingly contingent upon the decisions of a relatively independent finite world, since, by definition of the process school, God's "body" or sphere of actual existence has to be some physical universe or other everlastingly.

Not only does this doctrine say more than needs to be said for us to conceive of God as temporally relevant, but it also leads Whitehead and Hartshorne into serious logical and empirical difficulties which will be examined in the following pages. For now, let me simply say as a convinced biblical Christian that it is much more satisfactory logically, and certainly more faithful to biblical revelation, to hold to the doctrine that God has by a miracle of grace created this world of spacetime, not out of need but out of the fullness of his abundance, and has graciously shared a portion of his power with human beings, having created them in his own image. Human freedom for the duration of this world order is not a metaphysical right, nor does it justify a creaturely claim against God. It is a gift of divine grace with all the privileges and responsibilities that attend it.

Anthropodicy or Theodicy?

The process position amounts to both a theodicy and an anthropodicy; it is, respectively, a defense of God against evil and a defense of man against determinism. It is not clear which takes precedence, although I am tempted to suggest that in the end it is the defense of speculative human freedom that is foremost in the minds of both its leading advocates.

Whitehead inveighs against the "deeper idolatry" of fashioning God in the image of oriental despots which, he says, has been the fallacy of Christianity and Islam: "When the Western world accepted Christianity, Caesar conquered."[4] Classical Christianity, he says, adopted Aristotle's notion of the unmoved mover and merged it with its own favorite doctrine of God as "eminently real": "The combination of the two into an aboriginal, eminently real, transcendent creator at whose fiat the world came into being, and whose imposed will it obeys, is the fallacy which has infused tragedy into the histories of Christianity and Mohammedanism."[5]

The words *whose imposed will it obeys* are the nub of the problem (although Whitehead's criticism refers more accurately to Islam than to biblical Christianity). If God is absolute in all respects, he asks, where do man's dignity and freedom come into the picture? Accordingly, Whitehead rejects the Christian doctrine of the sovereignty of God and avers that "the concrescence of each individual actual entity is internally determined and externally free."[6] Not only is this so, but also God, the indispensable primordial lure for the creativity of temporal creatures, is himself dependent upon them: "But of course, there is no meaning to 'creativity' apart from its 'creatures,' and no meaning to 'God' apart from the creativity and the 'temporal creatures,' and no meaning to the temporal creatures apart from 'creativity' and 'God.'"[7] God in his own actuality is "consequent" upon and derivative from their creativity.[8] Creaturely freedom is indispensable to God's own concrete existence. God in his consequent or concrescent nature is contingent.

Similarly, when Hartshorne in *The Divine Relativity* entitles the first chapter "God As Supreme, Yet Indebted to All," he sounds his principal philosophical theme, namely, that God is supremely relational in terms of the universe and is indebted to all its relatively free agents for the content of his actual experience. God's "concrete knowledge is relative, the generic abstract property of being-all-knowing is strictly absolute."[9] That, in shorthand, is Hartshorne's position. God is Absolute (A) only in the abstract sense of his generic mode of being; he is Related to the universe (R) in his concrete or actual experience and knowledge.[10] Thus God is AR, where A is no longer his absoluteness in the biblical sense, but his abstract characteristics as they remain the same in an everlasting procession of finite universes. This view of God, says Hartshorne in the

4. *Process and Reality*, p. 519.
5. Ibid.
6. Ibid., p. 41. See also pp. 30, 74f., 255, 344.
7. Ibid., p. 344.
8. Ibid., pp. 523f.
9. Hartshorne, *The Divine Relativity*, p. 11.
10. Ibid., pp. 82f.

opening lines of his first chapter, addresses the fundamental theological problem: "The question is whether and how God (or, if you prefer, the Supreme Being) can be conceived without logical absurdity, and as having such a character that an enlightened person may worship and serve him with whole heart and mind."[11]

The anthropocentric emphasis of this sentence should not be missed. Hartshorne establishes three criteria by which a conception of God either stands or fails: (1) it must be free of logical absurdity; (2) it must appeal to an enlightened person; (3) such that he judge the Supreme Being worthy of worship and service with whole heart and mind. All three criteria lie within the control of the person: the enlightened finite creature judges the logical suitability and worthiness of doctrines about God. Such a view is the legacy of the Enlightenment with its demand that human reason be the final test of truth. God's own revelation of his nature and of his ethical demands in sacred Scripture plays no more part in Hartshorne's process theology than it does in Whitehead's. Hartshorne emphatically rejects the biblical basis of historical Christianity and refers to the theory of infallible revelation as the confusion of deity and humanity.[12]

My first criticism of this rejection of God's self-disclosure in sacred Scripture is that it leads to a confusion of deity and humanity, for now human reason becomes the final arbiter of what God may be conceived to be and of his worthiness to be worshiped. The first and last court of appeal is the enlightened person who numbers himself among those "men of the highest integrity and wisdom" who have attempted "to worship the objective God, not our forefathers' doctrines about him."[13] This is anthropodicy, a defense of human autonomy and reason against the claims of biblical revelation. Hartshorne might want to call it a theodicy, or defense of the only justifiable view of God as he conceives of him.[14] But I think the charge of anthropodicy will stand. Reason is the final arbiter for Hartshorne. At the age of seventeen, he tells us, he made up his mind to trust reason to the end.[15] He also allows in the same passage that rational criticism and objectivity are not merely individual matters but a process of mutual correction and inspiration. My view is that reason enlightened by biblical revelation leads to real objectivity about the nature of God and reality, but that dialogue even in the realm of fallen

---

11. Ibid., p. 1.
12. Ibid., p. 149.
13. Ibid., p. 148.
14. For a similar view, see David R. Griffin, *God, Power, and Evil: A Process Theodicy* (Philadelphia: Westminster, 1976), passim.
15. Charles Hartshorne, *The Logic of Perfection and Other Essays in Neoclassical Metaphysics* (La Salle, IL: Open Court, 1972), p. viii.

and unaided reason may be of benefit because of God's providential gift of logic, which is the ground of discourse, whether we use it well or poorly.

Accordingly, I will challenge Hartshorne's notion that biblical Christianity is illogical and will argue instead that the finite deity of process metaphysics is itself illogical and in the end not so much a theodicy as a justification of the claims of speculative human reason. The anthropodicy of Enlightenment philosophy, with its virtual deification of human autonomy, I find necessary to reject on the grounds of what I consider the rational superiority of classical Christian theology; this argument I hope to make convincingly in the following pages. As for the suggestion that the finite deity of process thought is alone worthy of worship with whole heart and mind, I have to say from personal experience is untrue, for such a limited deity does not invite my wholehearted devotion. My reason for saying this is based upon my own awakening to the weakness of finitist theology. It simply does not have holding or staying power. I have observed the same effects in others who have tried to work out the implications and problems of process theology. If it argues for a God who cares, it does not offer a God who can do very much with a world that in one form or another will be everlastingly recalcitrant to God's ordering patterns. The limited deity of process theology is rather like the demiurge of Plato's *Timaeus*, or Ahura Mazda in Zoroastrianism, or the principle of light in Manicheism. In these speculative dualistic philosophies, deity is necessarily limited in power by a universe ultimately independent.

Logical Problems in the Finitism of Process Thought

This prompts us to turn to logical problems in the finitism of process thought. First let us look at the logic of divine power and human power.

The Ratio of Power

In process metaphysics the central question seems to be, who has the power? Processionists reply that if God has all the power, we have none; hence our decisions are meaningless.[16] The opposite possibility, that we have all the power, is equally absurd, says Hartshorne, for then all would be ruled by chance and chaos, which would lead to nothing at all. Thus logically, he reasons, a compromise is needed between providence and chance, or between God's power and our power.[17] But at this point he is faced with a serious problem. What is the relation of God's power to ours in numerical equation? How much is his and how much is ours? To what

16. Hartshorne, *The Divine Relativity*, pp. 50, 52, 116, 134-39.
17. Ibid., pp. 136f.

extent is God able to establish the equation? Hartshorne writes as though God really has the power to assign the limits of our power: ". . . [God] takes account of the freedom of others, and determines events only by setting appropriate limits to the self-determining of others, of the local agents."[18]

In this passage Hartshorne clearly asserts that God decrees the outlines of human freedom by setting "appropriate limits," but he does not indicate what those limits are and what criteria would define the word *appropriate*. Several pages later he specifies the ratio somewhat less vaguely:

> The radical difference between God and us implies that our influence upon him is slight, while his influence upon us is predominant. We are an absolutely inessential (but not inconsequential) object for him; he is the essential object for us. Hence God can set *narrow* limits to our freedom. . . . Thus God can rule the world and order it, setting optimal limits for our free action, by presenting himself an essential object, so characterized as to weight the possibilities of response in the desired respect.[19]

Creativity, Hartshorne allows, has narrow limits:

> As James Clerk Maxwell said, not without a touch of exaggeration, "if there is any freedom it is infinitesimal." I sometimes think of an individual's freedom as the fraction of which the numerator is the momentary experience of the individual, and the denominator is the past of the universe, so far as effectively involved. The value of this fraction is small, but still not zero.[20]

Here Hartshorne seems to set the limits of human freedom as radically as anywhere in his writings. It is clear to me that the logic of divine and human freedom should compel Hartshorne to say that it is God who gives freedom to his creatures as a gift, rather than their having it or claiming it as a metaphysical fact or right. If God sets narrow and optimal limits to our freedom and if once we have that freedom it is only infinitesimal, then logically God has optimal power in the universe and by sheer grace shares a small fraction of it with his creatures.[21] He is always optimally in control whether the creature uses that small measure of freedom creatively or not.

18. Ibid., p. 138.
19. Ibid., pp. 141f. His italics. Compare pp. 51, 135–37.
20. *The Logic of Perfection*, p. 180. If this equation is $\frac{1}{\infty}$, it does in fact equal zero. The question is whether this qualifier "effectively" equals infinity, as it should in the organic scheme of a social universe.
21. For Hartshorne's view of grace, see *The Divine Relativity*, p. 146.

With the notion of God's self-limitation I have no trouble at all, and I think it eminently biblical. God, through the "Grand Miracle" of love, as C. S. Lewis calls it,[22] shares a minute fraction of his power with his creatures, and so loves them still when they abuse that divine gift that he empties himself in his Son and humbly bears their rebellion upon a cross to redeem a lost freedom (Phil. 2:1-13). He remains in control, however; the prerogative of power is his to order and to share as he pleases. Of course, this view of God and his creatures is according to sacred Story and the higher logic that attends it. It is not something human reason would have thought of. In any event, to confine God to human logic is reductionist and limiting of God's privileged access to his own transcendence.

Hartshorne's attempt to formulate a theodicy therefore fails, it seems to me, because he has already allowed God to set the limits of creaturely freedom. His theodicy fails because God, with such enormous power, could at any time revoke that freedom, rid the world of evil, or destroy this present evil world and create a better. But he does not. Accordingly, Hartshorne seems to face the same problem as the classical Christian: Why does God allow freedom to be misused and suffering to continue if he both desires the best for his creatures and has the power to destroy evil? The answer of both classical Christianity and Hartshorne would logically appear to be the same: Because the gift and limits of freedom are optimally set for the response of the creature to God's loving persuasion. God respects the freedom that he has given to his creatures and will bring optimal good to those who freely respond to his love. Those who choose to use the gift of freedom egocentrically and destructively necessarily face the tragic view of life in final entropy.

Yet Hartshorne only *seems* to infer that God ultimately has all power and elects to share a small fraction of it with his creatures. That would be the logical conclusion of his arguments regarding God's setting narrow limits to human freedom. But he now makes a curious and illogical move. He argues that God has *always* had some universe or other and has *always* been limited by the freedom of some creatures or other. The doctrine of God's ultimate sovereignty over finitude is sacrificed to the notion of the eternal partial independence of the creatures from God.[23] Although Hartshorne holds that God can contain any relational pattern and remain himself,[24] his relational pattern or sociality is always necessarily with some finite universe or other:

> That the human creator always has a given concrete actuality to work with does not of itself establish a difference between him and God, unless it

22. See *Miracles: A Preliminary Study* (New York: Macmillan, 1973).
23. Hartshorne, *The Divine Relativity*, pp. 29-30.
24. Ibid., pp. 81f.

be admitted as made out that there was a first moment of creation. For if not, then God, too, creates each stage of the world as successor to a preceding phase. Only a dubious interpretation of an obscure parable, the book of Genesis, stands between us and this view. What does distinguish God is that the preceding phase was itself created by God, so that he, unlike us, is never confronted by a world whose coming to be antedates his own entire existence. There is no presupposed "stuff" alien to God's creative work; but rather everything that influences God has already been influenced by him, whereas we are influenced by events of the past with which we had nothing to do. This is one of the many ways in which eminence is to be preserved, without falling into the negations of classical theology.[25]

This is an important passage for process theology, for it avers that God is everlastingly related to some phase of the processing world. As Whitehead says, "Metaphysics requires that the relationships of God to the world should lie beyond the accidents of will, and that they be founded upon the necessities of the nature of the World."[26] David R. Griffin supports the process view on this crucial matter and approvingly quotes Whitehead:

> Furthermore, that there be an actual world of some sort or other is not a contingent matter. There would simply be no meaning to "God" apart from "creativity" and the worldly "creatures" (*Process and Reality*, 344). The notion of creation out of absolute nothingness, so that creation would be "the beginning of matter of fact," is rejected in favor of the creation of order out of chaos (*Process and Reality*, 146–147, 159).
>
> Accordingly, it is impossible for God to have a monopoly on power. There must be an actual world; and every actual world will necessarily contain actualities with power—some power of self-determination and some power to influence others.[27]

These passages from Hartshorne, Whitehead, and Griffin bristle with logical problems. One obvious contradiction is the disparity between the dogmata that God sets the optimal limits of creaturely creativity, yet is limited *necessarily* by those perimeters. One cannot have it both ways. If God sets the limits of finite freedom, he does so of his own volition; he limits himself for however long and to whatever degree he chooses to limit himself (in our system, for the tenure of this particular world epoch). Such would be my own position, and the biblical classical view. But if it is in the metaphysical nature of things that God is *necessarily*

25. Ibid., p. 30.

26. Alfred North Whitehead, *Adventures of Ideas* (Cambridge: At the University Press, 1933), p. 215.

27. *God, Power, and Evil*, pp. 279f.

limited by power other than his own in every actual world system everlastingly, then we are talking about an entirely different matter. This is no
longer biblical theism but a speculative dualism, with its eternal series of
worlds in which there are two eternal powers—God, and the power(s)
over which he has no final control. In this system, God has been and will
be everlastingly striving to bring order out of chaos, yet is supposed to be
able to set the optimal limits to the power that is other than his.

Observe the contradiction in the following statement by Griffin, which
is based on Whitehead's metaphysics:

> "Creativity" (by which the many become one and are increased by one) is
> a universal feature of actuality. It is inherent in actuality (*Adventures of
> Ideas*, 230). This does not mean that creatures derive their creative power
> from themselves, or that they are not dependent upon God for their exis-
> tence. But it does mean that to be an actuality is to exercise creativity, and
> that there is necessarily a realm of finite actualities with creativity of their
> own.[28]

How could there *necessarily* be a realm of finite actualities with creativity of their own who do not derive their creative power from themselves
and are not independent of God for their existence? To put it the other
way around, how could creatures derive their power not from themselves
but from God and at the same time comprise a realm of finite actualities
with creativity of their own *necessarily?* The two statements are logically
contradictory.

The credibility of the process school is at stake on this issue. If it
acknowledges creaturely dependence upon God for its creative power,
then classical Christian theism has already said this, and God remains
ultimately and metaphysically the sovereign source of all power, the sharing of which is solely his prerogative by grace. But if process doctrine
emphasizes the necessary metaphysical independence of finite actualities
with creativity of their own, then a whole new set of problems arise. Of
course, this is where process thought finally does settle; it is in fact the
raison d'être of process metaphysics. As Griffin says, speaking for the
school and its rejection of divine self-limitation:

> According to process thought, the reason is metaphysical, not moral.
> God does not refrain from controlling the creatures simply because it is
> better for God to use persuasion, but because it is necessarily the case that
> God cannot completely control the creatures.[29]

28. Ibid., pp. 276f.
29. Ibid., p. 276.

A Dualistic Metaphysics

Aside from the question I have already raised regarding the relative ratio between God-power and creature-power (is it a fraction of 1 percent? 2 percent? 10 percent? or larger or smaller?), the really damaging question is, what finite power or aggregation of finite powers can necessarily guarantee their being present in any possible or actual worlds forever? Finitude cannot be self-subsistent; by definition, no finite actuality is *necessary*. Process thinkers must know that they are talking about a dualism of powers, one eternally and divinely good (God), and one that is the source of everlasting finite power; and that this dualism is a very old school of thought. Griffin's attempt at theodicy follows Whitehead and Hartshorne very closely and is essentially a dualistic metaphysics. There are only two alternatives to dualism, both of which they reject: classical Christian theism, in which God is the metaphysical sovereign Lord or power who graciously shares a small fraction of this power for a limited time with his creatures, who are responsible for the use or misuse of that power; or pantheistic monism, which views ultimate reality as beyond good and evil, either as some spiritual substance, as in Hinduism, or as the process of nature itself, as in modern materialistic naturalism. One might be tempted to place process metaphysics in the category of pantheistic monism, especially since Hartshorne calls his view panentheism.[30] But Hartshorne takes care to point out that pantheism denies the personality of deity and identifies it with the cosmic collection of entities. Such is not the case, he says, with panentheism or surrelativism:

> The total actual state of deity-now as surrelative to the present universe, has nothing outside itself, and in that sense is the All. But the individual essence of deity (which makes God God, or the divine divine) is utterly independent of these All. . . . For since the essence of God is compatible with any possible universe, we can allow some power of decision, as between possibilities, without infringing the absolute independence of God in his essential character or personality. . . . True, the actual state of deity will be determined partly by the creatures; but this is simply the social character of the divine self-decision. . . .[31]

Here, too, there are serious logical problems in Hartshorne's view of God as person, a difficulty we will have to consider later in some detail. He divides God into two dimensions: his divine essence, which is his abstract character, as constant in any possible or actual world; and his divine existence, which is his actual, concrete, processing experience as

---

30. *The Divine Relativity*, pp. vii, xv, 88f.
31. Ibid., p. 89.

he interacts with the myriad free agents of this actual world and continually surpasses himself. If we focus on God as social actuality we might be
tempted to call Hartshorne's view a form of pantheism, for he suggests
that we actually comprise the brain cells of God himself:

> Everything contributes equally directly to the cosmic value. This means
> that the world mind will have no special brain, but that rather every indi-
> vidual is to that mind as a sort of brain-cell . . . and thus the cosmic
> analogue of a brain will be simply the entire system of things as wholly
> internal and immediate to the cosmic mind.[32]

Leaving aside for the moment the question, what is this cosmic mind
apart from the brain cells of finite individuals? we might say of the preceding passage that strictly speaking Hartshorne is avoiding classical
pantheism since he is careful to distinguish God's mind from the brain
cells which are somehow "in" the cosmic mind and contribute concrete
data for its experience, as reciprocally the cosmic mind seeks the integration and prosperity of the parts in a sort of creative synthesis.[33] The
proper term, says Hartshorne, is panentheism: that is, everything is *in*
God, but not everything *is* God, for he has an independent and absolute
modality of his own.[34] Accordingly, we may allow that there are modified
pantheistic strains in Hartshorne's metaphysics, but it is more properly a
dualism, as I have suggested, comprising God's abstract modality or
essence and some partially independent finite universe.

We have explored the logical difficulties of sorting out the ratio of
power between God and his universe and to what degree he sets the
limits of creaturely freedom. Judging from Hartshorne's speculations on
the matter, I conclude that he considers God's power to be very great
indeed. I fail to see, then, how Hartshorne and Griffin can consider their
rather similar process theism any great advantage over classical Christian theism as a theodicy, for in either system God apparently could
destroy this present evil world and its fragile citizens at any moment and
fashion another from the raw materials. That God has not yet done so
suggests to me not that he cannot, but that he does not will to, for the
reason biblical Christianity suggests, namely, that in God's infinite wisdom greater optimal good accrues from his continuing to sustain the
world in its present course ("The Lord is not slow about his promise as
some count slowness, but forbearing toward you, not wishing that any
should perish, but that all should reach repentance" [II Peter 3:9]).[35]

32. *The Logic of Perfection*, pp. 197f.
33. Ibid., pp. 198f. See also Hartshorne's *Creative Synthesis and Philosophical Method*
(La Salle, IL: Open Court, 1970), passim.
34. *The Divine Relativity*, pp. vii, xv, 88f.
35. See Griffin's virtual agreement in *God, Power, and Evil*, pp. 308f.

Of course, if process theologians were to argue that God has no power to put an end to the world, then such a deity would have no qualifications for meeting either the test of a God worth worshiping or the test of God as that than which nothing greater can be conceived. But Hartshorne wants to meet those tests[36] and argues consistently that God is all-powerful in the sense that he has all the power the greatest conceivable Being could possibly have, given a social universe that necessarily exhibits some power independent of God. What Hartshorne and his followers fail to develop logically and clearly (and what is humanly impossible to articulate with precision) is just how powerful God is, and conversely, just how powerful the world is, individually and aggregately as independent of God in-some-sense-or-other.

I conclude, therefore, that Hartshorne has not followed reason to the end, and I suspect that the hidden presupposition that compels him to hold a logically contradictory position on power is motivated more by anthropodicy than theodicy. Hartshorne, Whitehead, Griffin, and others in the process school employ biblical language only in a peripheral way, but do not theologize from within the biblical Story. As a biblical interpreter I see their attempt to democratize God ontologically as a program of substituting a modern anthropocentric story for the theocentric story of Scripture.

The Issue of Human Freedom

Unfortunately, the question of the ratio of God's power to human freedom remains a fascinating and perplexing matter for many evangelicals who, unlike process theists, do take the Scriptures very seriously as the revealed Word of God. Recently I participated in a panel discussion on process theism at which evangelicals and nonevangelicals were present and was concerned to see how attractive the school appears to be to a number of evangelical scholars, especially those of Arminian backgrounds whose heritage has emphasized the freedom of the individual to choose above the sovereignty of God over creation. The search by one of the participants, Richard Rice, for a compromise between these two doctrines illustrates the attractiveness of the process model to certain schools of evangelical thought. In a recent study Rice poses the thesis that reality itself and God's experience of reality are essentially open rather than closed.[37] God experiences the events of the world as they happen, not in some timeless eternity. Accordingly, not even God knows

---

36. See *Anselm's Discovery: A Re-Examination of the Ontological Proof for God's Existence* (La Salle, IL: Open Court, 1965).

37. *The Openness of God: The Relationship of Divine Foreknowledge and Human Free Will,* Horizon series (Nashville: Review and Herald, 1981).

the future in all its details; otherwise, the idea of freedom would be meaningless. Rice realizes that this thesis varies from the conventional Christian view, but claims that it has the support of both the Bible and religious experience and that it makes more rational sense, indeed, enriches our understanding of divine providence, prophecy, and foreknowledge.[38]

Having been through this before on my own, I know how attractive the whole operation looks to the evangelical. But I want to point out that if the question is framed in this way ("Either the future is open for God or I am not really free"), then it is virtually certain that the biblical teaching on God's sovereignty is going to have to be radically modified. Rice accepts a human-centered definition of freedom as the norm for discussion. From a biblical perspective, that is a mistake. He declares, *"An act is free precisely to the extent that it renders definite something otherwise indefinite."*[39] This is precisely the way the nonevangelical frames the question: freedom entails indefiniteness, and since this is logically incompatible with the doctrine of a sovereign God, God therefore must have an indefinite or open future if creatures are to be free. But the problem for an evangelical saying this is that the Scriptures define freedom not in terms of freedom from God but as faithful fellowship with God. Over the face or understanding of the natural person there is a veil, and only in Christ is it taken away: "But when a man turns to the Lord the veil is removed. Now the Lord is the Spirit, and where the Spirit of the Lord is, there is freedom" (II Cor. 3:16–17). This is a radically different view of freedom from that of the natural person, but it is fundamentally biblical and is consummately expressed by Jesus in his challenging word:

> "If any man would come after me, let him deny himself and take up his cross and follow me. For whoever would save his life will lose it; and whoever loses his life for my sake and the gospel's will save it. For what does it profit a man, to gain the whole world and forfeit his life? For what can a man give in return for his life? For whoever is ashamed of me and of my words in this adulterous and sinful generation, of him will the Son of man also be ashamed, when he comes in the glory of his Father with the holy angels." [Mark 8:34–38]

Here, as throughout the Old and New Testaments, freedom is not defined as autonomous power apart from God, but rather as the creature's willingness to be faithful and selfless in service to God and to Jesus Christ. True Christian freedom is always to choose Christ, but one cannot choose Christ until God graciously removes the veil of rebellious nature. For if

38. Ibid., p. 8.
39. Ibid., p. 18. His italics.

one has a nature, and the nature is fallen (a very biblical view, as Romans 3:9–20 attests), is he really free to choose good? If he is not determined by his fallen nature, then his "I" has no substantial identity; that is, he is whatever he chooses to be at any moment, and thus is merely a succession of "I's." That is the process, but not the biblical, view. Accordingly, I will observe that Rice's definition of freedom does not qualify as a faithful exegesis of what God defines true freedom to be in Scripture.

Let us see how well Rice does with the argument from logic. For God to have an open future (which is necessary, he says, if we are to be genuinely free), time must be real for God: events must enter his experience as they happen, not before. Hence the views of Whitehead and Hartshorne are claimed to be valid interpretations of God's experience, especially Hartshorne's analysis of dipolar theism, namely, that God is both absolute and relative, necessary and contingent, eternal and temporal, changeless and changing.[40] But there is one important difference between process theism and the process theology Rice is advocating. He wants to make the claim that God is not ontologically dependent on the world. In this he is correct, and one of my major arguments throughout this book is on that very theme. But can Rice say this and at the same time agree with process theism that the future of the world is also future to God? As an evangelical he wants to agree with traditional Christianity that God sustains all history, is an agent within history, and interacts with finite historical agents, supremely in the life, death, and resurrection of Jesus; God created the world and does not need finite creatures to make up for his deficiencies. Yet, he says, God created an open world in terms of which his own knowledge is dynamic, open, and constantly developing. Hence, God not only affects the world, but the world also affects him.[41]

If we lay aside for the moment those biblical texts that indicate the certainty of God's plan for the world redemptively and eschatologically from the very beginning (e.g., Gen. 3:15; Rom. 8:18–31), how logical do we find Rice's attempt to conceive of God as ontologically independent of the world yet dependent on spacetime contingency for his knowledge of the world? I would say that the two are incompatible logically. If God is necessarily beholden to the process of time to experience the novelty of free creatures in the world, then to that extent he is not ontologically independent of the world. I have the same difficulty with this novel attempt at bipolarity as with Hartshorne's effort to provide a theodicy of distributed power where God has all the power he could possibly have, given a social universe in which he shares available power necessarily with finite creatures. The best Rice could do would be to argue that in

40. Ibid., pp. 22–28.
41. Ibid., pp. 29–33.

some sense God is not dependent on the world for his ontological experience (whatever the Trinity might experience on its own), while in another sense (as far as the world is concerned) he would be contingent upon its independence for worldly data. This sounds very speculative and raises once more the question of the ratio of God's independent knowledge to his dependent knowledge.

The Issue of Divine Foreknowledge

Since one of Rice's purposes in writing the book has been to defend God against the charge of responsibility for evil, it would be well for us to consider whether his defense of God fares any better than Hartshorne's. A common argument against God's sovereignty is advanced by Rice, namely, that if God foreknew what an evil turn this world was to take following its creation, but went ahead anyway, then he is ultimately responsible for evil. Accordingly, Rice suggests the following scenario to defend the notion that future free decisions are indefinite until they occur and are therefore in principle unknowable in advance; thus God's moral integrity is supposedly protected.

> God decided to create a world containing morally free beings. These beings had the choice of serving Him or not. Since their obedience or disobedience was something He left up to them to decide, it was not definite. Therefore their future decision was not knowable until they existed and made the choice themselves. God knew they *could* rebel when He created them. But it was not certain that they *would* rebel until they decided to do so. Thus, God is responsible only for the possibility of evil (simply because He created morally free beings). But He is not responsible for the actuality of evil. The creatures are entirely to blame for that.[42]

Again, biblical passages come to mind that militate against God's not knowing definitely what would ensue from his creation, verses such as Ephesians 1:4 ("even as he chose us in him before the foundation of the world, that we should be holy and blameless before him") and I Peter 1:18–20 ("You know that you were ransomed from the futile ways inherited from your fathers, not with perishable things such as silver or gold, but with the precious blood of Christ, like that of a lamb without blemish or spot. He was destined before the foundation of the world but was made manifest at the end of the times for your sake"). These are disclosures of God's redemptive purpose before the fall that anticipate his radical response to evil even before it happens. But perhaps, as I shall argue later in the book, our concept of time is too linear to fathom such odd but marvelous language, and perhaps in the end we shall have to

42. Ibid., p. 43. His italics.

admit that we know more than we can tell, as Michael Polanyi has reminded us is true of most tacit beliefs to which we are committed.

We need to consider the logic of Rice's argument more closely. If, as he suggests, God took an enormous risk in creating man with free will, is he absolved from responsibility for evil if he continues to sustain the world in which so much evil continues to be perpetrated? If he cannot put an end to the world, then he is very contingent indeed and is hardly worthy of our worship. If he can put a stop to evil, why doesn't he? The argument is circular, and we seem to have made no progress at all since the introduction of the initial problem. I made the point earlier with Hartshorne and will make it again with Rice that it does no good simply to redistribute power from God to finite creatures in order to gain a theodicy unless the ratio of transferred power is great enough to render God incapable of putting an end to an evil world. Only then would God be absolved of responsibility for evil. But then he would be such an impotent deity as to be unworthy of worship. Any lesser ratio of transfer of power would not suffice. It is a serious dilemma and logic alone will not solve it.

Yet Rice continues to play the percentages as though somehow a little limitation of divine foreknowledge will defend God's integrity and guarantee our human freedom. But observe what sort of difficulty this gets him into when he tries to explain the distribution of power between God and creation, and how similar his dilemma is to Hartshorne's:

> The open view of God is therefore entirely compatible with the view that God knows a great deal about the future course of events. Certainly some of what will happen in the future is determined by factors that already exist. This forms the basic presupposition for all scientific endeavor. In fact, the vast majority of future events may be the inevitable outworking of past and present causes. All that our open view of reality requires is that the future be *indefinite to the extent that* the world contains *genuine freedom*. And the openness that genuine freedom entails may actually constitute a small proportion of what will happen. Possessing *exhaustive knowledge of the past*, God therefore knows all that will happen as the result of factors already in existence. In other words, God knows infallibly (or foreknows absolutely) all the future consequences of the past and present. . . . Therefore a great deal of the future that appears vague and indefinite to us must be vividly clear to Him.[43]

I have italicized points of logical difficulty in this argument. First, what is the actual percentage of open power we as creatures need to be genuinely free? What is the cash value of the phrase *indefinite to the extent that?* Obviously the sense of the larger passage suggests that we

43. Ibid., p. 47.

have very little freedom indeed. What I want to know from Rice, as from Hartshorne, is what small quantitative percentage of freedom apart from God constitutes genuine freedom? I do not think a logical answer can be forthcoming, or that it is even conceivable. Second, what is the definition of "genuine freedom"? Creatures make many decisions, but is it possible to define genuine freedom simply in terms of choosing quantitatively? Or is genuine freedom something rather different and qualitative? Third, is it logically possible that God can have "exhaustive knowledge of the past" if he does not sovereignly know the present immediacy of the creature who chooses? But this he cannot know exhaustively if the creature is in some respect independent of God as he moves into the private moment of decision. This is an argument I want to make at greater length later on, but suffice it to say at present that the cost of adopting a process model is very expensive theologically; for whatever immediacy of private freedom the creature enjoys cannot be shared by God and so cannot be remembered by him, hence is lost forever.

My feeling is that Rice, like other evangelicals who are inclining toward process theism, has not thought through the consequences of the system, and for that he and they might be excused for a while, since it took me a long time to see what I had bought into and how great was the cost. To be sure, Rice is very cautious when he is talking percentages (even more so than Hartshorne because he has more to lose), and he repeatedly draws back from allowing the creature too much freedom. He goes so far as to say, for example, that "there is no possibility of God's being caught by surprise by any development in the creaturely world. . . . Nothing can happen that He has not already envisioned and for which He has not made adequate preparation. Consequently, although God does not know the future absolutely, He nevertheless anticipates it perfectly. He faces the future with complete foresight." He knows what *will* happen and what *might* happen, yet he does not know everything that *actually* will happen.[44]

This seesawing back and forth between taking from God and giving back to God indicates an unease about the way the question is framed. Since the question of ratios of power cannot be determined logically or philosophically, it is much better (and certainly more faithful to the revealed Word of God) to approach the question quite differently. It is God who should be the focus of biblical exegesis and theology, not the fallen creature who demands to be free. Freedom in biblical terms is a gift of God and can only be attained indirectly by forsaking the demand for one's rights and negotiations over power. Whenever theology focuses on a defense of human freedom, God's sovereignty will be subtracted from and

44. Ibid., p. 49.

modified to accommodate the rights of the creature, but never will a satisfactory ratio be arrived at. The problem will be particularly aggravating for the evangelical and he will find himself, like Rice, fluctuating back and forth like alternating current between what he knows he must say on biblical terms about God's sovereignty and what he wants to say about human freedom.

The logical improprieties of the following passages are perhaps a fit conclusion to my warning that process theism is more trouble than it is worth if one is looking for a helpful hermeneutic to apply to biblical exegesis and theology. Employing William James's analogy of two chess players to illustrate the compatibility of divine providence and human freedom,[45] Rice suggests that while the beginner is free to do whatever he chooses, the master knows exactly how to respond to any possible move; hence the eventual outcome of the game is a foregone conclusion. This does not mean that God knows or plans everything in advance: "God maintains ultimate sovereignty over history. But He does not exercise absolute control."[46] I find this a very difficult and contradictory analogy since it will please neither the biblical exegete, the traditional theologian, nor the nonevangelical process theist. If on the one hand "nothing can thwart the eventual realization of God's objectives,"[47] then it seems to me that in the end God is sovereign; but if the creature is "genuinely free" in the sense in which Rice wishes to use the expression, then the phrase means nothing unless God's plans can be thwarted by contrary human choices. The halfway house of conservative process theism is not in a very defensible position; it would be better to pay the price and take the consequences of the autonomous demand for one's rights, which is a necessarily finite God. But it is better still to follow faithfully the biblical disclosure that God is absolutely sovereign over his creation, and because he is, holds his creatures responsible for their thoughts and actions. That may be logically odd language, but it has the advantage of being what God says about what really is the case. If he says he can do it, he can do it. I take that to be a distinct advantage indeed, for it begs us to get on with the job and not complain about the language game God has established for our salvation. We are not, after all, in a position to bargain with God over the distribution of power in his universe. It would not be wise for an ant to try to negotiate with God from the top of a blade of grass when there is an untamed Lion walking about.

45. William James, *The Will to Believe and Other Essays* (London: Longmans, Green, 1897), pp. 181f., cited in John H. Hick, *Evil and the God of Love*, rev. ed. (New York: Harper and Row, 1978), p. 344.

46. Rice, *The Openness of God*, p. 57.

47. Ibid., p. 85.

2

Whitehead and the Problem of God As Person

An Identity Crisis in Process Theology

Another logical "incompossibility" in process thought is as problematic as the question of distribution of power between God and the world. The problem we will deal with in this chapter concerns the Whiteheadian and Hartshornean concepts of God's absolute, unchanging essence. In what sense do these doctrines allow that God is the eminent Person, the absolute "I," who as consummately conscious Agent stands behind reality with intentional fidelity, makes continuous cosmic decisions, sets optimal limits to creaturely power, and lures the universe onward in creative advance as the One than which nothing greater can be conceived? If God is eternal and unchangeable in his primordial nature only, as Alfred North Whitehead argues, and only in his abstract essence, as Charles Hartshorne believes, how is the transcendent pole of God truly the supreme *Agent* of conscious, personal activity? For both philosophers the problem is a large and serious one.

Whitehead contends that God like any subject (but eminently so) is dipolar; that is, he has a mental pole (his primordial nature) and a physical pole (his consequent nature):

> The mental pole introduces the subject as a determinant of its own concrescence. The mental pole is the subject determining its own ideal of itself by reference to eternal principles of valuation autonomously modified in

their application to its own physical objective datum. Every actual entity is "in time" so far as its physical pole is concerned, and is "out of time" so far as its mental pole is concerned. It is the union of two worlds, namely the temporal world, with the world of autonomous valuation.[1]

In God's case, however, unlike ours, his pure conceptual prehensions are underived and are therefore free to be radically nontemporal; God's envisagement of pure possibilities is neither past, present, nor future. Whitehead claims, however, that God's mental pole or primordial nature is unconscious: "This side of his nature is free, complete, primordial, eternal, actually deficient, and unconscious."[2] It is only when the physical pole or consequent nature of God acquires integration with the primordial side that it becomes "determined, incomplete, consequent, 'everlasting,' fully actual, and conscious."[3]

What sense does Whitehead make of God as transcendent and personal? Certainly God must in some special sense be above the world of spacetime if he is primordial, and eminently personal as ultimate Agent if he is "the unconditioned conceptual valuation of the entire multiplicity of eternal objects."[4] Yet here we encounter a very serious contradiction in Whitehead's concept of God as primordial Agent. Any being who is the "determinant of [his] own concrescence," who is "the subject determining its own ideal of itself," "the primordial superject of creativity," "the unconditioned conceptual valuation" can legitimately be described as such only if he meets the requirements of *personal* modality. That is, to describe God as conceptually valuating and self-determining in his mental or primordial pole should lead logically, on analogy of our own finite conceptual valuating and self-determining which is conscious on its highest level, to the view that God is the chief exemplification of *conscious* conceptual valuating and self-determining. How can a supposed *unconscious* primordial nature of God be described legitimately through models drawn from conscious human agents?

My criticism of Whitehead is that he has a faulty view of persons as agents and of what it means for us, and what it must mean even more so for God, to use the personal pronoun *I*—for example, "I conceive of this," "I valuate that," "I choose to do this," "I am who I am." What could Whitehead's description of God possibly mean?

Viewed as primordial, he is the unlimited conceptual realization of the absolute wealth of potentiality, . . . [but] so far is he from "eminent reality,"

1. *Process and Reality: An Essay in Cosmology* (New York: Harper and Row, 1957), p. 380.
2. Ibid., p. 524.
3. Ibid.
4. Ibid., p. 46.

that in this abstraction he is "deficiently actual"—and this in two ways. His feelings are only conceptual and so lack the fulness of actuality. Secondly, conceptual feelings, apart from complex integration with physical feelings, are devoid of consciousness in their subjective forms.[5]

'If ever there were a "ghost in the machine," here is one! The language is full of inconsistencies and illegitimate use of models. Whitehead employs the personal pronoun *he* to describe an abstraction that has no consciousness yet is somehow capable of the unlimited conceptual realization of the absolute wealth of potentiality. Now potentialities are possible actualities, and the highest actuality we experience as persons is consciousness. Is it then possible for God to realize conceptually the high potential of consciousness without being conscious? Can an unconscious abstraction conceive of consciousness?

I confess that such language makes little sense to me. What would "conceptual feelings . . . devoid of consciousness" be for God, unless they are the old forms of Plato's world of ideas? But then Plato never made the categorical mistake of positing the forms in the unconscious mind of a being referred to as "he." Plato is accordingly more consistent than Whitehead in that the eternal forms are purely abstract, although he too is faced with the insuperable problem of explaining how there can be independent and abstract ideal forms without some actual Agent who conceives of them. Can pure abstractions be self-subsistent?

Whitehead tries to explain God's consciousness as synthetic feeling that integrates physical and conceptual feelings. Consciousness is therefore the subjective form of an intellectual feeling of God whereby he synthesizes, effecting a contrast between an actuality and a real possibility; that is, he brings together the primordial and consequent natures in synthesis.[6] Thus it is clear in Whitehead's theory that God's consciousness depends upon a real physical world. We may ask, however, how Whitehead can sustain the notion that God's consciousness arises only upon his intellectual synthesis with some physical world, when he claims that God as primordial "is the unconditioned actuality of conceptual feeling at the base of things."[7] How does an abstraction "feel"? What could an abstract "feeling" possibly be? Moreover, the modifying word *conceptual* is the adjectival form of "conceive," from the Latin *concipio* (*com + capio*), "to take together, hold together." Likewise to be conscious or to have consciousness is "to have knowledge together, to know together" (Latin, *com + scio*). In both cases the primordial meaning is verbal action

5. Ibid., p. 521.
6. Ibid., pp. 286, 326, 371-72, 407-8.
7. Ibid., p. 522.

by an agent; it is action (*capio, scio*) performed by the agent that results in unity (*com*).

So it must be with God as primordial. If "His unity of conceptual operations is a free creative act,"[8] then it is illogical to deny that in freely and creatively acting God is conscious, for only a personal agent can actively bring about such a highly sophisticated unity of conceptual operations. God is, after all, envisaging all conceivable possibilities, including possibilities of consciousness. Can he do that without being aware of what he is doing, without being aware of "awareness"? Whitehead is all the time using personal models in his definition of the primordial nature of God; but on analysis of what it means to be a person I judge that he is using personal models illegitimately. The difficulty in Whitehead's system is that he defines God's mental pole as the realm of pure possibilities. This primordial nature is "the unlimited conceptual realization of the absolute wealth of potentiality." But because the primordial nature is "deficiently actual," that is, it lacks the experience of a real world, it is really only an abstraction.

Now, my question is, since the primordial nature is described as potentiality rather than actuality, *who is doing the conceptualizing?* Can unconscious abstract potentiality *do* anything? How can Whitehead legitimately speak of the primordial nature as "he," and ascribe to "him" inexhaustible unconscious conceptuality? To speak of God's primordial "envisagement" as "unconditioned conceptual valuation" is to use a whole series of analogies drawn from conscious human experience. "Conceiving," "envisaging," and "valuating" are all terms that are drawn from the empirical experience and observation of what thinking, seeing, and valuating human beings do in their conscious activity as persons. What is this primordial nature of God that is not only the objective, fixed, atemporal hierarchy of all eternal objects (that would be strictly Platonic), but also the *subjective envisagement* and *valuation* of those eternal objects, and the one who provides the physical world with its initial aims? How could God be unconscious and yet primordially be a single actual entity with the attributes of person-subject-agent?

Consider the following passage in which Whitehead describes God's subjective primordial nature:

> The "primordial nature" of God is the concrescence of a unity of conceptual feelings, including among their data all eternal objects. The concrescence is directed by the subjective aim, that the subjective forms of the feelings shall

8. Ibid.

be such as to constitute the eternal objects into relevent lures of feelings severally appropriate for all realizable basic conditions.[9]

Here we seem to have an actual "agency of comparison"[10] which brings about the togetherness of the eternal objects *by its own decision.* This decision is necessary to fulfill the requirements of Whitehead's ontological principle, or principle of efficient and final causation: "This ontological principle means that actual entities are the only *reasons;* so that to search for a *reason* is to search for one or more actual entities."[11] He continues his argument:

> The notion of "substance" is transformed into that of "actual entity"; and the notion of "power" is transformed into the principle that the reasons for things are always to be found in the composite nature of definite actual entities—in the nature of God for reasons of the highest absoluteness, and in the nature of definite temporal actual entities for reasons which refer to a particular environment. The ontological principle can be summarized as: no actual entity, then no reason.[12]

I would agree that actuality precedes potentiality, preeminently so in God; it is another way of saying that behind reasons are actual agents, and behind the totality of reasons for the universe is, in the highest sense, God himself as Agent. But how does the primordial nature of God in any sense qualify as an actual entity or agent, since it does not have any consequent actuality through the real world of actualities? Proponents of Whiteheadian metaphysics might reply (and have replied to me) that one cannot separate the primordial nature from the consequent nature of God: the two natures comprise an indissoluble unity. But that is to beg the question, for Whitehead gives the primordial nature if not a temporal yet certainly a logical priority, and the logical priority begs us to ask how it is possible for this primordial nature, to which are assigned personal attributes of agency, to act as agent when it is nonpersonal and without actuality?

My own view, with biblical, historic Christianity, is that God in himself *is* the highest Actuality, the infinite personal God, the Supreme Agent, than whom nothing greater can be conceived. His own "time," his own "space," if we may speak analogically, is beyond imagining, but are best understood in terms of his self-contained sociality within his own triunity. God's nature is defined in biblical Christianity as the "process" of eternal

9. Ibid., p. 134.
10. Ibid., p. 48.
11. Ibid., pp. 36f.
12. Ibid., p. 28.

love between Father, Son, and Holy Spirit (John 14). Even Thomas Aquinas, who is most under attack by process thinkers as the principal advocate of the immutable God, hints at God's "inexhaustibility."[13] This divine process is quite independent of any created finite process, although Love's Gift has brought the world into being and he sustains it by the word of his power. Biblical classical Christianity does not admit any claim to independent power on the part of the created universe, other than what God has freely given it. Whatever existence and freedom creatures possess is a gift of divine grace. The alternative of process theology leads directly to a metaphysical dualism where the finite creation brings God to consciousness and provides the concrete material of his experience. The dualistic metaphysics of Whitehead and Hartshorne requires that God have some universe or other forever. I challenge this speculative notion on logical as well as biblical grounds and defend the classical Christian doctrine that God is self-contained sociality within his own triunity, eternally conscious and actual.

What then, we ask, would Whitehead's primordial nature of God be, this nontemporal act of becoming that seems to have most of the essential characteristics of an actual entity and yet is not? As Lewis S. Ford has remarked, it would be a mistake to interpret God's primordial envisagement as a merely passive contemplation of a realm of eternal objects inherently ordered and quite independent of God's own activity. On the contrary, Whitehead argues that the very ordering is God's primordial decision.[14] This opens up another problem in Whitehead's view of God, for when he says that God "does not create eternal objects; for his nature requires them in the same degree that they require him,"[15] he fashions a double dualism by placing God in debt to two external givens: the eternal objects on his primordial side and the physical world on his consequent side. This sounds very Platonic, with the demiurge sandwiched between eternal forms and eternal matter.

In what sense is God, primordially speaking, an actual agent? Whitehead has him ordering and differentiating the basic, bare, given, uncreated "sensa," or pure emotional forms, "the lowest category of eternal objects," whatever these might be.[16] Following his fundamental metaphysi-

---

13. See Aquinas, *Summa Catholicae fidei contra Gentiles* 1. 22; Frederick Copleston, *A History of Philosophy*, 5 vols. (New York: Doubleday, 1962), vol. 2, pt. 2, pp. 75–81.

14. *Process and Reality*, p. 392.

15. Ibid.

16. Ibid., p. 174. See Whitehead's discussion of the sensum/sensa in *Process and Reality*, pp. 100, 172–78, 185, 193, 257–67, 479, 496. Whitehead is very vague as to the content of sensa, allowing that they are both simple as pure emotional forms, and complex in that they represent potential patterned relationships with other eternal objects, and ultimately with actual entities in the world. I have not a clue, however, to the meaning of a bare sensum in the primordial realm of eternal objects. How can one speak of pure "feeling" when there is no actual thing or person who feels?

cal principle that higher levels rise from lower by means of ingression, and that consciousness is the result of what begins with basic atomicity ("the ultimate metaphysical truth is atomism"),[17] Whitehead posits primordial atomic sensa as the ultimate uncreated givens with which even God must work in his primordial state; but he never defines these low-category eternal objects. What would these sheer qualities be, and how could they have independent status logically prior to God himself? The clue to Whitehead's thinking on ultimacy is his notion of creativity:

> In all philosophic theory there is an ultimate which is actual in virtue of its accidents. It is only then capable of characterization through its accidental embodiments, and apart from these accidents is termed "creativity"; and God is its primordial, non-temporal accident.[18]

This speculative system repudiates the classical Christian belief that nothing is prior to God, and that if we are to speak of eternal forms at all, they are to be conceived as generated by God's own conscious creativity.

But not only is Whitehead's notion of uncreated sensa a serious problem. More difficult is how an unconscious God creates relationships between the lowest category of eternal objects, the bare sensa; generates the higher categories of eternal objects out of complex integrations of conceptual prehensions of these sensa; differentiates and contrasts the sensa and thus brings an integrity of inner unity and distinctiveness; makes decisions (literally "cutting off") by discriminating, envisaging, and valuating all conceivable possibilities, including the most sophisticated possibilities of consciousness: and he does all this without consciousness! Yet surely the necessary Being and First Cause cannot be less perfect than what proceeds from it and depends on it.[19]

I think Whitehead's metaphysical principle of incurable atomicity is basically at fault here, and is philosophically untenable. He does not have a truly satisfactory concept of "person," of what it means to refer to the first person pronoun *I*. Like ourselves, says Whitehead, God concresces as a unity of conceptual feelings. This concrescing primordial nature of God is directed by his subjective aim and constitutes the eternal into relevant lures for feelings for all possible conditions.[20]

But what is this "subjective aim" of God? What is this "unity" of conceptual feelings? And how, logically, does it concresce? (Of course, in the realm of God's nontemporal nature we can speak only of logical, not

17. Ibid., p. 53. "Actuality is incurably atomic," p. 95. See also pp. 104, 178, 188, 213, 359, 365, 471.
18. Ibid., p. 11; see also pp. 30f., 46, 130, 135, 197, 249, 324, 339, 528.
19. See Copleston, *A History of Philosophy*, vol. 2, pt. 2, p. 116.
20. Whitehead, *Process and Reality*, p. 134.

temporal, relationships.) What is God's "subjective aim"? At what point logically does it appear, and how, since the incurable atomicity of the bare sensa, the lower order of eternal objects, is logically prior to the concrescing subject, God? Do the sensa logically concresce so as to produce God? But how could they possibly do that? Where does the subject, the "I," of God's subjective aim come into the picture? It is much the same problem (only on a larger scale) that Whitehead and Hartshorne face with the concept of human persons and the meaning of the personal pronoun *I*. Buddhism, to which the process school is rather similar, shares many of the same difficulties with respect to the concept of person.

Is it possible to conceive of the primordial nature of God as unconscious, considering that he does all the personal ordering and envisaging that conscious human beings do, and infinitely more? Indeed, God orders *all conceivable possibilities*, whereas human beings order only a finite and immediate number of situations. If God as primordial orders all conceivable possibilities,[21] then among these possibilities are possibilities involving consciousness on all levels of intensity. To entertain possibilities of consciousness, God must be primordially conscious. But he cannot be, because Whitehead complicates the problem by insisting that "consciousness only arises in a late derivative phase of complex integrations with the physical world."[22] Consciousness, he says, is the negative perception, the feeling of negation, of "the contrast between the 'theory' which *may* be erroneous and the fact which is 'given.' Thus consciousness involves the rise into importance of the contrast between the eternal objects designated by the words 'any' and 'just that.'"[23]

Whitehead illogically attributes this definition of consciousness only to the consequent nature of God as God contrasts his primordial aims with the actual physical world, and thus becomes conscious and aware.[24] A key line, however, is Whitehead's remark that "a pure concept does not involve consciousness, at least in our human experience."[25] The qualifying words *at least* must be taken for their full value. It would seem to me that the primordial nature of God must be functioning at an extremely high level of consciousness to do its ordering, deciding, valuating, and envisaging of all conceivable possibilities. If it is true (and I would agree that it is true) that "in some 'decisions' consciousness will be a factor,"[26] then with God it must be consummately so in his primordial nature.

It is my contention that God's primordial nature must be conscious, first, because to fulfill the ontological principle God has to be an actual

21. Ibid., pp. 46, 245.
22. Ibid., p. 245.
23. Ibid. His italics.
24. Ibid., pp. 369–70.
25. Ibid., p. 371.
26. Ibid., p. 68.

entity; secondly, because God's primordial "decision," in the root sense of "cutting off," makes valuations that require high-level consciousness; thirdly, because the actual eternal forms and God as primordially actual fulfill, respectively, the relativity of decision "whereby every decision expresses the relation of the actual thing, *for which* a decision is made, to an actual thing *by which* that decision is made."[27]

In spite of Whitehead's claim that God is devoid of consciousness in the abstraction of his primordial actuality,[28] I hold that a proper use of personal models, which Whitehead is continually employing, requires God's primordial consciousness. What actually is decided by God's primordial, nontemporal decision? According to Whitehead, God avoids chaos by "cutting off" certain possible relations of eternal objects as impossible possibilities. God distinguishes, in other words, between possibility and impossibility,[29] thus making negative as well as positive decisions. God's pure, conceptual prehensions of the bare sensa require not only positive decisions as he includes their data in the synthesis of his subjective envisagement of the real possibilities, but also must (contrary to Whitehead's system) require negative decisions as well, as God primordially "decides" upon the order and importance of formal combinations of possibilities.[30]

But I am unhappy about the use of prehensions as a description of God's primordial working on the bare forms; for prehensions are in Whitehead's analysis the general and lower levels, devoid of consciousness, on which an occasion includes other actual entities or eternal objects. Whitehead is really using personal models of *com*-prehension when he speaks of God deciding, ordering, and envisaging all conceivable possibilities. Certainly God must be primordially conscious to an eminent degree to achieve such a highly sophisticated ordering of all conceivable possibilities. The fundamental problem in Whitehead's metaphysics, it seems to me, is his doctrine of atomicity: discrete atomic units are prior to God's consciousness as they are to our consciousness, only to an eminent degree. But the system does not work, either for us or for God.

My conclusion is that Whitehead's description of God as primordial is impossible in view of the personal qualities required by all the activities he assigns him. The consequent nature of God fares little better: while God is conscious because of the effect the physical world has upon him, he remains deficient in that he is forever incomplete, due to the everlasting flow of time and the unknown novelty of the future.[31]

27. Ibid. His italics.
28. Ibid., pp. 521f.
29. Ibid., pp. 28, 64, 522.
30. On the matter of prehensions, see *Process and Reality*, pp. 35, 88f., 133.
31. See ibid., p. 524.

It is troubling, but not surprising, to find two of the foremost interpreters of Whitehead carrying on his legacy of God as abstraction, and I find in their metaphysical speculations the same tendency to misuse person language. The first, Ford, develops a "process trinitarianism" in terms of abstract principles.[32] The formula of classical Christian trinitarianism, "one substance in three persons," is dismissed as "a fatal ambiguity," for either it means, Ford says, "one actuality having three distinct aspects" or "three distinct subjectivities inherent in one divine substratum." But if it is the latter (which is the true classical doctrine), then, says Ford, Whitehead has precluded that possibility by his insistence that there cannot be a vacuous actuality; that is, there is an intrinsic connection between substantial unity and subjectivity in the sense that every substantial unity enjoys its own subjectivity. The divine substance or substratum in which the three persons inhere is the very vacuous actuality devoid of its own subjectivity that Whitehead rejects. Whitehead's doctrine would require that three persons entail three substances, while one substance entails a single person.[33]

Now the curious thing about this argument is that Whitehead's view of person, whether of human person or of divine person, has no place for the word *substance* at all. There is no substantial self that unifies all processive occasions of experience, but only the processive occasions themselves. It is illicit for Whitehead or Ford, therefore, to argue that three persons require three substantial unities, when the central doctrine of process thought is that there is no substance that underlies the concrescing occasions. This is the most damaging deficiency in process metaphysics. Who is this "I" who continually surpasses "himself," this "actual entity" that is forever perishing and being taken up into a new "actual occasion"? Where is the identity of the "one," the continuity that is signified by the personal pronoun *I* or the other personal pronouns *you*, *he*, or *she* that indicate a conscious, creative, and responsible agent who continually stands in back of spoken and acted language? Although Whitehead does speak sparingly of the actual entity as activated by its own "substantial form,"[34] he does not have in mind a substantial subject with predicates. Rather, the predicates or "the feelings are inseparable from the end at which they aim; and this end is the feeler. The feelings aim at the feeler, as their final cause. The feelings are what they are in order that their subject may be what it is. . . . An actual entity feels as it does in order to be the actual entity which it is."[35]

32. Lewis S. Ford, "Process Trinitarianism," *Journal of the American Academy of Religion* 43 (June 1975): 207, 213.
    33. Ibid., p. 207.
    34. *Process and Reality*, pp. 336-60.
    35. Ibid., p. 339.

But surely this is circular reasoning. It doesn't really pin down the subject (or "superject," as Whitehead prefers to call it)[36] in any substantial way as the creative agent who stands in back of the process. The actual entity, whatever it is, is characterized by self-causation, says Whitehead.[37] But it is the word *self* that troubles me: what or who is this "self" which seems to emerge into personhood through the confluence of myriad lesser actual entities that comprise the body of feeling? How is it even possible for the unity of a subject to emerge as the result of the integrations of atomic feelings? For Whitehead's primary doctrine is that there is not first a subject, which then sorts out feelings; there are first feelings which, through integration, acquire the unity of a subject. "Process doesn't presuppose a subject; rather the subject emerges from the process."[38]

Yet Whitehead realizes that something does not come from nothing. Sheer chance will not produce a unity of feelings, much less a complex unified organism like a conscious human being. There is, therefore, a subjective aim in the process which is God's lure or ideal for that emerging actual entity. The subjective aim has to do with the direction to be taken by the concrescing subject that characterizes its very being.[39] But as Whitehead insists, this subjective aim is only God's lure, is only a divine proposition of potentiality seeking fully determinate actuality in the concrescing entity.

Two serious problems arise from this description. The first we have already considered: To what extent is process thought willing to grant that God's subjective aim for the concrescing subject is efficacious; that is, what is the ratio of his control to the freedom of the emerging agent to accept it or reject it? Surely a good deal rides on the answer to this question if God is not to emerge as a tyrant (Whitehead's greatest phobia), or as inconsequential and impotent.

But let us put that aside for the moment. Assuming that God's subjective aim has some efficacy in holding the physical world together and guiding it to some intensity of harmonious feeling, our second question is, who or what is this independent *causa sui* that Whitehead calls the subjective form, the "how" a feeling is felt by the concrescing subject of that feeling? How does this independent self-caused subjective form come into being if it is produced by the less actual entities that comprise it (each of which has its own subjective form), and by the subjective aim which derives from God's lure for ideal unity? Whence does the actual

36. Ibid.
37. Ibid.
38. Donald Sherburne, *A Key to Whitehead's Process and Reality* (New York: Macmillan, 1966), p. 244. See his synopsis of subjective aim and subjective form, pp. 244f., 28ff.
39. Whitehead, *Process and Reality*, p. 342.

subject-superject emerge, who or what is it, and how does it claim independence from or authority over its constituent parts? What is the mechanism in process by which a conscious actual entity called a person can claim atomic independence of God and of the constituent assembly of actual entities that comprise its body? Whitehead says that "the subject, thus constituted, is the autonomous master of its own concrescence into subject-superject."[40] Where does this autonomous energy come from, and who is the autonomous master who emerges as the result of the concrescing process, peaks, perishes, and is succeeeded by an endless series of self-surpassing selves until it finally perishes in death? Where is the continuous subject-superject who can claim substantial identity from beginning to end? How does Western process thought avoid the same problem of personal identity that plagues Eastern Buddhism?

40. Ibid., p. 374.

3

From West to East

Neo-Buddhist Tendencies
in the Process Theism of Hartshorne and Cobb

I t is not surprising that process theology shares some of the same weaknesses in its concept of persons and the personal pronoun *I* as Buddhism, with which it acknowledges many affinities. John B. Cobb, Jr., remarks in a recent article how Alfred North Whitehead early on "noted that every philosophy requires an ultimate that is actual only in its instantiation."

> In *Science and the Modern World* he called this ultimate "substantial activity," and he related it specifically to Spinoza's substance. But by the time he wrote *Process and Reality* the note of substantiality was gone. The ultimate is creativity, and creativity is nothing other than the many becoming one and being increased by one. Creativity is neither a being nor Being. It is remarkably like the ancient Buddhist dependent co-origination.[1]

The Buddhist term for dependent coorigination is *pratitya-samutpadha*, where "all the elements jointly constitute the new event which is then an element in the constitution of others. Both as event and as an element in other events it is empty."[2] Cobb speculates that a

1. John B. Cobb, Jr., "Buddhist Emptiness and the Christian God," *Journal of the American Academy of Religion* 45 (March 1977): 16.
2. Ibid., p. 15.

Christian theology of ultimate Emptiness is compatible with the Buddhist doctrine of Emptiness, and he brings them together in terms of Martin Heidegger's Being and Whitehead's doctrine of creativity, the pure potentiality and possibility of creative advance. Insofar as God is, he is empty of substantiality:

> That would mean recognizing that God does not possess a being different in kind from the being of other entities which has been displayed as Emptiness. God, too, must be empty, just as the self, and all things are empty—empty of substantiality or own-being, and lacking in any given character of their own. God like all things must be an instance of dependent co-origination.[3]

Aside from Cobb's rather dogmatic insistence on what God "must" be, what is really questionable is his assumption that the self, any self, is empty of substantiality or own-being and therefore lacks any given character of its own. It is difficult to imagine what a reference to the personal pronoun *I* could possibly mean when the substantial self is dissolved into sheer "empty process." This is the triumph of Protagoras with a vengeance, and has long been my principal criticism of the Buddhist analysis of the self. What is the value of "co-" in dependent cooirigination if the substantial self is dissolved? This is not to mention the peculiar difficulty Buddhism faces when it tries to explain the continuity of the "self" that is held to be responsible to the law of karma in its transmigration from one life to the next.

But Cobb realizes that an empty ultimate that is "freedom from all distorting perceptions and concerns and perfect openness to all that is, human and nonhuman alike," opens the door to all kinds of ethical problems.[4] Accordingly, he posits a second ultimate. If Emptiness or Creativity is the metaphysical ultimate, then God is the second ultimate, the principle of rightness.[5] Hence we are back again to my original criticism of process thought—that it is essentially a dualism—only this time Cobb has explicitly stated it as a dogma. In his speculative system the metaphysical ultimate is Whitehead's creativity and Buddhist Emptiness combined, which means that "God" in this sense (if the term is at all appropriate) is completely undiscriminating, like the enlightened Buddhist, only supremely so. Creativity and Emptiness simply receive all things for just what they are in their suchness:

3. Ibid., p. 22.
4. Ibid.
5. Ibid., pp. 22-25.

God is constituted by the progressive unification of all actuality with all possibility. Each actuality and every possibility is allowed to be just what it is in the process of dependent co-origination or concrescence. God is undiscriminatingly benevolent towards all. There are no distortions in God's perceptions and concerns preventing God's perfect openness toward all that is, human and nonhuman alike. Thus "God" can be freed from the note of substantiality and dualism that makes this concept offensive to the Buddhist.[6]

Here Cobb has departed, I think, from Whitehead's original definition of creativity as the potentiality for novelty in everlasting creative advance. For Whitehead it is the category of the ultimate that brings the many into complex and novel unity forever—"to the crack of doom in the creative advance from creature to creature."[7] The "crack of doom" passage is a curious contradiction in itself, for the metaphor of doom bespeaks the inevitability of entropy, while the metaphor of "creative advance" characterizes the evolutionary optimism that is central to Whitehead's process metaphysics. The two notions are mutually incompatible and disclose the most serious problem of contemporary materialistic scientism. Evolutionary advance and entropy can be reconciled only in a pulsating view of the universe, or in an endless sine wave of peaks and valleys. In an infinity of time all possibilities (which would have been arranged in priorities and limited by the primordial nature of God) would already have been realized (an infinite number of times?).

But in classical Hinayana or Therevada Buddhism the doctrine of *pratitya-samutpadha* does not suggest a metaphysical basis for everlasting creative advance (a modern Western idea that has its roots in evolutionary doctrine). Quite the opposite. It is designed to show that since there is no substantial self, or anything substantial at all, there is no reason to suffer through attachment to anything in the processing world, for suffering (*dukha*) is the result of craving (*tanha*), and craving can be eliminated only by realizing that the whole process of the "self becoming" is empty of substantiality. Salvation, if it may be called that, comes from the enlightened realization that one must not impose self-interest upon what is, but simply allow everything to be what it is—pure processive emptiness, devoid of any substantiality. The fire (*vana*) of deluded attachment to things as though they were substantial must be blown out (*nirvana* = "no fire or flame"). Nirvana is cessation of attachment to the substantiality of being and the loss of becoming. It is nonattachment and emptiness. When one achieves the realization that all is empty

6. Ibid., p. 23.

7. *Process and Reality: An Essay in Cosmology* (New York: Harper and Row, 1957), p. 347. See also pp. 31f.

insubstantiality—no God, no self, no-thing enduring—then one is said to have found peace from the attachment that brings sorrow.[8]

Whitehead conceives of creativity quite differently. For him the emptiness or potentiality of creativity leads to the *satisfaction* of the actual entity in terms of the process itself. Satisfaction involves the fulfillment of the actual entity as superject, including the intensities of individual emotions in a narrow dimension, and the savoring of the complexity of the universe in a bond of wider dimension.[9] The goal of creativity is therefore not the empty nonattachment of Buddhism but the attainment of peculiar definiteness and objective immortality.[10]

But since positive and negative prehensions and conscious distinctions between good and bad are involved in realizing the goal of satisfaction, it is necessary for Cobb to introduce a second ultimate, this time an ultimate of discrimination, which he terms the principle of rightness, or (properly) God. Otherwise, to acknowledge only the ultimate metaphysical Emptiness is to admit of no guidelines as to good or bad, desirable or undesirable. Whitehead, too, as we have seen, saves sheer creativity from meaningless randomness by introducing the order of eternal forms and the primordial nature of God, who arranges the raw forms in priorities of desirable possibilities and functions as the divine lure to creaturely activity.

In the following passage Cobb defends his transition from the formless and undiscriminating metaphysical ultimate of creativity to the necessity of the ethical God:

8. See Edward Conze et al., eds., *Buddhist Texts Through the Ages* (New York: Harper and Row, 1964), pp. 90-102: "The stopping of becoming is Nirvana" (Samyutta-nikāya II, 117); "Wherefore is the world called empty because it is empty of self and of what belongs to self" (Samyutta-nikāya IV, 54); "To the extent that the freedoms of mind are immeasurable, are of no-thing, are signless, of them all unshakable freedom of mind is pointed to as chief, for it is empty of passion, empty of aversion, empty of confusion" (Majjhima-nikāya I, 297-98). It is precisely the doctrine of creative advance and its culmination in continual self-surpassing satisfaction that distinguishes Whiteheadian creativity from Buddhist Emptiness. The former sees creativity as the source of satisfaction (indeed, as the source of reality), while the latter views it as the source of pain and unreality. No Whiteheadian would ever express the following Buddhist sentiment: "But if we neither will nor intend to do, are not occupied with something, there is no object for the support of consciousness; hence no foothold for it; with consciousness having no foothold or growth, there is no rebirth or recurrent becoming in the future" (Samyutta-nikāya II, 65f., in Conze, *Buddhist Texts*, p. 71). Accordingly, Cobb's translation of *pratitya-samutpadha* as "dependent co-origination" is better rendered simply "conditional genesis," or "dependent origination," without the "co-." See Conze, *Buddhist Texts*, pp. 65, 70.

9. Whitehead, *Process and Reality*, pp. 251f., 71. Compare pp. 38, 129, 233, 335.

10. Ibid., p. 340.

Buddhism teaches that this ultimate is indeed devoid of form and beyond good and evil, as mystics have often said. It is exemplified without discrimination in a cockroach, a human child, God, and an atomic explosion. It is not evident that this is the one ultimate that should guide all human attention, effort and reflection. If there is importance in the shape that dependent co-origination or concrescence takes, if it matters whether the universe is full of life or allowed to die, then we should attend to God.

Then he adds: "It is meaningless to speak of Emptiness as superior to God or of God as superior to Emptiness. They are incommensurable."[11]

Yet surely if the components of this ultimate dualism are "incommensurable" (that is, having no common measure or standard of comparison, utterly disproportionate), Cobb has not really honored the incommensurability. In the passage just quoted he lists God as one item in a random list of items, including a cockroach, a human child, and an atomic explosion. If that is so, then comparatively speaking, creativity includes God and is therefore commensurably greater. That this is the case seems clear from his earlier definition of God as empty:

> That would mean recognizing that God does not possess a being different in kind from the being of other entities, which has been displayed as Emptiness. God, too, must be empty, just as the self, and all things are empty— empty of substantiality or own-being, and lacking in any given character of their own. God like all things must be an instance of dependent co-origination.[12]

The logic and clarity of this argument are patently deficient. If God is empty, how can he in any sense be the principle of rightness, since rightness means discriminating between right and wrong, better and worse? God is not an exception to the categories of creativity, says Cobb, since the principle of universal relativity includes God. Indeed, in Buddhist terms,

> ... God may be conceived as the totally enlightened one, the supreme and everlasting Buddha, who does not juxtapose self-interest and the good of others, but as the enlightened one is equally benevolent toward all. Emptiness is freedom from all distorting perceptions and concerns and perfect openness to all that is.... God is undiscriminatingly benevolent towards all. There are no distortions in God's perfect openness toward all that is, human and nonhuman alike. Thus "God" can be freed from the note of substantiality and dualism that makes this concept offensive to the Buddhist.[13]

11. Cobb, "Buddhist Emptiness," p. 24.
12. Ibid., p. 22.
13. Ibid., pp. 22f.

Having bent over so far backward to please the Buddhist, however, Cobb has totally forsaken the Christian by defining "God," supposedly the saving principle of rightness, in terms befitting Whitehead's metaphysical ultimate of creativity—except for one inconsistency that also mars the Buddhist description of the enlightened one: namely, that he is "undiscriminatingly benevolent" toward all. That is an impossible combination of words, for one is either undiscriminating, in which case it would be as improper to say that he is benevolent as to say that he is malevolent toward all; or that he is benevolent, in which case he has already willed (*volo*) to be loving or well-intentioned (*bene*) toward all. Thus both the Buddhist and Cobb have imported discriminating notions or ethical principles of rightness (in the case of the Buddhist, the Eightfold Path) into what should be pure undiscriminated "thatness."

How, then, is God the principle of rightness that Cobb sees as so necessary, since we assume it matters to him "whether the universe is full of life or allowed to die." That question is not answered, nor is it at all clear in what sense God has any power to impose "his" principle(s) of rightness upon the "suchness" of the creative process if he is no exception to the process, but is, like ourselves, empty of substantiality, own-being, or any given character.

Cobb's suggestion of two ultimates is fraught with problems and contradictions; but since we have been dealing with neo-Buddhist concepts of the self in this chapter and the difficulty of pinning down the meaning of the personal pronoun *I* in process theism, it would appear that Cobb is farther away than even Lewis S. Ford in allowing any conscious personality in God. My major objection to Cobb's speculative dualism is that neither his metaphysical ultimate of emptiness and creativity nor his ultimate principle of rightness, God, is capable of being or doing anything remotely resembling the God of the Old and New Testaments. In the sacred Scriptures, which I take to be the trustworthy self-revelation of God regarding his own being and redemptive activity on behalf of humankind, he is the supremely righteous Actuality who benevolently "makes his sun rise on the evil and on the good, and sends rain on the just and on the unjust" (Matt. 5:45), and thus is the one Source of life and process (sun and rain), Cobb's metaphysical ultimate, and the personal source of righteous discrimination (the just and the unjust), Cobb's principle of rightness.

Persons Act As Agents; Principles Are Abstractions

It must be remembered that principles do not do anything; persons do. Principles are merely abstractions that persons use to describe certain behavior, and must not be mistaken for the agent who is acting. Whitehead warned against committing "the fallacy of misplaced concreteness," and was himself eminently guilty of it when he ascribed personal activity and personal pronouns to the unconscious and impersonal primordial nature of God. Ford is also guilty of the fallacy when he reduces the Trinity to abstract principles, as is Cobb when he offers two sheer abstractions as ultimates. This simply will not do. It is illicit use of language drawn from actual persons acting as agents. But it does illustrate the modern penchant for reducing wholes to abstract and impersonal parts. It would be well to remind Whiteheadians what their mentor himself said of the fallacy of misplaced concreteness:

> This fallacy consists in neglecting the degree of abstraction involved when an actual entity is considered merely so far as it exemplifies certain categories of thought. There are aspects of actualities which are simply ignored so long as we restrict thought to these categories. Thus the success of a philosophy is to be measured by its comparative avoidance of this fallacy, when thought is restricted within its categories.[14]

According to biblical revelation, God is the consummate actualization of the personal pronoun *I*, the "I AM WHO I AM" (*'ehyeh 'ašer 'ehyeh*, from *hâyâh*, "to be" [Exod. 3:14]). The beauty of the Hebrew imperfect verb form in this passage is that it allows a comprehensive meaning that satisfies the requirements of being and becoming: He is the supreme personal "I" (John 1:1, 12), not the abstraction or the principle, but the infinite Person himself who creates and sustains the creation; engages in the redemption of his people in the process of history (the God of Abraham, Isaac, and Jacob [Exod. 3:15]); and is defined as the substantial and changeless "I am who I am," the sovereign Creator ("I cause to be what I cause to be"), and the processive yet autonomous and changeless Lord of redemptive history ("I will be who I will be"). All these translations are correct and are contained in the original tetragrammaton *YHWH*, which discloses the God who is radically different from an abstract and impersonal metaphysical being or becoming. He is the eternal, autonomous, living God who also writes his signature as a promise that he will be faithful to his people in every time present and future, as he has been in the past.

God is without change, and yet he is the supreme creator of and participant in change. The theophany of the burning bush powerfully symbolizes this merismus or paradox of polarities: "The bush was burning, yet it was not consumed" (Exod. 3:2). Metaphorically God burns with creative power, yet he does not change. The divine appellation *Yahweh* is

---

14. Whitehead, *Process and Reality*, p. 11.

purposely mysterious because it contains a panoply of attributes that are used in speculative metaphysics of seemingly disparate powers or principles; but the name also serves warning against such speculative systems, for God can be known only as he chooses to disclose himself. And he, the infinite personal God, has chosen to reveal himself in a way that is analogous to the self-revelation of human persons who are made in his image. In the New Testament the consummate self-revelation of God is through the person of his Son, who is both the preexistent and eternal Word (being) and the incarnate Word in spacetime (becoming): "In the beginning was the Word, and the Word was with God, and the Word was God. . . . And the Word became flesh and dwelt among us, full of grace and truth" (John 1:1, 14).

This is the reason I am now convinced that a far better route, in fact the only possible route, to travel in resolving the question of the relation between the one and the many, being and becoming, of "thatness" and "rightness," is to follow canonical biblical revelation. This heuristic commitment allows one to appreciate the power of biblical merismus, namely, that mystery or apparent paradoxes in religious propositions are perfectly legitimate, especially when they derive from the self-disclosing Agent, God himself. The questions with which we are dealing in this book are unavoidable paradoxes, but they are logically explorable. They are logically explorable because they are anchored in God's empirical disclosure in history and are recorded propositionally in the Holy Scriptures. There is a logical character to religious language because of its empirical anchorage in the disclosure situation. As I. T. Ramsey says:

> The logical behavior of "I" then, being grounded in a disclosure and ultimately distant from all descriptive language while nevertheless associated with it, is a good clue to that of "God," and we can expect the paradoxes of "I" to help us somewhat in our logical explorations of unavoidable religious paradox, to help us distinguish the bogus from the defensible.[15]

Biblical theology, which focuses on the mystery or merismus of personal models, is more reliable than a paradoxical theism that uses impersonal models. Whitehead, Cobb, and Ford all end up with largely unexplorable paradoxes in their doctrines of God because they insist on employing impersonal analogies. As Ramsey says, "'I' is the best (perhaps the only) clue to all genuine mystery, all sublime paradox. . . ."[16]

---

15. "Paradox in Religion," *Proceedings of the Aristotelian Society* (suppl. vol. 33, 1959), reprinted in Dallas M. High, ed., *New Essays on Religious Language* (New York: Oxford University Press, 1969), p. 159. See also Ramsey, "The Systematic Elusiveness of 'I,'" *Philosophical Quarterly*, vol. 5 (July 1955): 193–204; William H. Poteat, "God and the 'Private I,'" in High, *New Essays on Religious Language*, pp. 127–37.

16. In High, *New Essays on Religious Language*, p. 161.

An analysis of the use of "I" by God in the Old Testament and by Jesus in the New Testament gives far clearer disclosure of the nature of God than speculative metaphysics, since the latter begins with finite assumptions and employs (in the case of Whitehead, Cobb, and Ford) abstract, impersonal models of God, while biblical faith has long been characterized by its confidence that God is personally speaking in the scriptural texts. As William H. Poteat has argued, God is not a thing, any more than a human person is a thing, since a *thing* can be exhausted by predicates in a sentence. What cannot be exhausted is the "I" who stands in back of his words and acts with his own privacy, mystery, and paradox. "Person" is not a concept that can be logically assimilated to "thing" language without remainder.[17] The pronoun *I* always functions reflexively, in that it names the namer who is systematically elusive.[18]

Thus, if God's "I" is not exhausted by his words and acts in Scripture, although his words and acts adequately disclose his nature for our salvation, then even less is he reducible to speculative abstractions, such as the word *principle*. As C. S. Lewis wisely observed,

> [I]f God is the ultimate source of all concrete, individual things and events, then God Himself must be concrete, and individual in the highest degree. Unless the origin of all other things were itself concrete and individual, nothing else could be so; for there is no conceivable means whereby what is abstract or general could itself produce concrete actuality.[19]

Lewis continues with this compelling argument:

> God is basic Fact or Actuality, the source of all other facthood. At all costs therefore He must not be thought of as featureless generality. If He exists at all, He is the most concrete thing there is, the most individual, "organised and minutely articulated." He is unspeakable not by being indefinite but by being too definite for the unavoidable vagueness of language. The words *incorporeal* and *impersonal* are misleading, because they suggest that He lacks some reality we possess. It would be safer to call Him *trans-corporeal, trans-personal*. Body and personality as we know them are the real negatives—they are what is left of positive being when it is sufficiently

---

17. As Schubert M. Ogden tried to do in *Christ Without Myth: A Study Based on the Theology of Rudolf Bultmann* (New York: Harper, 1961), when he proposed that "Christian faith is to be interpreted exhaustively and without remainder as man's original possibility of authentic existence as this is clarified and conceptualized by an appropriately philosophical analysis" (p. 146). The ponderous and abstract (not to mention arrogant) language of this enterprise almost condemns itself, but the attempt to remove God's "private 'I'" and reduce it to nonparadoxical and unmythological language is still very much in evidence in contemporary liberal theology.

18. Poteat, in High, *New Essays on Religious Language*, pp. 130f.

19. *Miracles: A Preliminary Study* (New York: Macmillan, 1973), p. 89.

diluted to appear in temporal or finite forms. Even our sexuality should be regarded as the transposition into a minor key of that creative joy which in Him is unceasing and irresistible. Grammatically the things we say of Him are "metaphorical": but in a deeper sense it is our physical and psychic energies that are mere "metaphors" of the real Life which is God. Divine Sonship is, so to speak, the solid of which biological sonship is merely a diagrammatic representation on the flat.[20]

The implications of this line of thinking are enormously fruitful, for Lewis helps us to conceive of God analogically as the ultimate Fact of unity and variety, being and "becoming" *within his own* transpersonal, transtemporal, and transspatial "time and space," as it were—the Source of the creative joy that is unceasing and irresistible. Moreover, God's personal disclosure by himself in biblical history has led to what we would not otherwise have guessed, although Paul says that if our minds were not rebellious and blind we should have been able to see the creative hand of God in nature, evidencing his very nature: "Ever since the creation of the world his invisible nature, namely, his eternal power and deity, has been clearly perceived in the things that have been made" (Rom. 1:20). The astounding truth of this passage is that God's ontological unity in society and society in unity as Triunity is derivatively evidenced in everything we can name in nature, for there is nothing we can name that is not at once unity in variety and variety in unity. God is the Archetype, nature is the ectype. For me, this suggests an ultimate solution of the problem of the one and the many which has perplexed philosophers since the days of the pre-Socratics and is yet in evidence today, unsolved by the naturalistic mind in the predominant philosophies of the many and becoming. Rather, as biblical faith affirms, God is ultimate Actuality and Fact, the supreme exemplification, analogically speaking, of what we see in his handiwork, namely, the mysterious union of the many and the one—from the world of the atoms to the human self to the vast universe around us.

Person Analysis:
A Means of Understanding the Nature of God

The analysis of persons lends itself, I think, as the best model by which to understand the complexity and unity of God, primarily because we are ourselves persons and have a privileged access to the experience of being a person. For this reason I have postponed a discussion of Charles Hartshorne's view of persons and God as person until now, since Hartshorne

20. Ibid., pp. 93f. His italics.

has argued as persuasively as any process thinker for the primacy of person analysis as a clue to the nature of God. God, he says, is a supreme person.[21] Hartshorne suggests that the Hebrew verb *hâyâh* in Exodus 3:14 be used to fashion a new word, "hayathology" or "hayathontology," to replace the old term *ontology*, and thus imply the creativity of the personal, living, and acting God.[22]

The Identity of the Self

In Hartshorne's metaphysics, God is a personally ordered, self-surpassing series of experiences in the social setting of some universe of other. With the doctrine of God's sociality I have no problem, for that is the principal significance of the Trinity—God is the Supreme Sociality. But I do object to Hartshorne's view that God requires a world for his experience of sociality. This is a whole universe apart from what the Scriptures and the church fathers have in mind when they speak of the intimate relationship between Father, Son, and Holy Spirit. Hartshorne's commitment to the principle of becoming forces him to attach God's experience exclusively to the changing processes of the material world. God, he says, is the most concrete and inclusive Self; but he

> can only be the divine Self-now as inheriting our momentary selves, Itself to be inherited by subsequent divine selves. A kind of neo-trinitarianism can be worked out from this—with, however, an infinity of Holy Spirits, rather than just one. There must indeed be a kind of "begetting" in the divine life.[23]

But in what way, I have to ask, is Hartshorne's God a self at all, in the sense of the personal pronoun *I* that denotes an enduring, substantial person who stands in back of changing experiences, words, and acts, and remains identical in some foundational sense through the continual process? Hartshorne does not give a satisfactory answer to this question, for with other process thinkers, he takes the category of creativity or becoming as absolute and is forced to speak of the identity of the self as a mere abstraction from the process. Thus he writes of "divine selves," in the plural, as though the processive movement from one state to the next necessitates an endless succession of selves, tied together only by anticipation and memory.

Yet once again we must ask the question, *who* is doing the remembering

---

21. See, for example, Hartshorne's *Logic of Perfection and Other Essays in Neoclassical Metaphysics* (La Salle, IL: Open Court, 1973), p. 4; and *The Divine Relativity: A Social Conception of God*, new ed. (New Haven: Yale University Press, 1964), pp. 142f.

22. *The Logic of Perfection*, p. 8. More accurate terms would be "hayatheology" or "hayontology."

23. Ibid., p. 122.

and the anticipating, since the old self is constantly being succeeded by a new self? Hartshorne is really a neo-Buddhist, by his own admission.[24] The characteristics of identity in the "self" Hartshorne terms abstractions from the concrete process of becoming. The ego is not a single entity that endures through a person's lifetime.

> No such ego is ever literally "conscious of itself." The self-now is the individual subject actually enjoying the present consciousness; later selves will enjoy it so far as they remember it; past selves did enjoy it only so far as they anticipated it. Any "timelessly the same" self, birth to death, is a mere abstraction. It does not literally do or know anything.[25]

Yet surely this will not do. If there is no sense in which the self is a contiguous and continuous identity over its tenure of life, other than as an abstraction that does not literally do or know anything, then we can speak only of an I-I-I-I-I series of unrelated actual occasions. What accounts for the identity of the self and the sense of the transcendence of the ego? A remark made not so long ago in my presence by a prominent process theologian illustrates the uncertain doctrine of the school. "I look inside myself," he observed, "and find only the processes of change; I see no changeless substance called the ego or the soul." My question was, "Who is the 'I' who is doing the looking on at 'myself' in the process?" There is an ordered continuity in the self that is more than the mere chance collocations of atoms or monads from which consciousness finally supervenes. The personal pronoun *I* is something we legitimately use for a lifetime, in spite of the continual metabolism of the body. It does not help to call this "I" or "ego" a mere abstraction from a series of "self-nows," when the point in question is *how* a series of self-nows is related in continuity so as to enable the processing self to refer to himself in some sense as the same today as he was yesterday.

A fundamental point that needs to be made here is that abstractions are not necessarily lifeless, although the term usually connotes that for most people. An abstraction is simply the description of an aspect of something whole and concrete. My point would be that the changeless characteristics of a person's life, that is, his mode of existing, or style, is very much alive and describes the actual manner in which he experiences his life—because his personal existence is comprised of both the change-able and the changeless. This brings us back to Ramsey's and Poteat's insistence that legitimate language must make room for paradoxical

24. Ibid., pp. 10, 17f., 122, 146, 273. He repudiates the pessimism of Buddhism and its blurring of past and future events with the present, but affirms its doctrine of the insubstantiality of the self.
25. Ibid., p. 122.

statements about ourselves and about God: I am becoming, and I am also being; I experience change, and I also experience identity. Otherwise, as Poteat reminds us, "person" becomes a concept logically assimilable to "thing" language without remainder.

The Question of Being and Becoming

There is an even more serious question that Hartshorne's process metaphysics must face, however. If the whole system is not to reduce to the sheer chaos of becoming, it must allow that God sets certain limits to creaturely becoming and in some sense lures the creature to divine ideals in the creative advance. The question is this: If God himself is conceived of along the lines of the becoming self (although eminently so), and if his becoming is necessarily dependent upon the concrescing material universe, in what sense and to what degree does he give prior and sovereign order to the direction the evolving process will take, since he seems to be more the consequence than the cause of what is? We earlier asked Hartshorne to what extent he sees God directing the process of creativity by setting its limits and ideals. We concluded that he feels God has very large prerogatives indeed, and that creaturely freedom is very small, although not insignificant.

Now my question is, who is this God who establishes the ideals of the world process and maintains its order, when his actual concrete existence is contingent upon the same processing physical world? Hartshorne argues that the world mind, God, has no special brain, but that every individual contributes to the "mind" of God as a sort of brain cell.[26] Thus, he writes, "the cosmic analogue of a brain will be simply the entire system of things as wholly internal and immediate to the cosmic mind. A special world-brain, so far from confirming the supposition of a truly cosmic mind, would negate it."[27]

This, I think, is the most difficult and unsatisfactory doctrine of Hartshorne's process metaphysics from the standpoint of biblical theism. It allows no independence for God external to the world. It allows no identical and independent substance to God, other than as an abstraction from the physical world: "The abiding ever-identical agent is an abstraction."[28] Hartshorne reasons that as one's finite self has a dominant member that is the synthetic act, or act-sequence, which derives its data from the nervous system, so God is the eminent dominant member of the cosmic body. But then Hartshorne avers that our finite dominant member

26. Ibid., p. 197.
27. Ibid., p. 198.
28. Ibid., p. 201.

may not be actualized in deep sleep.[29] If that is the case, may we not conclude that God, the eminent dominant member of the cosmic body, might be eminently "asleep" and unactualized as conscious influence of the body during the vast stretches of evolutionary and entropic time before and after conscious human beings appear and bring the conscious cosmic mind into being? But then how is the cosmic body ordered by "God" in these pre- and posthuman stages, and how are the vast symmetries held together which order the process in its onward thrust to "creative synthesis"?

This is much the same irrationality that we found in Whitehead's notion of God's primordial nature, which cannot possibly do all he requires of it because it lacks the actuality of the personal "I." Hartshorne's God is only an abstraction drawn from the stream of procession, on the analogy of the human "I," which is also an abstraction: "The abiding ever-identical agent is an abstraction." The underlying problem with this neo-Buddhist view of the self and of God is the doctrine that "the higher is compounded of the lower."[30] It is the notion of incurable atomicity. The problem is particularly severe in the case of God because, at least in theory, the finite self is supposed to be guided in large by the divine lure to creativity. But God has no one to guide his coming into being; and since he is no abiding, ever-identical agent in any substantial sense apart from the physical world, but is in fact concretely constituted by the physical world, his emergence as dominant cosmic monad is more of a mystery than the emergence of the dominant monad called the self in the finite person.

Accordingly, the doctrine of "incurable atomicity" needs to be challenged. It really is not a *working* doctrine anyway in either Whitehead's or Hartshorne's metaphysics, except on the very small level of finite freedom, for that freedom is substantially limited by the God of ideals, forms, order, and lure. For the most part, the creative process works from the top down. Pure chance and natural selection can produce nothing meaningful on their own. The attempt of process metaphysics to force God to subscribe to the doctrine that "the higher is compounded of the lower" fails in actual practice, for God must at least be spoken of as the "dominant" member, the "lure," or the "orderer," all of which signal a priority that is not logically entailed in the doctrine of atomicity. The only solution to this logical impasse as I see it is to subscribe to the biblical view of God as the Supreme Actuality, the infinite personal "I" who is prior to the created world of procession and gives to it its life, order, and freedom. Thus the order is reversed: "The lower is compounded of the Higher." This

29. Ibid.
30. Ibid., p. 202.

does not mean that in our finite existence we do not come more fully into being as the myriad parts and feelings of our bodies combine to give us conscious experience on a highly sophisticated level. The point is that this could not happen were it not for the prior conscious activity of God in directing the whole process toward creative synthesis.

Yet if that is the case, then God cannot be dependent upon the same emerging finite world for his own actuality. He cannot be both the product of the world and the orderer of the world at the same time. This acute anomaly is illustrated in the following passage where Hartshorne considers the need for order, unity, and control in the world organism:

> What is needed for supreme control is obviously that every organ should be directly, and not via some other organ, such as a nervous system, responsive to the whole. The idea of a perfect yet special brain-organ is a contradiction in terms, but the idea of a perfect mind, a mind co-extensive with existence and thus omniscient, is not for all that a contradiction. For such a mind must have, not a world-part as brain, but the whole world serving as higher equivalent of a brain; so that just as between a brain cell and the human mind there is no further mechanism, so between every individual in existence and the world-mind there is no chain of intermediaries, not even a nervous system, but each and every one is in the direct grip of the world-value. The higher the organism, the larger the part directly responsive to the whole; the highest organism must be the largest organism as all brain, so to speak.[31]

The argument begs the question. If God the all-world-brain is the *result* of every organ being responsive to the whole, how can we account for that responsiveness without the *prior* lure of God that is assumed in the process system? Moreover, since the neo-Buddhist concept of person is operative—namely, that there is never any substantial self that remains identical throughout the process—what explains the appearance of and guarantees the continuance of this emergent cosmic mind that is perfect, coexistent with existence, and omniscient? If Hartshorne replies that this is the eternal, absolute modality of God's mind which he has everlastingly, regardless of the changing fortunes of some processing universe or other, then I would reply that something substantial has been introduced into the discussion that cannot be logically induced from the creative process itself.

If Hartshorne were speaking of God as an independent self, partially limited by the freedom of finite selves, that would be one thing. But he is arguing that God's mind is actually *comprised* of finite "cells." The analysis of the human mind and brain discloses that different states and qualities

31. Ibid., p. 198.

of behavior follow from the quality of the brain cells themselves. Why then should God be an exception to this principle of analogy and himself not suffer radical differences in mental experience, depending upon the quality of his brain cells at any particular moment, or in any particular phase of the world system? All Hartshorne ought to say, given his metaphysical commitment that the divine actuality must be contingent, is: *That* God exists is a necessary truth; *how* he exists is contingent upon the state of his body, the world.[32]

On this premise it would be illicit to say, therefore, that God is everlasting love. How could we possibly know that, except by God's revealing himself as the loving God? But the problem goes deeper: *What* is there about God that loves everlastingly—unless his is substantial personal love, quite apart from the fluxing cosmos? Hartshorne opines that it is one of the great oddities in human development (he is thinking of orthodox Christians) that certain persons can believe God loves his creatures while remaining in the same state. Yet Hartshorne himself says something even odder, in view of his notions on the cosmic brain: God's "degree of lovingness, its perfection, would of course not vary with varying worlds; but by definition, to 'love' is to care about differences and to respond to them differentially."[33]

With the last clause I would not disagree; nor with the first. But how does Hartshorne introduce an absolute *how* ("love") into the absolute *that* of God's everlasting existence? What explains an absolutely loving mode or character in God if his mind is comprised of his creatures who function as his brain cells? What guarantees that God's loving-kindness will not vary with varying worlds? It is not sufficient to argue that God's changeless and absolute modality (A) is an abstraction from the procession of relativity (R),[34] for the abstract essence or character is the point in question, and there is no way that pure relativity can produce a constant. To say that *"Being* is intelligible as the abstract fixed aspect in *becoming*, and eternity as the identical element in all temporal diversity" does not explain what must be explained, namely, how Hartshorne accounts for the presence of a fixed aspect and eternity in becoming and temporal diversity.[35] It is not an advance in philosophical thought to substitute for

---

32. See ibid., p. 158. But it is even questionable whether he could affirm the *that* without the *how;* certainly not logically. Perhaps, then, by appeal to internal, ineffable feeling?

33. Ibid., p. 36.

34. Ibid., p. 248.

35. Ibid. His italics. See also Hartshorne's "Personal Identity from A to Z," *Process Studies*, vol. 2, no. 3 (Fall 1972): 209-15, in which he further elaborates on the neo-Buddhist theme that process is inclusive and being is a constituent of this inclusive reality. Continuity, he says, is a matter of possibility or ideality, not of actuality. This means that

Parmenides' or Shankara's absorption of becoming into being the reverse position, which attempts to derive being from becoming. It simply cannot be done, although the attempt is at least as old as Heraclitus. The quality of being must be present on its own terms, not as something derivative from processive chance.

Moreover, as I pointed out earlier, abstractions should not be construed as dead elements, but as substantial and living aspects of an existing person. Thus, to say of God that he is eternally loving is not to describe him through a dead abstraction but to point out that he is always that kind of person, who stands behind his words and acts with intentional fidelity as the infinite "I AM," and who is systematically elusive and unreducible to "thing" language. On a smaller scale, our personal identity cannot be explained as the chance collocation of processing atoms, but only as the result of God's gift of identity through lure, character, and free will, which comprise the uniqueness of the embodied self. In biblical terms, each person has a fallen nature until it is tranformed in spiritual rebirth through the work of Christ ("All have sinned and fall short of the glory of God, and are justified freely by his grace through the redemption that came by Jesus Christ" [Rom. 3:23-24, NIV]). Rebellion against God characterizes the substance of the natural man, while love for and worship of God characterize the substance of the man reborn.

Although it is best in my opinion to hold being and becoming and the one and the many together in inseparable and paradoxical union, for the sake of argument it is interesting to turn Hartshorne's argument around and argue that the substantial being of a person actually constitutes his becoming, as Frank G. Kirkpatrick has done in a trenchant criticism of Hartshorne's concept of identity. Kirkpatrick makes a crucial point regarding the notion of the personal subject: "If deciding is what a subject does and if the subject has no being until the process of becoming ends, then the decisions within the process are not the decisions of a subject, but the decisions which *produce* a subject."[36] Kirkpatrick argues instead for the primacy of the subject as being and the process of becoming as the abstraction:

> The concrete reality is the being: the abstract reality is the process by which it came to be in the sense that conceptually we need the notion of the being before we can think about that which creates it. . . . Therefore, notions

---

personal identity is no more than the persistence of certain defining characteristics which, as far as my own sense of "I" is concerned, turn off in dreamless sleep and reappear in consciousness, but all the same (if one may so speak) is involved in continual processive self-surpassing.

36. "Subjective Becoming: An Unwarranted Abstraction?" *Process Studies*, vol. 3, no. 1 (Spring 1973): 22f. His italics.

assuming self-creativity, self-determination, decision, and intention (since they suppose rootage in *a* being) can be applied to the process producing a self only abstractly, i.e., only as lifted out from the completed subject.[37]

I conclude that the neo-Buddhist view of the self and of God is seriously lacking in logical consistency and empirical verifiability, and moreover takes no account of the biblical disclosure by God of his own nature and of the fallen and redeemed natures of human beings. But the worst is yet to come for Hartshornean metaphysics. His position is in serious trouble with regard to time, the very core of the system, and to that question we now turn.

37. Ibid., pp. 23, 25. His italics. For a similar criticism see Edward Pols, *Whitehead's Metaphysics: A Critical Examination of Process and Reality* (Carbondale: Southern Illinois University Press, 1967); Lewis S. Ford's reply, "Can Whitehead Provide for Real Subjective Agency? A Reply to Edward Pols' Critique," *The Modern Schoolman*, vol. 47, no. 2 (January 1970): 209-25; and Pols's reply, "Whitehead on Subjective Agency: A Reply to Lewis S. Ford," *The Modern Schoolman*, vol. 49, no. 2 (January 1972): 144-50. See also Peter Bertocci, "Hartshorne on Personal Identity: A Personalistic Critique," *Process Studies*, vol. 2, no. 3 (Fall 1972): 216-21.

4

Process and Simultaneity in God

Logical Difficulties in the Process View of Time

$\mathbf{M}$y first serious difficulty with process thought arose with the realization that God's rate of speed is crucial if his actual experience is necessarily bound up with time. A second question then appeared: What is God's frame of reference, his position of perspective with respect to the whole universe, if his concrete existence is limited to space? (Most readers will find this chapter hard going. Indeed, most scientists are baffled by the complexities of time. All I can do is ask the reader to understand as much as is possible, but to appreciate the fact that the view of time in process thought is too simplistic and raises more problems than it solves.)

Charles Hartshorne has argued that God is "a perfect mind, a mind co-extensive with existence and thus omniscient. . . ."[1] The problem with this doctrine in view of the first is that if God is processive in spacetime he must move at the speed of light (C)—the approximate velocity of 186,000 miles per second. But then he could not be coextensive with existence, for light from distant sources would take millions of light years to reach any kind of coordination in his cosmic mind with light from other sources in different segments of the universe (depending, of course, on God's frame of reference—the other question). If, as Hartshorne suggests, the total physical

---

1. *The Logic of Perfection and Other Essays in Neoclassical Metaphysics* (La Salle, IL: Open Court, 1973), p. 198.

universe comprises God's brain cells, then (by analogy of the delay rate that occurs in the human body between the injury in the finger, the subsequent registration of hurt in the brain, and the resultant conscious coordination of this feeling with all other feelings in the body) one can only conclude that God, moving at the speed of light, could have a coordinated and unified experience of the whole universe perhaps only once in an entire universal cycle. Hartshorne actually suggested this in a letter to Mileč Čapek as early as 1955, and repeated it in a lecture that I attended.

The problem is not ameliorated by assuming that God's speed is faster than the speed of light—say, the speed of a hypothetical supertachyon—for the length of time required for a coextensive, omniscient mental perspective would then be only fractionally reduced. Indeed, for Hartshorne to argue that God's perfect mind is coextensive with the totality of existence actually requires a God *beyond* time and space who can coordinate instantaneously all relative speeds and spaces. But this is precisely what classical biblical Christianity has always believed: God is not limited by the relativities of time and space, but is the Creator who has called this universe of relativities into being (Gen. 1:3ff.—"let there be . . . , and there was") and who "uphold[s] [it] by his word of power" (Heb. 1:3). He is also the God who is absolutely relevant to his creation because he participates in its process as Redeemer ("God was in Christ reconciling the world to himself" [II Cor. 5:19]; "the creation itself will be set free from its bondage to decay and obtain the glorious liberty of the children of God" [Rom. 8:21]).

God is not bound to our time and space by necessity, as process metaphysics insists; rather his experience of our world and his participation in our suffering as Redeemer is of his own sovereign and gracious choosing:

> For thus says the high and lofty One
> who inhabits eternity, whose name is Holy:
> "I dwell in the high and holy place,
> and also with him who is of a contrite and humble spirit." [Isa. 57:15]

If the biblical claim—that God is above our time and space, yet is its Creator, Sustainer, and Redeemer—sounds paradoxical, I would refer to I. T. Ramsey's argument that the analysis of the human self leads to analogous unavoidable paradoxes that are nonetheless explorable and meaningful.[2] The alternative to the mystery that is couched in the divine

---

2. See "Paradox in Religion," *Proceedings of the Aristotelian Society*, suppl. vol. 33, 1959, reprinted in Dallas M. High, ed., *New Essays on Religious Language* (New York: Oxford University Press, 1969), p. 161, where Ramsey ends his argument by remarking: "What I have tried to allow for is genuine mystery in the sense that 'what there is' is not

"I am" is not a true rationalism, in spite of Hartshorne's early commitment to "uninhibited rationalism" and his promise "to trust reason to the end."[3] As we have seen, process thought is quite irrational at a number of points, especially on the matter of time and simultaneity. As concerns its claim to satisfy the empiricist demands of modern scientific theory, we can only attempt to show in brief compass how the notion of a finite and temporal God runs into insuperable difficulties with contemporary concepts of time and space.[4]

Relativity Theory and the Creative Power of God

If God is moving forward in creative advance at the velocity of light, is his experience of all the myriad data of the universe, all of which are past when they reach him, also at the speed of light? If they comprise his brain cells how could he have an instantaneous and simultaneous experience of all of them? Hartshorne speculates that "the notion of a 'creative advance of nature' seems to imply a cosmic 'front' of simultaneity as short as the shortest specious present. I suppose God to have this *now* as his psychological simultaneity."[5]

But if Hartshorne's naturalism aims at consistency with contemporary theories in physics, it runs aground for several reasons. First, as Čapek argues, in relativity physics there is no such thing as an instantaneous configuration of the world at a given moment.[6] Instantaneous cuts across

---

restricted to observables, and to suggest that it is as apt currency for such mystery that there arises 'mysterious paradox,' which is then neither a vicious muddle nor an inaccessible incantation, but paradox whose structure can be investigated and explored under the guidance of the logical behaviour of 'I.' 'I' is the best (perhaps the only) clue to all genuine mystery, all sublime paradox, and all revealing impropriety."

3. Hartshorne, *The Logic of Perfection*, pp. x, viii.

4. An important article that considers the serious problems of process metaphysics is John T. Wilcox's "A Question from Physics for Certain Theists," *The Journal of Religion* 41 (October 1961): 293–300. (See also my note 10.) Hartshorne's reply appears in Sidney and Beatrice Rome, eds., *Philosophical Interrogations* (New York: Holt, Rinehart and Winston, 1964), pp. 324f., and in Hartshorne's *Natural Theology for Our Time* (La Salle, IL: Open Court, 1967), pp. 93–95. See Lewis S. Ford, "Is Process Theism Compatible with Relativity Theory?" *The Journal of Religion* 48 (April 1968): 124–35, for a novel approach and a criticism of Hartshorne. For a full bibliographical list of works by and about Hartshorne through 1973, see Dorothy Hartshorne, "Charles Hartshorne: A Second Bibliography," *Process Studies*, vol. 3, no. 3 (Fall 1973), pp. 179–223.

5. In Rome and Rome, *Philosophical Interrogations*, pp. 342f. His italics. See also John B. Cobb, Jr., *A Christian Natural Theology* (Philadelphia: Westminster, 1965), p. 192. For a trenchant criticism of the position, see John Baker, "Omniscience and Divine Synchronization," *Process Studies*, vol. 2, no. 3 (Fall 1972): 201–8.

6. *The Philosophical Impact of Contemporary Physics* (New York: American Book Co., 1961), pp. 152, 361, 383f.

a four-dimensional world history are impossible to conceive. No total simultaneity in the objective sense is possible in timespace, and that would have to include Hartshorne's finite God whose experience moves at the speed of light. The crux of the matter is this: Any kind of simultaneity for a finite being has to be a relative one, depending on one's frame of reference. God's choice of a frame of reference is necessarily restricted in process thought by the notion that he is limited by the processing universe which presumably moves at the speed of light or some equivalent speed. Does God make use of some unique spacetime system? What would that be? If God's experience travels at the speed of light then we can only conclude that he receives information only after his creatures have experienced it, and cannot receive all of it all at once. There simply is no way of determining any absolute simultaneity within a finite system, unless God is not limited to our spacetime system. And this is the position of biblical Christianity I am defending.

Hartshorne's own argument for a cosmic present works against the logic of his process metaphysics and against the views of contemporary relativity theory:

> Must there not be a cosmic present, in spite of relativity physics, the *de facto* totality of actual entities as present in the divine immediacy? As Parker and Bergson have said, the inability of human beings, by signalling methods, to determine a unique cosmic present or simultaneity need not prevent God, who knows things directly, from experiencing such a present.[7]

As I have already mentioned, Hartshorne suggested to Čapek in a letter dated December 22, 1955, that God might have one specious present every cosmic epoch and retrospect the whole vast history of the cosmos at a single blink. But such a notion, even if it were to be taken seriously (although it is the only logical way to reconcile a specious present with a finite God), eliminates the possibility of any worshipful relationship between persons and God (God's response to prayer is rendered impossible), and practically reduces God to passivity and logical absurdity. One of the major doctrines of process metaphysics is supposed to be God's continual influence on every finite creature, not only as the one who established and sustains the physical laws of order, but also as the omnipresent lure to creativity. How, then, could God be the universal orderer who sustains the order of laws throughout the universe, including the speed of light itself, yet himself be limited to the speed of light? Similarly, how could he act as immediate lure to every finite creature if he himself were processing at a finite rate?

7. In Paul Arthur Schilpp, ed., *The Philosophy of Alfred North Whitehead*, The Library of Living Philosophers (New York: Tudor, 1956), p. 545.

The problem is unresolvable by the canons of human logic. That is why Hartshorne has to resort to illogical arguments on behalf of simultaneity. The God of simultaneous experience and omnipresent relevance must, by definition, be a Being who is supratemporal and supraspatial. And this is what biblical faith maintains: God has created timespace, sustains it by the word of his power, and participates in it as Redeemer. In him the two necessary poles of the paradox are held together, not irrationally, but suprarationally in a way that is explorable and meaningful, if unimaginable. Hartshorne has often criticized positivistic thinkers for holding that "God is not intelligible unless he is imaginable." I would present the case for biblical faith with a similar argument: God is absolutely actual within his own uniplurality or triunity; he is above created timespace, the inexhaustible and creative Archetype, by whose sovereign grace we are created ectype. God has his own unimaginable "timespace," if we may speak analogically, which may be explored meaningfully if not exhaustively in terms of the exchange of love within the Triune God, compared to which our love is but a small copy.

God, accordingly, has his own divine present or divine system which is capable not only of comprehending the entirety of events in the created universe, but also each creature within its own frame of reference. The latter point is important, for God continually creates and upholds the laws of nature throughout the universe, the universality of which cannot be accounted for in the process model where God is temporally limited. Only the biblical God who transcends time and space can guarantee the universally supportive laws of time and space. Only by viewing God as beyond our timespace and fully actual and inexhaustible in his own absolute sociality-unity, the Trinity, can we appreciate how God can create, sustain, and participate in our universe with its vast reaches on the macrocosmic level, and its equally tiny spaces and moments on the microcosmic level. A finite deity of process whose very brain is comprised of finite entities cannot experience all of the universe at once, much less create, sustain, and influence. Millions of light years or microscopic events in the duration of a millionth of a second for a deity limited to the speed of light render that deity logically absurd and religiously irrelevant. In a remarkably powerful statement of the role of Christ in creation, the writer to the Hebrews declares that God's Son, "through whom also he created the world. . . , uphold[s] the universe by his word of power" (Heb. 1:2–3). Anything less than that kind of divine creative power is incapable of explaining satisfactorily the transcendence and immanence of God over and within the world. The logical absurdities of a wholly temporal deity in the Whiteheadian-Hartshornean system now need to be explored in greater detail.

Figure 1

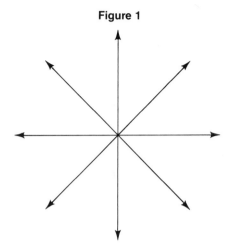

Potential Models of Time

Perhaps a somewhat strange but quite possible model of time and space derived from contemporary speculative scientific theory will suggest the complications of viewing time as flowing in only one direction.[8] In his work in physics and theology, a former student of mine, Earl Wajenberg, observed that it is quite possible under the known laws of nature to speak of negative entropy in thermodynamics, or time flowing backward. Furthermore, scientists are postulating the possibility of particles called tachyons ("speedy" particles) that always move faster than the speed of light, just as ordinary particles ("tardyons"?) move at a slower speed. The combination of these possibilities leads to a view of multidimensional time and space that is quite bizarre compared with the usual view of physics. If our own time may contain universes with a common beginning that age away in opposite directions, then postulated tachyon universes may do the same. Using our relative frame of reference we may speak of time flowing radially in eight directions: past to future, future to past, east to west, west to east, north to south, south to north, top to bottom, bottom to top, fanning out from the center (the "big bang") like the rays of a star, but at different rates and directions. Some would move in titanic beams of tachyons that flash away out of all possible ken at the initial creation. An observer in any one of the eight universes would not view the whole, nor could he, since no event in any of the others would ever reach the observer by normal relativistic methods. All seven of our postulated sister worlds would be closed to us forever, and we to them, in perfect symmetry (Fig. 1).

8. See Martin Gardner, "Can Time Go Backward?" *Scientific American*, vol. 216, no. 1

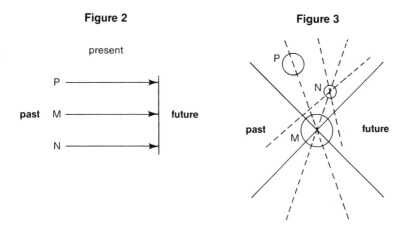

Figure 2

Figure 3

This is a strange but quite possible model of what might be; but whether it be true or not, it illustrates the absurdity of limiting God to one velocity or sequence of time, when as Creator and Sustainer of our own universe and of whatever other universes there may be he must be above the limitations and conditions of finitude, the possessor of absolute perspective, while capable of entering into every conceivable relative perspective. Any lesser concept of God is inadequate logically, scientifically, and religiously. As Creator, God has all velocities, hence all reference frames, and is accordingly above any particular frame of reference.

But to return to our own world of spacetime. If we configure contemporaneousness as I have in Figure 2, we discover that the term *future* is itself relative; for the future does not move forward with a contemporaneous front like an army on the move (an incorrect model). Rather, insofar as we are able to diagram relativity theory at all, contemporaneousness would resemble the model in Figure 3.[9] The two wedges formed by the solid lines that intersect M represent the area of M's contemporaneousness. The duration of M's immediate present includes the duration of P and N, but P and N do not include the totality of M's duration. This observation is based on an empirical examination of our present world epoch. The broken lines intersecting N represent the limits

(January 1967), pp. 98–108; Gerald Feinberg, "Particles That Go Faster Than Light," *Scientific American*, vol. 222, no. 2 (February 1970), pp. 68–77; Michael N. Kreisler, "Are There Faster Than Light Particles?" *American Scientist*, vol. 61, no. 2 (March/April 1973), pp. 201–8. On the present affecting the past, see Charles Williams, *Descent into Hell* (Grand Rapids: Eerdmans, 1975), pp. 152–75, especially p. 157. See also Hans Reichenbach and Marie Reichenbach, *The Direction of Time* (Berkeley: University of California Press, 1971).

9. The figure is adapted from Donald Sherburne, *A Key to Whitehead's Process and Reality* (New York: Macmillan, 1966), p. 111.

Figure 4

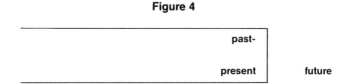

of N's contemporaries. P is not a contemporary of N, and vice versa, although P and N are contemporaries of M. In other words, there are many durations through M.

Now the question is, how wide is a wedge of duration allowed to become and how inclusive the nexus of contemporaneouness? Hartshorne correctly holds to the doctrine of divine simultaneity, along with his incorrectly held notion of finite divine relativity, but seems to envision the two intuitively rather than logically, for they cannot fit logically together as long as God is limited to temporal succession. The best he might do with the diagram would be to extend the lines of the past to form a partial figure. Thus God's past-present contemporaneousness would look something like Figure 4. God's present would be the totality of past data which are held eternally in his contemporaneous present without loss.

Of course there are serious problems here for Hartshorne, since the processing deity would have a line of vanguard contemporaneousness with finite contemporaries, all of which are supposed to be causally independent of each other (else, supposedly, they would not be free). But to delineate exactly what that region of causal independence would be is one of the central difficulties for Hartshorne's view of a processing deity. Genuine contemporaneousness would include all actual atomic occasions in a unison of becoming within the extensive continuum.

But is there a divine duration that is more than just a cross section of the world and that includes the immediacy of the entire universe or universes? Only if God is not limited to spacetime. How, for instance, would Hartshorne's imagined deity handle the question posed by John T. Wilcox, who demonstrates the logical problems of indeterminacy in the time order of two events? For example, a light signal, leaving at the moment of its occurrence as one event at one location, cannot reach the location of a second event before the second event occurs. Thus, while from our privileged hypothetical perspective event 1 happens before event 2, from the perspective of event 2, event 1 is future. And light emitted from "later" event 2 will be future to "earlier" event 1. Only by using an arbitrary frame of reference (a sort of God's-eye view) can we speak of one event preceding the other in the example. The arbitrary language ("before," "after," "future," "past") of event 1 and event 2 is

Figure 5

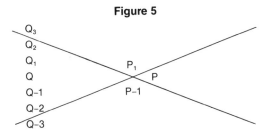

relative to our position as observers and to our choice of a frame of reference. From our limited perspective as finite creatures there is no absolute simultaneity to which we can appeal. Although there is, of course, a psychological simultaneity in which we recognize a cohappening of sense impressions in our consciousness and from which we calculate physical simultaneity in certain objective events in space, we have no purely human access to an absolute objective criterion of simultaneity.

Wilcox illustrates the problem with a diagram of relativistic simultaneity, where light leaving P or Q just as either occurs could not reach the other before *it* occurs. The interval between the two events makes it impossible for a body to be present at both events simultaneously, even if it moves at the speed of light. Q is located relative to P in what Sir Arthur Stanley Eddington called the "Absolute Elsewhere," not in some "Absolute Past" or "Absolute Future."[10] (Refer to Fig. 5.) The figure represents relativistic simultaneity, for a light signal leaving event Q_{-3} can reach P but not P_1 before it occurs, and a light leaving P can reach Q_3 but not Q_2 before it occurs.

Four Meanings of "Present"

What then is the meaning of the word *present*? Wilcox discusses four different meanings of the "present" of an event, the first being the *causal present* of P. The causal present simply means the causal independence of P and all the events Q_{-2} through Q_2 in the figure, since they occur in such a framework of contemporaneousness that a causal influence, even at the speed of light, could not reach P from them or reach them from P. They are in the contemporaneous zone of P's absolute elsewhere. Wilcox argues that truth here is absolute even for God, for what absolutely precedes P does precede it, what absolutely succeeds P does succeed it, and what does neither of these does neither.[11]

Yet one should be careful of using the word *absolute* here, I would

10. See John T. Wilcox, "Relativity, Simultaneity, and Divine Omniscience," master's thesis at Emory University, 1955, p. 6. (See also my note 4.)

11. Ibid., p. 7.

remark, for this is a truth relative to our empirical observation of events and hypothetical beyond our limited observational powers, In biblical history, for example, Abraham precedes Moses, and Moses precedes Christ. Yet there is a supratemporal sense in which Christ precedes and superintends creation. The mixture of tenses in Paul's declaration that "he is before all things, and in him all things hold together" (*autos estin pro pantōn kai ta panta en autōi sunestēken* [Col. 1:17]) indicates that for God there is no absolute elsewhere, for *in* him all things were created, including light itself. The "normal" sequence of causal events obtains only relatively in our created world order, for there is also the sense in which our "future" is already "present" in the absolute simultaneousness of God's eternity. This is denied by Hartshorne, but his desire to hold on to God in process yet absolutely simultaneous with the universe is fraught with enormous logical difficulties and is no more than human specula tion, while Holy Scripture is God's revelation of objective propositional truths about himself. Thus Paul in Ephesians 1:3–4 expresses the paradox of created sequential time and divine supratime: "Blessed be the God and Father of our Lord Jesus Christ, who has blessed us in Christ with every spiritual blessing in the heavenly places, even as he chose us in him before the foundation of the world (*pro katabolēs kosmou*), that we should be holy and blameless before him." And Jesus in John 17:24 prays, "Father, I desire that they also, whom thou hast given me, may be with me where I am, to behold my glory which thou hast given me in thy love for me before the foundation of the world (*pro katabolēs kosmou*)."

The early Christians were given to see that while there is a created temporal sequence for us and for the work of the incarnate Christ, there is an Absolute Presence that transcends the niceties of our human verbal tenses and the velocity of light. For us and for God in his incarnate self-limitation in Christ and in his immanent presence in the experience of the sparrow and in the "occasions" of the hairs on our head there is sequential time and relative elsewheres, but not for God in his absolute suprapresence. Hence Wilcox's causal present is true for God only in the sense that God participates in the whole spectrum of relativities, but not for God in supraspacetime. The biblical theologian must not accede to the naturalistic doctrine that the speed of light is absolute, as Wilcox seems to assume. This would amount to a new although more sophisticated worship of the sun, a new heliocentrism, a modern photocentric idolatry.

The second of the four meanings for "present" may be called the *influential present*. This includes whatever influences P, such as Q_{-3}. Wilcox feels that this is absolute even for God,[12] although I would object again that this is true for God only relative to his participation in the

---

12. Ibid., p. 8.

sequential time pertaining to P. But in respect to God as creator of space-time, nothing in that spacetime is absolute for him. He alone is absolute, and all created "absolutes" (such as the velocity of light) are therefore relative absolutes. The process view of the absoluteness of light and temporal sequence is, in light of biblical Christianity, one of the most ultimate and sophisticated modern idolatries. The central Christian proclamation regarding the forgiveness of sins through Christ's death on the cross means that past event influences the present in such a way that a person's past deeds of wrong are forgiven and forgotten, and therefore their effects reversed by God. The past can be changed by divine grace so that it no longer has a tyrannical influence upon the present or the future. Is time reversible in the realm of divine forgiveness, and thus the truth of the influential present only relative to us and not an absolute for God?[13]

Writing of the once-for-all (*ephapax*) character of Christ's suffering for sin which fulfills the sequential Old Testament sacrificial system of sin → sacrifice → sin → sacrifice, the author of Hebrews says:

> But when Christ had offered for all time a single sacrifice for sins, he sat down at the right hand of God, then to wait until his enemies should be made a stool for his feet. For by a single offering he has perfected for all time those who are sanctified. And the Holy Spirit also bears witness to us; for after saying,
>
> > "This is the covenant that I will make with them
> >   after those days, says the Lord:
> > I will put my laws on their hearts
> >   and write them on their minds," [paraphrase, Jer. 31:33]
>
> then he adds,
>
> > "I will remember their sins and their misdeeds no more."
> >   [paraphrase, Jer. 31:35]
>
> Where there is forgiveness of these, there is no longer any offering for sin.
> [10:12–18]

The implications of this doctrine are enormous. Only Christ's atoning death can remove the weighty burden of the nontheist who attempts to find self-forgiveness from the past by turning his back, like Jean-Paul Sartre, on *en soi*, being itself or past essence, and by existing in the self-ish fringe of *pour soi*, for oneself, where the ego continually transcends the past. For as the Scriptures teach, if the past is not in some sense reversible then our sins are unforgiven and unforgiveable, and that is the beginning of the tyranny of hell. One of the unhappiest doctrines in

13. See ibid., p. 8.

Hartshorne's process eschatology is his belief in "objective immortality," whereby God remembers everything we have ever done forever.[14] Hartshorne intends this to be a consolation and a viable substitute for the discarded Christian belief in subjective immortality. But I concur with a friend of mine who, when we were discussing the implications of Hartshorne's doctrine of objective immortality, remarked that it was the most awful thing he had ever heard of—that God would remember everlastingly *everything* one had ever done? One would have to have a very high opinion of himself indeed to take satisfaction in that kind of immortality. The doctrine is certainly bourgeois and gnostic and could only arise if one has the impression that he has brought great delight and satisfaction to God throughout his life and is eminently worth being remembered forever. Biblical faith sees the matter differently, however, and infers that the influential present, although real enough on the relative level of finitude, is not absolute for God. He does forgive the repentant sinner by sheer grace, "reversing" the past through the present.

A third meaning of "present" is a relative one, and is called the *apparent present*, in this case of P. It may be illustrated by an observer who is in a position to observe P and other events at the same time. But since this depends upon his particular position and motion, it will differ in content from one observer to another. Biblical theology would agree with relativity theory that individual observers have relatively "true" perspectives but would remind us that as we ascend the ladder from relatively unimportant observations in the physical realm, such as a man rowing a boat in a lake which appears oddly above a hammock suspended between two trees (my perspective on a summer day), to the observation of a nuclear weapon exploding over a city, to observing the narratives that relate the crucifixion and resurrection of Jesus Christ, the relative perspectives become more complex and what might appear to be an apparent present in one respect (a believer reading the Scriptures) is really an absolute in another (what the Scriptures say about God and the world). An apparent present, although in general relative, may very well contain under the right conditions God's own absolute perspective on the nature of things (the crucifixion of Christ, for example, and my reading of his cosmic meaning in the New Testament).

A fourth meaning of "present" may be called the *calculative present*. It includes those events that can be calculated, once they are observed, to have been simultaneous with P when P occurred.[15] Light that reaches P from a distant star on a starry night might seem to be simultaneous with a light signal nearer by (apparent present), but by scientific calculation P

14. *The Logic of Perfection*, p. 259.
15. Wilcox, "Divine Omniscience," pp. 8f.

could determine that the light from space was emitted one hundred million light years ago. This raises an interesting question for process thought regarding the future. How much of what seems to us to be present is already past, and how much that seems to us to be future is already present, or even past? Process philosophy has never been very precise in calculating the differences and discrepancies between the various kinds of "presents" in order to determine how much actual freedom lies within the causal present of P and how much P is actually determined by other factors, although he might mistakenly consider himself free in those respects. We have already discussed the haziness of Whitehead and Hartshorne concerning the degree to which God sets the laws and limits of finite freedom and what that free area really amounts to.

A crucial question in this section is to determine to what degree our future is known by God and what, on process grounds, might be "absolutely" unknown even to him because it belongs entirely to our free and novel subjective creativity. In other words, in what sense might we create a genuine future for God and thus render him finite and dependent upon our decisions, as process thought insists is the case? Wilcox concludes that there is an acceptable resolution within the framework of a temporalistic theism if God has a privileged spacetime system.[16] While I would agree that God's ability to number all the hairs on our heads and to experience the fall of every sparrow requires his absolute relativity in spacetime, I do not agree with Wilcox that it might be possible to map out a velocity and acceleration that would yield a system equivalent to the divine.[17] The divine present would then be mainly calculative, for the relationship between this high-speed processive divine system and the spacetime system of any enduring object would be changing at every moment. This would not imply that God is located at some point but that at his "infinite" velocity (what would that be?) he would know every causal present, every influential present, every apparent present, and every calculative present. When Wilcox concludes that God's knowledge of simultaneity in this world would therefore be complete, he asks what evidence there might be for such a unique divine cosmic system. He replies that there is no evidence for the divine present and that no evidence is anticipated.

But then I would ask whether finite human beings would ever be able to understand how the composite natures of the organic actualities of the world obtain adequate representation in the divine nature. This is a serious problem in Alfred North Whitehead's ontology.[18] There are effects

16. Ibid., pp. 28–40.
17. Ibid., p. 31.
18. See *Process and Reality: An Essay in Cosmology* (New York: Harper and Row, 1957), p. 19.

that are knowable only to God and are forever humanly undetectable. Wilcox ends his discussion on a note of uncertainty. He is dealing, he says, only with analytic assertions, not empirical ones. The full and concrete meaning of "the divine present of P" would be known only to God. Thus there is no empirical evidence for a divine present, he allows, although it does make sense to talk about it. Even though we cannot know what the divine presence contains we can know what it is like by analogy, for we have our own human experience of memory, sequence, and simultaneity of events to draw on.[19]

It seems to me, however, that Wilcox has not gone far enough in solving the problem. For one thing, he holds on to the basic tenet of temporalistic theology; that is, viewing God as limited by time, to be sure in some realm of supervelocity, but nevertheless limiting him ultimately to spacetime. This commitment to an autonomous speculative metaphysics dismisses the propositions of biblical revelation which describe God as transcendent over spacetime, indeed as the Creator of temporality, space, and matter while immanent within it. In the Scriptures there is a paradox of tension between God's redemptive participation in fallen spacetime, superlatively expressed in the kairos of Christ's redeeming ministry, and the supratemporal and supraspatial reality of God as Creator and Sustainer of spacetime matter. An intellectual solution to the question of the relativities of spacetime and God's simultaneity cannot be resolved by unaided reason, especially since, in the biblical view, human reason is bent by rebellion and will always skew the data of thought to its own advantage and to the disadvantage of God. Only when the rational powers of the human intellect are regenerated away from rebellion against God toward worship and praise of his awesome transcendence and immanence can the divine paradox be fully accepted and intuited, and the mind be at peace. Even the naturalistic process theist who takes spacetime creativity to be coequal with God comes to paradox in the end—Whitehead with his intuitions, Hartshorne with his "insights," John B. Cobb, Jr., with his two principles, Wilcox with his apparent paradoxes. We might as well begin with the biblical merismus that God is sovereignly above spacetime, yet by a grand miracle of grace within it redemptively.

Exploring the Future

The Growth of God's Knowledge

We return once more to our large question. If God is supremely above created spacetime then he knows not only past and present but future as

19. Wilcox, "Divine Omniscience," p. 40.

well. In further exploring what the future is it is important to appreciate the incredibly large number of occasions of experience which, on the process model, occur for God in a second's time, as the future possibility moves into the present and becomes actual fact, then perishes and becomes a past datum. John Baker has calculated that if we consider a pattern of twelve temporal extensions, all approximately $\frac{1}{10}$ of a second, such as

$\frac{1}{9}$	$\frac{1}{10}$	$\frac{1}{11}$
$\frac{2}{19}$	$\frac{2}{21}$	$\frac{2}{23}$
$\frac{3}{28}$	$\frac{3}{31}$	$\frac{3}{34}$
$\frac{4}{37}$	$\frac{4}{41}$	$\frac{4}{45}$

then the temporal extension of the divine experience, in order to function separately in relation to each individual in this series, must be $\frac{1}{2^2 \times 3^2 \times 5 \times 7 \times 11 \times 17 \times 19 \times 23 \times 31 \times 37 \times 41}$, or $\frac{1}{4,842,179,260,380}$ of a second.[20] While a divine temporal extension of nearly five trillionths of a second is unimaginable, although not logically impossible, the divine experience of overlapping electrons with extensions of thirty microseconds would be even incredibly smaller in duration.

But then the question of the growth of God's knowledge comes into focus in such a process model, for the central doctrine of process theology is that God depends upon the finite universe for his concrete experience, and eternally self-surpasses his past knowledge. But as Baker observes, a curious problem arises at this point:

Arranged in increasing magnitude of temporal extension, the actual entities appear [in the table] as $\frac{2}{23}$, $\frac{3}{34}$, $\frac{4}{45}$, $\frac{1}{11}$, $\frac{2}{21}$, $\frac{3}{31}$, $\frac{4}{41}$, $\frac{1}{10}$, $\frac{2}{19}$, $\frac{3}{28}$, $\frac{4}{37}$, $\frac{1}{9}$. Assume that there are twelve actual entities, each uniquely possessing one of these values. Further assume that all of these actual entities commence simultaneously at some time t. Arbitrarily select any two contiguous fractions, such as the third and fourth in the series, $\frac{4}{45}$ and $\frac{1}{11}$. After the completion of the actual entity with a temporal extension of $\frac{4}{45}$ of a second, God will have 9,780,160,124 successive experiences before the satisfaction of the actual entity with a temporal extension of $\frac{1}{11}$. This means that God has nearly ten billion successive experiences before there exists an actual entity whose satisfaction he can prehend, thereby increasing his knowledge. This assumes that all of God's successive experiences are equal in temporal duration. If this is true, it is incorrect to think that each successive experience of God increases his knowledge.[21]

20. "Omniscience and Divine Synchronization," pp. 201-8.
21. Ibid., p. 204.

Such is Baker's specific criticism of Hartshorne and Cobb and the process school in general. But I would take the figures in a different direction. Observing that a vast amount of person P's experience is comprised of actual occasions of atomic and cellular nature which occur prior to the synthetic experience of P himself, we must allow that God has prior exhaustive knowledge of all these ingredients that are sending or are about to contribute their myriad experiences or feelings to the synthesizing and creative center of the organism, P himself. Now if for the moment we employ the process model, what does P contribute to God that is genuinely new, when God knows beforehand down to the trillionth of a second or better every single environmental and organic datum that is still future to the dominant monad P and that will affect P's new emergent occasion? Whatever P contributes, if much at all (the determinist would say nothing at all; Hartshorne, that it is 1 over all contributing data), is certain to be very small indeed and certainly not surprising to God. The horns of the dilemma for process theology are really sharp, and fortunate is the process theologian who does not become impaled on them. Relativity theory does not allow us to think of a unified front of moving time called the future, along which we are all, including God, supposedly processing at the same rate and in the same direction, but of many occasions happening in different and often unrelated contexts, relative to their own spheres of experience. Yet Hartshorne wants to speak of a simultaneity of God's experiencing all occasions along such a front, as God processes in a superlative way along with the finite order.

But this is an irrational argument, and all the more serious since Hartshorne claims to be a rationalist. On the process model, and following relativity theory, God is going to know vast numbers of past occasions that are still future for the other occasions; yet there is no way that a finite deity that is limited to time can really experience all occasions throughout the vast universe simultaneously. If process theologians have been hard on classical substance theology, particularly on Thomistic thought, and have argued that the processive cannot be derived from the static, then the process theist is equally challenged by the problem of how to derive the static—in Hartshorne's case the simultaneity of divine experience across the board—from relativity and process. Process thought makes spacetime an absolute and places God within its procession and limitations, especially with regard to the future. Biblical theology asserts that God has disclosed himself as the creator of spacetime and hence beyond it, yet is its sustainer and major participant. Only when God's *supra*natural character as the infinite personal God is given pride of place in terms of the propositions of divinely revealed Scripture can both elements of the paradox be held together. God is the sovereign creator who experiences the simultaneity of past, present, and future in his superior and comprehensive sphere of supraspacetime, yet is also the God who is with us as Immanuel in our sorrows and joys, down to the trillionth of a second duration of each datum that contributes to the human self. He knows the future exhaustively, for there is no unified front of time and no absolute direction of time, apart from eschatological time as divinely revealed in Scripture, and God knows them all exhaustively.

The Location of God

There is another serious problem with the Whiteheadian view of God that accentuates the difficulty described by Baker. This problem has to do with the question, where is God? Marjorie O'Rourke Boyle argues that if we relinquish the punctual locution model for God, whether in serial relation to other existents (thus, ...) or in absolute identification with them (.), God-and-the-world then form a gestalt that is not reducible simply to the sum of its parts.[22] Cobb contends on the grounds of White-head's organic cosmology that the human soul may occupy both the empty space in the interstices and the regions occupied by many cells: so by analogy, says Boyle, the region of God may include the regions comprising the standpoints of all contemporary occasions in the world. This hypothetical model for God-and-the-world may be termed an interpoint; that is, the total class formed by the linear real a (God) and the class of linear reals x, y, and z (world) would have a similarity of position that a intersects. The relation of God and the world in spacetime would thus be a complex point, a simultaneity of position, where God is not a member of the world, for he intersects all its realities simultaneously.

The logical difficulty with this hypothetical model projected from Whitehead's theory of interpoints is, says Boyle, that it would then be impossible to identify any part of earthly events as God's place and action, since his location in spacetime would be in the interstices or the intersection of all realities without his identification as a member of the world. This has also been a problem with traditional theism; hence Whiteheadian thought does not help to answer the question of God's location any better than the classical theism he opposed. But then Boyle concludes on a promising note. The advent of relativity physics has collapsed the logical criteria for verifying God's location in spacetime:

> What is required for understanding divine spacetime in process perspective is a logic which does not situate judgment restrictively in front of things and in sequence, as if the universal stuff were solids extended seriatim in rigid, empty space, but rather allows access to plenitude and simultaneity.

22. "Interpoints: A Model for Divine Spacetime," *Process Studies*, vol. 5, no. 3 (Fall 1975): 191–94.

> Theologians search vainly for God's exact location for he appears in a field
> which is not observable in itself but only as it coappears with the world.[23]

In other words, she is saying, "Let God occupy the same spacetime as the world without his being locatable in any single part or aggregate of parts, without being locatable as the whole."[24]

There would seem to be a considerable wisdom in this appeal for a nonrestrictive "logic" for alogical wholes; but I would observe, first of all, that biblical theology does claim the location of God specifically in his revelation to Israel in the redemptive Exodus, in Torah, in symbolic sacrifice and prophecy, and superlatively in the incarnation of Jesus Christ. Secondly, I would note that Boyle's speculative attempt to solve the riddle of God's location in a process theism underscores again the impossibility of autonomous human reason arriving at a logically consistent metaphysical system. Whitehead was unable to do it, and Hartshorne, since he pledges himself to reason at the very beginning, is even more obviously a logical failure with his demand that God be conceived of both as a finite society of occasions processing serially at a finite speed in time and as a simultaneity that embraces all the occasions of the universe. Boyle at least reminds us that we have to allow for a logic of paradox. Both polarities of divine procession and divine timelessness (or simultaneity) are required, but they are not logically reconcilable on the limited level of finite reason. We simply do not know enough about spacetime itself (to say nothing of God's own nature) to insist that God's primary mode of existence is temporal and serial. The relativity of temporal sequences in spacetime is so complex that it is meaningless and false to say that God moves simultaneously along the front edge of the future. The point I wish to make is that the "future" itself is a relative term in view of relativity thought. The future relative to whom, to what, and relatively where are the questions to be kept in mind when we speak of futurity for God. There appear to be an indefinite number of time systems and no way of rationally locating God if he is ontologically limited to finite process. Far better that we think of God in the biblical pattern of explorable paradoxes than in the dogmatic and illogical structures of process thought. God is essentially supraspacetime, while as creator and redeemer he is the righteous and gracious participant in all the relative spheres of spacetime. That he is both we acknowledge, because he personally reveals himself in Scripture to be both; hence, "we believe in order that we may understand," as Augustine said and as Michael Polanyi wisely reminds us in our own day. We know more than we can tell: that God does this we

23. Ibid., p. 193.
24. Ibid., p. 192.

know from Scripture; how he does it is beyond our ken. The problem is especially severe for process theism because it has defined God a priori as temporalistic and finite and cannot adequately explain the supratemporal aspect of his bipolarity.

As a matter of fact, as Jerome Ashmore argues in agreement with Boyle, a whole may exceed and differ from the sum of its parts.[25] The alogical whole that is intuitively grasped by the creative imagination cannot at the same time be reduced to a discursive attention to logical consistencies and inconsistencies. Ashmore suggests that the most decisive weakness of Whitehead's philosophy may be his acceptance of reversibility between a unity and its abstracted members, while Ashmore himself argues for the priority of the intuited whole. Whitehead, in spite of his strictures against the fallacy of misplaced concreteness, emphasizes abstraction in his theoretical examination of time. Spacetime itself is an abstraction, Whitehead allows,[26] as is a set of time systems derived from the whole set of spacetime abstractions that are supposed to express the properties of the creative advance.[27] There is also the abstraction of a simple time series derived from the former which is used for natural measurement.[28] Ashmore asks whether the datum from which these derivative abstractions are made—that is, the concrete passage itself—is not different in kind from the abstractions. Are the abstractions not idealizations generated out of ordinary subjectivity to assist language? Are the relations indigenous to facts or does Whitehead start with relations as ideal data and look for facts on which to impose the relations?

Whitehead recognized the failure of language as the great difficulty of philosophy,[29] and opined that language is only a series of squeaks.[30] That rather low estimate of language as the medium of our life together would not be shared by all, certainly not by the followers of the later Ludwig Wittgenstein. But Ashmore cogently asks whether Whitehead's investigation of time, which began with the abstract precision of mathematics, should be normative:

> Is the field of physical science an appropriate point of departure for philosophy? Are most philosophical questions adaptable to subjugation by bare

25. Jerome Ashmore, "Diverse Currents in Whitehead's View of Time," *Process Studies*, vol. 2, no. 3 (Fall 1972): 183-200.

26. *Science and the Modern World* (New York: Macmillan, 1925), p. 96.

27. Alfred North Whitehead, *An Enquiry Concerning the Principles of Natural Knowledge*, 2d ed. (Cambridge: At the University Press, 1925), p. 81.

28. Alfred North Whitehead, *The Concept of Nature* (New York: Cambridge University Press, 1964), p. 178.

29. Alfred North Whitehead, *Modes of Thought* (New York: Macmillan, 1938), p. 67.

30. *Process and Reality*, p. 403.

precision and persistent refinement of it? Can ingenuity exceed itself to the point where its result is a tour de force?[31]

The Future Freedom of the Self

Considering then the high degree of abstraction involved in process models of time, it seems to me very questionable to argue that if God knows the future we are therefore not in any sense free. This question lies at the heart of process theology's anthropodicy. As a matter of fact, in Whiteheadian thought there really is never an agent who has a future anyway, since there is no abiding selfsame subject who determines its destiny with relative freedom and acts and responds to others over a lifetime. Frank G. Kirkpatrick calls the subjective becoming of White-head's thought an unwarranted abstraction.[32] When process theology selects the becoming of a subject as the fundamental concept, to the neglect of the substantial and abiding unity of the subject, it simply cannot make sense of what it means to be a subject or a person. This problem has already been dealt with earlier, but since it bears upon the question of the future I bring it up again. Kirkpatrick charges that the model of Whitehead and Lewis S. Ford is an abstraction, for it has abstracted the notion of the process of becoming a being from the more fundamental notion of the basic reality of beings: "What I cannot regard as possible is the conception of a process which is both subjective and self-determining *and* not yet a being because any notion of self or subject already requires the notion of a being."[33] The *self*-determining, *self*-purposive agent cannot be separated from an enduring being:

> Our whole notion of self is predicated on the assumption that the self is in some sense a determinate being, an object capable of having predicates ascribed to it as it endures over a period of extensive time (the same self is asleep now, was awake yesterday, etc.).[34]

Accordingly, Kirkpatrick argues, the *process* of unification is really an abstraction from the acts of unification done by unified beings. This stands the whole process school of theology on its head, and is (I think) a correct criticism. The basic problem in process thought is its illogical doctrine that a process of unification has, in effect, subjective unity prior to the achievement of subjective unity. In process thought there never is a continuing subject who determines anything concerning his future selfhood. There are only new subjective becomings which continually perish. But if

31. "Whitehead's View of Time," p. 200.
32. "Subjective Becoming: An Unwarranted Abstraction?" *Process Studies*, vol. 3, no. 1 (Spring 1973): 15–26.
33. Ibid., p. 19. His italics.
34. Ibid., p. 20.

that is the case, then not only is the use of subject predicates illegitimate in process theology (unwarranted abstractions, Kirkpatrick calls them), but also *there is no future* for any subject or occasion, since none persists with subjective identity! The question whether we are free or not if God knows the future is therefore irrelevant. It might have some bearing on some emergent occasion or other yet to be, but that would be another "self," not *my*self. Obviously, process thinkers who are concerned that God's omniscience might impinge upon their future freedom are thinking inconsistently in the substance terminology of the enduring self, rather than working out the consequences of radical process thought. The radical processionist will, like the Buddhist, have no regrets about the past and no anticipations or anxieties about the future, for the passing moment of becoming is all there is, really, to what we call the "self." Ultimately all is emptiness because nothing endures.

Moreover, as Rem Edwards points out, in process metaphysics there are problematical gaps that occur between the emergent occasions. In his article, "The Human Self: An Actual Entity or a Society?"[35] Edwards asks whether it is possible that the "soul" is the dominant society of actual occasions in the human body, as the process school insists, or whether the human self is an actual entity? Whitehead and William Christian allow that there is at least one self that is an actual entity, not just one actual occasion or a society of actual occasions—God. The gist of Edwards's argument is this:

> The main point of thinking about God as *an* actual entity instead of a society of actual occasions is that *the epochal theory of time just does not apply to God at all.* I am raising the question *whether it fails to apply to man as well.* God is an actual entity and not a society of actual occasions at all, and I am wondering if human experience is so atomized.[36]

Edwards is concerned about what Whitehead means by God as an actual entity and actual *now*, as a being in unison with every becoming in the world whose divine succession does not mean loss of immediate unison.[37] The difficulty is that Whitehead's epochal or atomic theory of time, based on the discontinuous microscopic pulsations of energy which constitute the subject matter of quantum physics, leads to the problem of gaps between successive occasions during which nothing exists.[38] God must then be an exception to the vibratory theory of discontinuous experience,

35. *Process Studies*, vol. 5, no. 3 (Fall 1975): 195-203.
36. Ibid., p. 196. His italics.
37. Whitehead, *Process and Reality*, p. 523.
38. Whitehead, *Science and the Modern World*, p. 52; Edwards, "The Human Self," p. 197.

for there are no gaps in his existence. Edwards proceeds to argue that
this epochal theory of discontinuous vibrations is a mistaken model. The
human soul, on analogy of God's continuous existence, does not sputter
in and out of existence every fraction of a second, but is a continuously
existing actual entity with continuous immediacy.

This critique strikes at one of the pillar doctrines of process theology as
represented by Whitehead, Hartshorne, Cobb, and Christian. Edwards
considers their theory of human soulhood mistaken.[39] Human personality
is not essentially atomic but radically different from electrons and more
in kind like God. A human being is an agent of creativity who *endures*
from moment to moment. Accordingly, it is the Whiteheadian notion of a
given duration that is the abstraction from the continuous flow of
selfhood and that is less confirmed by experience and philosophical
reflection:

> The brand new and atomically existing subjects or selves appearing every
> tenth of a second or so with which the orthodox Whiteheadian confronts us
> are the empty abstractions from the continuous flow of human experience
> and activity. *They* are the ones who commit the "fallacy of misplaced
> concreteness."[40]

That Hartshorne views this as a serious problem is clear from his
admission that human experience seems to give strong empirical evidence for the continuity of process; yet he would counter this evidence
with a "non-empirical case,"[41] although he does not know how to solve
the problem. Edwards cogently argues:

> I suggest that solving it requires abandoning the view that the concepts of
> continuity and infinity apply only to the realm of the potential and not to
> the actual. But if this move is made, Hartshorne loses one significant "non-
> temporal" objection to the theory of human experienced time as a con-
> tinuum. Even the theory that God is a society of actual occasions will not
> help Hartshorne avoid the doctrine of an actualized infinity. If the past is
> infinite, and if God's present occasion perfectly prehends the past, then
> God's present occasion will be an actualized infinity; and furthermore, there
> will actually be an infinite number of such infinitely rich members of God's
> society of actual occasions.[42]

I would add to the argument the logical implication that in an infinity
of past occasions God would have experienced all possibilities as actual

39. Edwards, "The Human Self," p. 199.
40. Ibid., p. 200. His italics.
41. Charles Hartshorne, *Creative Synthesis and Philosophic Method* (La Salle, IL:
Open Court, 1970), p. 192. See also pp. 63, 65, 125, 135.
42. Edwards, "The Human Self," p. 201.

in a finite universe (unless the universe is considered inexhaustibly infinite, which raises other problems for process theology and its logic—for example, how could spacetime, limited to the speed of light, be inexhaustibly infinite, and how could we possibly know that such were even the case?). In an infinity of past occasions now held perfectly by God in his present processing occasion, all possibilities of a finite spacetime universe would already have been actualized, including future possibilities which are no longer possibilities for God. All past *and future* occasions would accordingly be infinitely actualized in God's present occasion. Edwards does not follow this logic, for he wants to hold to an essentially processing deity; hence he dismisses the classical supernatural view that God prehends the whole of time, past, present, and future, "all at once" in a single *totum simul.*[43] But I do not see how the logic can be resisted, given a finite universe, when the empirical evidence for an infinitely expanding and novel universe is far less convincing than for a finite universe that reaches the farthest extent of the original "big bang," then contracts.

Edwards, however, takes his argument in a direction that is still very helpful in our discussion of God and the future. The reason we fail to notice the supposed gaps between occasions is because the gaps are not really there to be noticed. Therefore he reasons that (1) the epochal theory of time should be given up because it is self-contradictory to begin with.[44] (2) Experience fails to confirm the doctrine of the phases. They are really high abstractions: "This becomes patently obvious when we realize that these 'phases' all are supposed to occur together all at once rather than sequentially and that the whole process is supposed to repeat itself many times each second."[45] (3) There is a serious problem with the length of the supposed gap between occasions—how long between occasions are we not in existence?—since orthodox Whiteheadians speak of the human actual occasion as enjoying a specious present which lasts about a tenth of a second. (4) If there is a gap between occasions, how can a completely perished occasion function causally to present data to its successor? God cannot be drawn in as the ground of the givenness of the past to bridge the gap, as Christian supposes, for Donald Sherburne reminds us that the process system allows no divine prehension of contemporaries. Moreover, a similar problematic gap exists between an occasion in the world and God as between two occasions within the world:

43. Ibid., p. 196.
44. See Whitehead, *Process and Reality*, pp. 108, 227f., 323, 335, 433f., where temporal succession of phases is affirmed, and pp. 107 and 434, where succession and temporal importance are denied.
45. Edwards, "The Human Self," p. 202.

The epochal theory of time actually seems to make it impossible for God to know the world and thus creates more problems for theology than it solves. Better in my opinion to give up the epochal theory of time than to give up God! Better God without Whitehead than Whitehead without God![46]

If there are no gaps between occasions but rather an overlapping, then time is a continuous flow and the atomic theory of time has to be jettisoned. But this also means that we are able to prehend contemporaries, since occasion A still exists when it is prehended by occasion B. An occasion does not perish before it presents its data to its successor.[47] This critique has tremendous implications, for it means that we deal with each other as living beings, not as objective perished data. It also means that God has the universe as contemporaneous, not as something always slightly past and perished. (5) Edwards's final point takes us back to my earlier observation that God's knowledge of micro-occasions in our own bodies of the duration of a fraction of a millionth of a second gives him future knowledge of data that the self as agent has yet to experience and act upon. He asks how long, or how short, God's specious present may be if, according to Hartshorne and Cobb, the human specious present is about a tenth of a second long? Surely it must be far shorter than ours in order for God to give each of our actual occasions a subjective aim at its inception and then to receive it as objectively immortal when it perishes. But how short? And how long are the supposed intervals between divine occasions? Baker's figure, cited earlier, would suggest God's having billions or even trillions of occasions of experience per second. Edwards concludes his paper with an appeal for a radical departure from orthodox Whiteheadianism:

We may project that in a much more complex universe (such as ours?) God's actual occasions would have to be infinitely dense! But an entity with infinitely dense actual occasions is a continuum! Such a God would simply be a continually concrescing actual entity![48]

This conclusion is remarkable and I think on the right track, except that Edwards is not radical enough in his scope or logic. As long as God is conceived of as necessarily processive in our complex and vast universe, he has to be limited to some relative velocities along many lines of novelty. But in a universe of relative velocities, positions, and temporal directions, what could it possibly mean to say that God is a continually concrescing continuum? It seems to me that once the radical rejection of Whitehead's

46. Ibid.
47. Ibid., p. 203.
48. Ibid.

epochal doctrine is made, the notion of time as a limitation of God's vastness is a manner of speaking that can be explained only in biblical terms of creation and re-creation. No amount of metaphysical speculation can begin to solve the dilemma. In fact, as Edwards has written, the Whiteheadian attempt to unravel the mystery of time and God has raised more problems for theology than it has solved.

Only the God who is above spacetime as its creator and sustainer and who reveals himself to the mind of finite human beings can make it possible for them to comprehend him at all, and then only in explorable paradoxes having to do with the mystery of his being and time. It is here that biblical revelation does so much more than metaphysical speculation by announcing that the God beyond time has taken on time redemptively in Jesus Christ. Hence the preferred perspective of time—God's time for us—is the kairos of the cross. In the biblical process of redemption there is past, present, and future that is couched in terms of recitation, prophecy, and eschatology. But even there, and especially there, the future of our little life on earth is known only to God in his beyondness, and as much as need be known of that future for our redemption is revealed to us through the inspired prophets and seers. As to the precise time of God's final closure on this finite and fallen spacetime, even Jesus allowed that in his role as servant he was not given to know (Mark 13:32). But the Father knows, and that is the point. There is no way that God, who holds the vast but created and contingent continuum of the universe in his absolute elsewhere, could be absolutely limited by the creation called time.

Even for the Hartshornean there is no past for God as there is for us. The term *past* is an abstraction referring to what we have lost or forgotten, due to our finitude. For Hartshorne, nothing is lost for God, who perfectly holds the past in his present immediacy. For the orthodox Christian there is past for God only in terms of the Scriptures which disclose the miracle of his speaking and acting redemptively on our behalf in salvation history.

I have contended in this chapter that the future is equally present to God with the present and the past in his absolute elsewhere. Only in the relative and subordinate realm of our redemptive history does "future" take on meaning. Paradoxically it is the biblical drama of salvation itself that has given the religious world, otherwise cyclical in theory, its intense concept of linear past, present, and future. But for God on the supranatural level there can be no absolute future. Future in regard to what? At what velocity? In what position relative to other positions? We have explored these questions sufficiently to demonstrate that contemporary process thinkers are stymied by the perplexities and logical contradictions and yet by the necessity of claiming for God some preferred simultaneity of experience, some absolute nowness, which sheer process and relativity cannot afford. We have discovered that for all its brilliance, the human mind is too inadequate, too bent and fallen, to gain an answer from below in terms of naturalist theology. Biblical Christianity comes off very well indeed in rational debate with the best the finite mind can offer, not to mention its superiority in salvation experience. It approaches the problem from above through God's self-disclosure as the infinite Person, the "I AM who I AM," who has revealed himself consummately and compassionately in Jesus of Nazareth, who said, "I am the bread of life." The self-revelation of the great "I am" as both above timespace and redemptively within timespace is the Christian answer to the wrenching problems of the human mind and heart. Process theology is articulate evidence that no satisfactory solutions are available from below through naturalism and finite human thought.

PART TWO

Twenty False Propositions in Process Metaphysics

A Summary Critique of Hartshorne's Theory of Divine Relativity

5

A Critique of the Cardinal Tenets
of Process Theism

Part One

It seems clear from our examination of current process studies that serious logical problems attend the doctrines of the school and that those doctrines need to undergo some kind of radical surgery. As I have already pointed out, the most philosophically untenable and the most unbiblical doctrine of temporalistic naturalism is its attempt to limit God ontologically to finite spacetime. If a theology of "God in the world" (the aim of process theism) cannot be derived from an Aristotelian notion of God as wholly apart from the world, neither can its desire nevertheless to hold on to some aspect of "God above the world" be derived from the notion of a deity wholly tied to the world of process. Every process thinker seems in the end to come to grief on this issue. In order for God to be God, he must be universally present in his experience of creativity and as lure to creativity, but this is not logically possible if he is limited to the velocities of process and to some relative spatial position(s) or other. Rem Edwards, as we have seen, applies the coup de grâce to process metaphysics by assailing the core idea of epochal jumps in human experience on which the process interpretation of past, present, and future depends. But since no gaps are observable in our experience of continuous duration, the assumed gaps between past, present, and future in process metaphysics must be considered mere abstractions superimposed upon something more basic and more fundamental to our ongoing experience, namely, the continuous ontological ground of our being which is represented by our use of the person pronoun *I*.

God is no exception to this ontological principle but rather its supreme Archetype, the consummate instantiation of the personal pronoun *I*, as the Judeo-Christian Scriptures have always insisted. God is the infinite personal Being above spacetime who has called this intricate network of times and spaces into being and who sustains them by the word of his power (Col. 1:15–18; Heb. 1:3).

Accordingly, the future (or futures, we should more correctly say) in spacetime is not some potentiality that lies "ahead" of God and limits his omniscience, omnipresence, and omnipotence. All possibilities and all possible actualities are known by God because he has directly or indirectly brought them into being by providing the ground for their becoming actual in their own relative times and spaces. The key to the problem of God and the future is the realization that there are myriad times and spaces in vastly different "places" throughout the universe which may be comprised of peculiar parabolic patterns intersecting, overlapping, or not even related at all in spacetime, and which move in a variety of velocities and directions that simply boggle the human imagination. What is future here is past there, and what is present in another position is future elsewhere, and past in another elsewhere. No front line or futurity can possibly mark such a complex universe, unless God specifically reveals a favored eschatological time line relative to his redemptive activity on our behalf in this world pattern. This of course is the biblical pattern; however, it is not arrived at by human speculation but by God's own self-disclosure, and therefore becomes normative for Christian faith. The reason why biblical revelation and Christian eschatology are normative is because God who is supratemporal and supraspatial is himself the creator, sustainer, and only trustworthy revealer of meaningful spacetime patterns.

Hence a temporal deity limited to some finite velocity and spatial system simply does not make sense. Only the infinite personal God who transcends the abstractions of past, present, and future (and who is therefore truly infinite), who knows each of us better than we know ourselves (and is therefore eminently personal) can satisfy the two polarities of unity and diversity, being and becoming. This is the claim of biblical faith which, in my opinion, cannot be bettered by metaphysical speculation unaided by divine revelation as to the nature and order of reality.

There was a time when I thought the metaphysical notions of process thought had radically improved upon the biblical polarities concerning God's transcendence and immanence. I no longer think so. In fact, having been thoroughly immersed in both epistemologies, I would now disclaim the ability of autonomous human reason, unaided by divine revelation, to understand the nature of God and creation without serious distortion. Such is Paul's declaration in Romans 1:18–3:20, which rules out any human self-justification or knowledge of ultimate things because of the moral and conceptual bentness of humanity. The logical contradictions in process naturalism, which assays the task of describing God and humanity apart from scriptural revelation, are truly enormous and were a shock to me as they appeared one after another following an initial reading of John T. Wilcox's critique of a fundamental problem in process theology regarding God's velocity and position is spacetime. I was further alarmed by the fact that more than a third of the articles in *Process Studies* were addressing serious difficulties in the process school of thought itself.

Of course there is no question that God is engaged in process. The Scriptures have always made that claim. God is the redemptive participant par excellence in human history and creation; and modern science has described a universe of such beauty, power, and awesome complexity that one is driven either to further praise God or to despair. But the limitation of God to time and space has to be considered a modern idolatry. Orthodox Whiteheadian-Hartshornean process theology has rejected the Judeo-Christian faith and its epistemology of scriptural revelation. I have already mentioned a number of passages in which Alfred North Whitehead and Charles Hartshorne reject classical Christianity because of its doctrine that God is omnipotent. This teaching is taken to be inimical to human freedom and to general creativity in nature. But what process theology has done—and this is a common hermeneutical failure, when one concept is selected in disregard of balancing and compensating concepts—is to depreciate the extremely important emphasis, indeed a hortatory emphasis, that Scripture places upon individual and corporate freedom and responsibility. God is sovereign, but he has also given his creatures a limited measure of genuine choice. This is the paradox that must be taken as a whole if justice is to be done to God's revelation of himself in the Bible. This is the "logically odd" language that is appropriate in Scripture, the merismus of a part here that is balanced by a part there. Where Islamic theology sacrifices the gift of human freedom in order to heighten the transcendence of God and ends up in fatalism, process theism sacrifices the sovereignty of God in order to heighten human freedom and ends up in relativism. Both are heterodoxies in light of historic Christian faith. The current attempt by a second and third generation of process theologians to wed the doctrines of process theism with traditional Christian thought I deem to be a fruitless undertaking. I know from personal experience, both in teaching and in Christian worship, that process theism has a way of intellectualizing God through speculative abstractions and compromising Christianity with other competing world views while dismissing biblical revelation on essential issues.

We have already noted how leading process thinkers have reduced the biblical personal infinite God to abstractions about potentiality, creativity, and rightness, and how John B. Cobb, Jr., in his desire to wed Christianity with Buddhism faces the problem of defining for Buddhists what his principle of divine rightness might be, without unduly offending the non-theistic Buddhist mind. But how do Christians react to this endeavor of a Protestant theologian to speak from a Christian context to another world religion? Gabriel Fackre, in his review of Cobb's *Christ in a Pluralistic Age*,[1] declares that in dismissing classical Christian doctrine Cobb has substituted a far less precise and satisfactory Christology. The Old Testament background of Christology is missing, as is any serious incorporation of Synoptic, Johannine, Pauline, or other early Christian proclamation about the significance of Jesus Christ. Cobb does not deal with fundamentally important questions as to how the depths of human perversity or the intractible powers of evil and death are met and overcome in Jesus Christ. Moreover, because Cobb's commitment to process thought prohibits his allowing any actuality of God prior to creation, he rejects the biblical belief in the universal work of the Logos and the incarnation at Bethlehem, both being the activity of the eternal Logos within the Triune God. The incarnation of the Logos in the personal and historical Jesus is "dissipated," says Fackre, by Cobb's confusion of "Logos ensarkos" or Logos incarnate in Jesus with the "Logos prophorikos" and "Logos spermatikos," which describe the more universal inseminating activity of the Logos in creation. Process christology is not able to do justice to the unique redemptive work of Christ and his lordship. Christ's defeat of the world's perennial foes is a revolutionary cosmic event that cannot be reduced to a static universal process.

Process theism, on the other hand, is committed to a soteriology of rational persuasion that cannot deal adequately with the real conflicts between competing centers of power. There is no eschatology of judgment in Cobb's reconstruction because his Buddhist-Whiteheadian view ultimately extinguishes personal accountability. As Fackre says,

> Accountability is a basic premise of both eschatology and Christology. Associated with this is the final reckoning with evil as well as sin, justice for the wretched of the earth and the accountability of the powers and principalities. The Whiteheadian understanding of the Kingdom of Heaven as the consequent nature of God does not deal profoundly enough with the

1. John B. Cobb, Jr., *Christ in a Pluralistic Age* (Philadelphia: Westminster, 1975); Gabriel Fackre, "Cobb's *Christ in a Pluralistic Age:* A Review Article," *Andover Newton Quarterly*, vol. 17, no. 4 (March 1977): 908-15.

adjudication of evil and therefore the pain of the world and its resolution in Christian eschatology.[2]

Fackre concludes that Cobb's failure to honor the particularity of the Christ of the incarnation reveals "an inadequate perception of the militancy of the powers of sin and evil and how they are finally confronted on Golgotha and Easter morning."[3]

In a similar vein Clark Williamson criticizes David R. Griffin's heterodoxy in regard to Jesus' resurrection.[4] Griffin declares that the resurrection of Jesus is "optional" for Christian theology. He does not view Jesus Christ as the Lord of the world but only as the Light of the world, and only then as providing a cognitive dimension for our outlook on the world. This is the gnosticism that is so obvious in much of process thinking today, as I have had occasion to point out earlier. But even this cognitive view of Jesus is for Griffin relative because of cultural and historical differences between New Testament times and our own. Williamson is correct, I feel, in expressing amazement that Griffin can consider the resurrection "optional" in light of the historical confession of the church that the risen Christ is Lord.

Such arbitrariness in regard to early Christian evidences and beliefs is typical of the process school, however, and brings into question the extent to which process methodology can helpfully inform the biblical scholar and theologian. As a Neutestamentler myself I modestly employed process categories in *Jesus, Persons, and the Kingdom of God*[5] a decade and a half ago, but I did not go so far as to deny the resurrection of Christ. Nevertheless, Griffin is consistently following Hartshorne's dismissal of resurrection teaching in general, since he does not believe in the possibility of subjective immortality (the gift of new conscious existence beyond death), but only in objective immortality (God's remembering without loss of any detail this one and only life on earth). The denial of the resurrection is also the denial of grace, for the one hope that is no hope at all, but rather horror, is that God would remember every detail of this life of mistakes, sins, suffering, and death! This is only one example of the substantial losses that are sustained when autonomous human speculation is made normative above the empirical evidence of biblical eyewitnesses and revelation.

The sum of my critique thus far is that process theism is epistemologically a speculative human enterprise which, depending on the individual

2. Fackre, "Cobb's *Christ in a Pluralistic Age,*" p. 315.
3. Ibid.
4. See Williamson's review of David R. Griffin, *A Process Christology* (Philadelphia: Westminster, 1973) in *Process Studies*, vol. 4, no. 3 (Fall 1974): 212–17.
5. (Siant Louis: Bethany Press; and Philadelphia: Pilgrim Press, 1967).

author, may or may not make use of certain Christian teachings. It is clear that essential Christian doctrines not only are considered unnecessary but also are largely rejected by process metaphysics. A philosophy that posits a fundamental dualism at the core of reality—God *and* the world—must define God in finite and naturalistic terms. In such a system, some universe or other is everlastingly necessary for God and is at least partly independent of him, thus rendering false the Christian teaching that God brought spacetime creation into being by his own command and sustains it by his sovereign word. God is therefore, according to process theism, everlastingly limited—a wholly unbiblical idea that undercuts the entire Christian drama of salvation by substituting a naturalistic dyscatastrophe for an eschatological eucatastrophe. Human salvation is by the good works of rational thought and philosophic persuasion, not by faith in the gracious sacrifice of God's own Son for a rebellious and fallen race. There is no special resurrection of Christ as forerunner of a new race, no general resurrection of believers at the final renewal of the heavens and the earth, no gifts of conscious eternal life for anyone. Biblical faith is simply left in shambles.

I confess sadly that although process thought was a fascinating preoccupation of mine for a dozen years, it has made no lasting contribution to biblical theology and classical historic Christian thought that is not already in the good news of God's gracious activity in Jesus Christ. Indeed, its presuppositions are essentially nonbiblical and non-Christian. A summary of Hartshorne's doctrines by a very dear friend of mine, Eugene Peters, who first introduced me to process thought, illustrates the truth of that criticism. In his festschrift article on the occasion of Hartshorne's eightieth birthday, Peters lists the cardinal tenets of the school with magisterial clarity.[6] Hartshorne remarked that it was the best summary he had seen of his thought. I find myself now in disagreement with every one of the twenty doctrines and will explain my differences by offering a critique, from a biblical point of view, of each of Peters's summary statements. The twenty doctrines are given (in quotation marks) together with my comments.

(1) "No experience has itself as a datum." But if there is never an identity between what is experienced and the experience of it, then there is no continuous self or personal pronoun *I* that refers to a substantial self. The agent *I* is the original and final agent of personal activity. Process theology's failure to account for the personal and continuous stream of experience is one of its most serious weaknesses.

(2) "A stream of experience is really a series or sequence of unit

6. Eugene Peters, "Philosophic Insights of Charles Hartshorne," *The Southwestern Journal of Philosophy*, vol. 8 (February 1977): 157-70. Dr. Peters, I was saddened to learn, passed away in May, 1983, at the age of fifty-four.

experiences." This is really a restatement of the first doctrine and is subject to the same criticism. *Who* is doing the experiencing? If experience is always asymmetrically backward—if we back into the future, as it were—what accounts for the unity of the unit experiences that never experience each other but experience only the perished and objective units that have preceded them? What is a personal "experience," except an abstraction from some more basic and continuous substratum called "I"?

(3) "Time is essentially the sequential actualization of unit experiences." But if there is no prior agent who experiences the continuous flow of actualization, how can there be any personal perspective from which the "I" can distinguish past, present, and future? Without the personal pronoun *I* as the prior reference point, there can only be discrete units with no relation and no perspective from which to judge that they belong to *a person's* past, present, or future. They would be just "there," unrelated. If a concrescing unit is said to remember or to anticipate then there is introduced the language of a continuous agent who underlies or transcends the process of time. If the personal agent *I* is admitted, then "time" is a useful manner of speaking, an abstraction from the unity of the subject's experiences that refers to what the enduring subject at present remembers and what he anticipates. If there is no substantial self, then it is illegitimate to speak of the individual as a self. The central failure of the process system is its inability to account for the reality of the person who is now becoming actualized and who is supposed to choose and freely act in view of the past and in anticipation of the future, and who does all this as the continuous person whose name he bears. Until this sense of continuity can be accounted for, there is no sense in using the word *time* to describe discrete units. The notion of time arises only against the background of a continuous person who can distinguish past, present, and future. Otherwise the "self" is simply locked into windowless monads that should have no sense of anything but of a momentary now.

(4) "Actuality is atomic, while possibility is continuous and homogeneous." This, I feel, is the fundamental error of process theism. It goes back, of course, to Whitehead's doctrine of atomicity. The same criticism applies here as in the preceding example. Without some prior organizing soul or mind that is a gift of God in creation (God himself being the absolute prior Mind behind all creation), no human personality could possibly come into existence. It is the great mythology and fiction of contemporary naturalism that atomic units can generate unity out of themselves. This cannot be done from the bottom up. Even the Whiteheadian and Hartshornean systems have to concede that there must be a divine lure working upon the atomic units from above for the creative

advance to occur, for pure atomicity and pure chance are pure chaos which can produce nothing creative of itself. This is also a criticism of pervasive naturalistic evolutionary doctrine. Where a controlled descriptive science dramatically discloses the amazing symmetry and unity in diversity of our universe, an incautious scientism claims that the system is self-contained and that aboriginal atomicity produces evolutionary order. At least this much can be said for Whitehead and Hartshorne and their followers, that they see the need for a divine Agent to order the process.

But then we have to ask not only about God's personal substantiality to order the world (he seems to be a mere abstraction himself), but also about the discrete finite units he is trying to lure to creativity. Who is it who receives the divine lure and does the resolving of possibility into actuality? Who experiences and feels except an agent who is named and identified as a substance or a person from his or her inception? From a biblical perspective that personal *I* is a creation of God and a gift, a soul who accounts for the unity of the so-called atomic events. The discrete events cannot of themselves produce a unified self. If "there is nothing that underlies experience," what accounts for the defining character of a sequence of events? It cannot be simply one of the atomic aggregates, a dominant monad, or some other part of the whole, else we are unaccountably left with a small unity in a sea of atomicity. The truth of the matter, I think, is the other way around. The atomic units are aspects of the substantial person who is doing the experiencing. This is the biblical picture of persons as portrayed in the opening chapters of Genesis. God the prior and consummate creative Agent breathes into atomic dust a living soul and gives this created person a name, Adam. The first human creature is thus seen to have a paradoxical nature which is processive and atomic on the one hand and substantial and personally responsive and responsible on the other. In no case is it true to biblical revelation to say that actuality is basically atomic and that continuity belongs only to the realm of possibility. Instead the human person is a child of God, an identifiable unity who bears a name and experiences his unity in spacetime. Of course the biblical picture of humankind also portrays the race as fallen and bent so that our present "nature" is always unnatural; that is, we always act as sinners in regard to the most essential relationship to God (Rom. 1:18–3:20). Indeed, in biblical terms the reduction of reality and therefore human beings to "incurable atomicity," as Whitehead put it, is to be classed with other forms of idolatry that absolutize the things of the created world. But in Christ, the Scriptures proclaim, a new nature is possible through faith in God's gift of forgiveness and reconciling love (Eph. 2).

(5) "Causality is crystallized freedom, freedom is causality in the

making." But how does a crystallized datum that has already perished affect a new becoming, and how does the new becoming appropriate what is crystallized, when its own individuality comes not at the beginning but at the end of the process? Here again the absence of a clear understanding of the personal pronoun I leads to a serious ambiguity. What does it mean to say "freedom is causality in the making"? Who is exercising the freedom? Causality? Not if it is in the making, for what is in the making is not yet fully itself and cannot be assigned the characteristics of agency and choice. At what point, then, does genuine choosing take over from "being caused" in the process of the emergent occasion? And by whose choosing do new possibilities keep opening up?

(6) "An event's causal ancestry has no initial terminus, but extends indefinitely into the past." This speculative doctrine implies the eternality of causal spacetime and thus leads to an ultimate dualism of God and the universe. It is one of the most anti-Christian teachings in process metaphysics because it necessarily denies that the infinite personal God alone is eternal and that he has brought the spacetime world into existence by his own act of creation. Since the world process is without beginning or end, the doctrine also denies the eschatological fulfillment of God's redemptive work in Christ. Hartshorne adopts the Christian doctrine that God is love, but having rejected the doctrine of the ontological Trinity, he has to give the world process eternal status in order that God may have an object of his love.

I have already commented on the logical problems of positing an endless world process. While Hartshorne, against Whitehead, argues that new possibilities arise with new actualities, nonetheless with the ebb and flow of finite spacetime stuff he cannot consistently argue for an infinite number of combinations, although he must if he is not to fall into the logical absurdity that if the past extends infinitely backward, then, as Hindu doctrine would have it, we have experienced the present and the future, as well as the past, endless times before, and every other actuality as well. I simply do not know what it means to say that the world process of new creativity extends infinitely before us, if it already extends infinitely behind us in actualized form. The latter should logically exclude the former.

Process theology is really a holdover from nineteenth-century evolutionary theory, but the notion of endless creative advance is sustained neither by recent human history nor by astrophysical theories that foresee the final exhaustion of the expanding universe and its eventual contraction. Does process thought then adopt a cyclical pulsating theory of the universe, similar to oriental cyclicisms? But then there could be no continuous creative advance but only an eternal repetition of old actualities. In a universe that faces eventual contraction, compressed perhaps

Figure 6   Figure 7

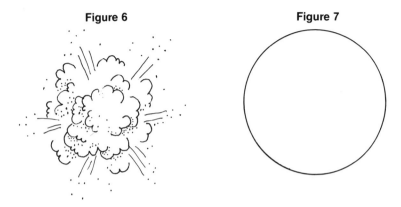

into a tiny black hole of unimaginable gravitational force (God's original created and compressed spacetime prior to the "big bang"?), there cannot be an infinite number of possibilities or actualities. It would seem to me then that Hartshorne's notion that an event's causal ancestry extends indefinitely into the past destroys the possibility of new creativity, as all finite possibilities would already have been infinitely repeated and actualized. Friedrich Nietzsche based his hopes of immortality on this cyclical belief. What is wrong with the logic? At any rate, if creativity-become-actuality extends infinitely backward in timespace, it cannot extend infinitely forward, not in the sense in which process theism wants to think of creativity as its own end, "each new concretion enriching the accumulated wealth of value, however slightly," forever.

The error of this humanly conceived theism lies in thinking of time as a straight line extending indefinitely into the past and into the future, even for God. But as I have suggested, if any given universe allows only a finite number of creative possibilities before it dies, time would be viewed in a push-pull configuration that produces a number of successive different universes infinitely repeated (see Fig. 6). Or it would resemble a circle, with each universe a unit on the circumference, infinitely repeated (Fig. 7). What cannot be entertained logically in a finite universe comprised of finite and limited components is an infinitely expanding configuration that affords everlastingly novel creativity. All novelty would have been long exhausted and already repeated innumerable times if the past extends infinitely backward. But in either pattern, time is then not linear but cyclical. I fail to see how Hartshorne's rejection of the biblical doctrine of spacetime creation by the sovereign God does not lead him logically to a cyclical view of time and, ironically, to the virtual denial of the very freedom and creativity he has sought to defend. Only when something is done once in a straight time line is there genuine freedom. And this is the biblical view. Spacetime has a terminus a quo and a terminus ad quo, and whatever is done between these points is once and for all, never to be repeated in quite the same way.

This means that spacetime belongs to God its creator and sustainer, not God to spacetime. This is the fundamental issue between biblical Christian theology and contemporary naturalist theism. For the former, the sovereign personal God is absolute; for the latter the abstraction of creativity and world process is ultimate.

(7) "The arrow of implication points from effect to cause, not from cause to effect (as in deterministic theories)." The problem with this attempt to avoid determinism and to insure novelty is that it denies what I have been arguing for all along, namely, that before we can speak of an effect we must identify a causal agent, a substantial subject who experiences the event and chooses the effect. For Hartshorne, the event or experience is not an attribute of a substance, subject, or agent, even though ordinary intellectual habits and language make the view a natural one. I would agree with other critics of this process doctrine that we ordinarily think and speak as though there were a subject experiencing an event because this idea is true to reality. Rather than the self-identical characteristics of the subject being abstractions from a sequence of experience-events, the experience-events are abstractions from the continuing subject, else how can we speak of a sequence or of experience? A sequence connotes an identity of relationships, and there is no such thing as an "experience" without a subject experiencing. Peters summarizes Hartshorne's view:

> These characters or structures do not possess the events; rather, they belong to the events. As Hartshorne insists, process, not fixity, is the inclusive category, for (as he succinctly puts it) it is impossible to insinuate novelty into identity.[7]

What is really impossible is to insinuate identity into novelty, for without a free and choosing agent, there is no thing nor no one to produce the novelty or newness in the process. The word *novelty* means new, but new relative to what? In the process system there is supposed to be a "new" event-experience every tenth of a second or so, but without a subject substantially the same who endures from one experience to another there is no relationship between events, no sense of continuity or of novelty, process, and time. It is not sufficient to appeal to an event-experience remembering or anticipating when there is no substantial identity that continuously remembers and anticipates. There are just discrete units essentially unrelated. There is simply chaos.

7. Ibid., p. 162.

Process thought has got the whole thing backward. It is impossible for sheer atomicity to generate subjects with characteristics of identity. By insisting on the priority of atomicity, process theism sacrifices identity horizontally in time, since the individual entity or person has no logical continuity from epoch to epoch; and it sacrifices sociality vertically in space because no actual entity is contemporaneous with another, for in order to be free it must be all alone and possess other entities only as past and perished occasions, including of course its past "selves." Moreover, in the process system, God is really only a deus ex machina, for without any substantiality independent of world process he nonetheless serves illogically to provide the world with a lure to creativity. He causes the world to take on certain configurations or effects, without total control, yet is himself with no actuality apart from the world.

But in that case why should process theism not say that cause precedes effect, at least in some substantial sense? Determinism is not necessarily implied when we view process in this manner, for according to biblical theology even God himself, the ultimate cause, accords human beings a measure of freedom to choose and to bear responsibility for the effects of their choosing (e.g., "Seek the LORD while he may be found, call upon him while he is near" [Isa. 55:6]).

To sum up: There are no "experiences" in and of themselves. Even if such blind, subjectless events could be imagined, they could not of themselves produce a subject. Reality does not process unaided from the bottom up, but from the top down, as process theism itself has to allow when it posits the supreme mind of God as the initial lure to creativity, even for atomic events. Only then can there be creative advance from the simple to the complex, as in the maturation of the human person. But, says biblical faith, God provides a basic level of identity and lure for the human being, the soul, which is the substantial unity of self that appears at the beginning of personhood and around which the experiences are oriented. Again, the meaning of "I" is the issue.

(8) "Space—unlike time—is a symmetrical order." That is, whereas data are antecedent to an experience-event and are therefore asymmetrical in time (the data can influence the experience-event, but not vice versa), in space two contemporary events are neighbors. Curiously, however, process theism does not allow these contemporary events to influence each other directly in their cocontemporaneity, for each creative event is alone in its moment of creative immediacy on the processing fringe of the future. Contemporary experience-events influence one another only as past data, just like everything else; but the contemporaneous events once they become past data are thought to mutually influence the new emergent experience-events that supersede the old.

Individual temporal experience-events move in one direction only, toward the future.

Now the past and perished data of several experience-events which have been contemporaneous are thought to influence each other vertically, producing a sense of space. This inviolate doctrine of temporal asymmetry and spatial symmetry in process theology is taken to be true of God as well. In his temporal line of experience the supremely processing God is everlastingly effected by his past experience data, but cannot reverse the process and influence those data; however, in his eminently spatial experience of the whole universe he is effected by all the past data of every perished occasion simultaneously.

If we set aside for the moment the serious problem we have already considered (i.e., how a processing God in a universe of relativity can simultaneously experience contemporaneous data everywhere), it is important to note that process theism denies that any experience-event, including God, can really enjoy genuine contemporaneity with anything or anyone. There can be no participation sideways at right angles in another's contemporaneity. Hence so-called spatial symmetry is not actually a vertical but a diagonal line, from the perished data of a to the living immediacy of b, and from the perished data of b to the living immediacy of a. Does this model really allow mutual symmetry in space? If we think for a moment of perished data a influencing the living immediacy of b, is it not the case that in temporal process by the time b has perished and its data is available for assimilation by a, a is no longer a living immediacy but has become a new emergent occasion; as has b by this time, so that no symmetrical exchange of anything is possible at all?

The point is this: while process theism seems to allow for spatial contemporaneity, in fact the content of anyone's immediacy is always of something past. Although other persons *seem* to be contemporaneous they are so only in a calculative sense. But this assumes that there are identical persons who can calculate, where the process system would seem to draw the shades on all the windows, both temporally and spatially. Two contemporary events, according to Whitehead and Hartshorne, are mutually independent and do not neighbor one another in the sense of being concretely related to one another in their present immediacy. They have only an abstract togetherness, since they experience one another only as past data. While this seems to allow for dialogue between two or more persons, such dialogue is always abstract since the person one hears speaking is already a past perished datum, while the "me" another hears is similarly already a past datum. God himself then works supremely with past data. Since everything has at some level its present immediacy which is independent of everything else, and since God is no exception to this metaphysical rule, God has no immediacy with the universe but only with his own lonely immediacy on the edge of time. All the concrete data of the necessary finite universe that contribute to his concrete experience are perished data, the past. Thus time in process theism is more basic than space, for the so-called contemporaneity of space is only a calculated abstraction, an apparent contemporaneity, since no experience-events, including God, are really interacting in the immediate present. Reality is comprised of independent monads with windows only on past dead data. This startling concept of timespace brings Gottfried Wilhelm Leibniz into our own century, with his independent and windowless monads locked into their own contemporaneity. I would say that that is quite a price to pay for "freedom." I would repeat my earlier criticism that process theology is a sophisticated anthropodicy, a defense of individual freedom at all costs.

A curious picture presents itself to us as we try to imagine what process theologians are saying about our experience. The implication of the system is that all conscious personal experience is necessarily of the past. The conscious self comes into being at the end of the emergent occasion, not at the beginning or somewhere in between. Accordingly, "I" (if "I" can be mentioned at all) exist unconsciously into the future, and consciously into the past. In other words, all of us are riding backward into the future with an unknown driver at the controls of events that are absolutely elsewhere in relation to each other. All sense of space and of time as actual is of the past. As conscious persons our relationship to ourselves, to others, to God, as actual, is in terms of the past. Even God's simultaneity of the entire universe would have to be with the universe as past. Only in the brief moment at the end of the emergent occasion when we become conscious do we anticipate the future and make choices for the next emergent occasion that will supersede us, but these conscious choices are only of what is possible, not of what is actual. And in the moment of choice we are all alone, without others, without God.

I conclude, then, that while space might seem at first to be symmetrical in its two-way traffic between seemingly contemporaneous entities, such is not and cannot be the case in process theism. Space is as asymmetrical as time; and the position of one who claims his freedom on grounds of human speculation rather than biblical revelation, frightfully lonely.

(9) "The human body is a society of event sequences, dominated by a superior, central sequence called the mind." Process theology has to be very careful here not to accord the mind any substantial character, otherwise it would give away its fundamental doctrine that experience-events are prior to and give rise to the self. They are not predicates of a soul or mind already there at the base of experiences.

What then is the mind in process theology? It is pointedly memory and perception which afford the causal connection that David Hume was not able to find between volition and bodily action. Hume was looking in the wrong direction from cause (volition) to effect (the action). Actually, says Hartshorne, it is the other way round. Memory and perceptions are narrow abstract functionings of the mind which is derived from the bodily cells that are data for the mind, the basic experience underlying all being sympathy or the feeling of feeling. But this attempted reversal from effect to cause, from basic bodily feelings to the superior and central sequence of feeling called the mind, fails to explain how the mind comes into being or what it actually is. If the mind (the cause) is subsequent to the experience-data of the body (the effect), how does one legitimately use the personal pronoun *I* as it appears in the following sentence, where "I" seems to be both the unity of the person yet only one entity in a body-mind dualism: "As Hartshorne puts it, my body is my friend, its parts my companions; I care about them and share their feelings"?[8] The point has been made before that the ordinary sense of identity and personhood and the use of "I" and "my" in ordinary language indicates that the mind is more essential than some "dominant and superior central sequence" that inexplicably appears in personal experience.

(10) "Hartshorne has seen that perception and memory belong to the same genus, for each is a form of inheritance. While memory refers retrospectively to events in the stream or sequence which I call myself, perception refers retrospectively to events in and around my body." Hartshorne calls the stream or sequence of a person his personal memory, while perception is his impersonal memory. Thus memory is both personal and impersonal. My question is, who is doing the remembering? It begs the question to reply that two types of memory comprise the person. Memory defies hypostatization because it is an abstraction from the substantial person represented by "I" and "my" who is doing the remembering. Furthermore, it is improper to refer to "impersonal" perception, because some personally ordered subject is supposedly doing the perceiving. It would be more accurate to speak of conscious and unconscious aspects of memory and perception, since both modes apply to the living "I." But most importantly, it is the underlying *self* who remembers and perceives, whether consciously or unconsciously, not some abstraction termed "sequence of events" or "dominant monad."

Hartshorne's epochal theory of existence by jumps leads to the curious notion that in dreamless sleep I have only a vegetative soul and that at that threshold personal unity is lost; in sleeping and waking I jump from and back to my selfhood. But surely that is the extent of absurdity to which the doctrine of atomicity in process theism leads one. If selfhood arises out of atomic experience-events, then it logically follows that it

8. Ibid., p. 164.

goes on and off, as one emergent occasion arises, peaks, and perishes, and another successive emergent occasion arises, peaks, and perishes. But that is contrary to ordinary experience and language usage, in addition to the fact that there is no empirical evidence that selfhood as such is posterior to atomic experience-events. A husband, gazing at his sleeping wife, never thinks of her as a selfless vegetable, or says, "I think I will restore this aggregate of vegetable experience-events to personal unity and bring it back to wifely selfhood by waking it up." Dreamless sleep is not a flitting out of personal unity, but an unconscious state of personal unity and identity which perseveres at various levels of intensity throughout a person's tenure of life. The husband would never refer to his sleeping wife as "it" but as "her," as the one who even in dreamless sleep retains her privileged access to her own unique and identified selfhood as she is viewed as a living person with a particular name by her husband.

(11) "The only individuals we directly experience in the outside world are animals, including, of course, one another (although not the dreamless sleeper)." I have already exposed the error of rejecting the dreamless sleeper as a person. What then of the remainder of the statement? Peters goes on to explain that Hartshorne views all other entities as groups or abstractions of some sort, but without individuality. Consider the logic of this explanation:

> A lake, for example, is a multiplicity of molecules, not a concrete singular entity. The molecules are imperceptibly small, so we do not perceive their movement or their makeup. Now, if we grant that there are imperceptible micro-individuals as parts of what is given, we may be willing to admit that our failure to perceive God (cosmic unity) is not a perceiving of his absence. For if at the micro-level there is individuality which is not perceived, there may also be unperceived megaloscopic individuality.[9]

How, we must ask, is a microscopic molecule an individual? And how do we get from unperceived molecular micro-individuals to the unperceived megaloscopic cosmic unity of God the individual if we deny that the intermediate sphere of lakes, trees, and rocks are also individuals with naiads or dryads inhabiting them as souls? What is the definition of an individual? If a dreamless sleeper has lost her individuality, how can it be said that an unperceived molecule is a micro-individual? Is a molecule awake or does it have its moments of dreamless sleep and cease to be an individual? Or is it superior to a human being in always being an individual as long as it exists? The discussion becomes rather silly at this point.

9. Ibid., p. 165.

Concerning God, since his brain is comprised of the bits and pieces of the universe which afford him concrete consciousness, what happens when these bits and pieces, blown into existence at the original "big bang," become subject to entropy, retreat, and compress into the final black hole at the doomsday of the universe? Does God then lose his individuality in the great dreamless sleep of the ultimate black hole? Does he awaken again and resume his individuality at the next pulsating explosion of a new universe, if there is one?

What does it mean to be an individual? Process thought does not answer that question. However, the process theist's view is certainly diametrically opposed to the biblical view of persons who are considered individuals within a divine covenant, even during conception. What does process theism have to say of the dignity and identity of the individual person that compares with the psalmist's inspired utterance:

> For thou didst form my inward parts,
> thou didst knit me together in my mother's womb.
> I praise thee, for thou art fearful and wonderful.
> Wonderful are thy works!
> Thou knowest me right well;
> my frame was not hidden from thee,
> when I was being made in secret,
> intricately wrought in the depths of the earth.
> Thy eyes beheld my unformed substance;
> in thy book were written, every one of them,
> the days that were formed for me,
> when as yet there was none of them. [Psalm 139:13-16]

(12) "Feeling belongs intrinsically to sensation." According to Hartshorne, there is a continuum within and inclusive of color, sound, taste, and so forth, since sensa (feelings that are more or less definite and localized) are continuous with the whole complex range of emotions and attitudes. In his system the taste of sweetness, for example, invites us to continue eating or drinking, while bitterness or sourness invites us to stop. Neither is a matter of association but is an innate impulse to accept or reject, arising from the sensation itself.

The question here is whether Hartshorne is speaking properly when he refers to innate impulses, invitations, and the whole complex range of emotions and attitudes. Unless we have assumed something more fundamental which experiences sensation feeling, namely, the person himself, we have committed the fallacy of misplaced concreteness. It is the self who is the continuity of the whole complex range of emotions and attitudes. Sensations and feelings do not somehow produce the person, but are aspects of the personal pronoun *I*. How is taste an innate invitation to accept or reject, except in terms of the continuum who is the person himself? In the process view, feeling lies at the base of reality. My contention is that individual *persons* feel—feeling is the predicate of some underlying unity that is experiencing the feeling. Feelings have no actuality on their own, any more than sensa. If the self is viewed in light of biblical theology, it is seen to be a body-soul unity, endowed by God the Creator with innate functions and ideas that provide the framework of limited freedom and creativity. But the self is always viewed in the Scriptures as a responsible unity, not as the supervening result of a complex of sensation feelings. Who is sensing, who is feeling, who is inviting? That is the question. Certainly not the sensa and feelings apart from their complex association in the living person.

6

A Critique of the Cardinal Tenets of Process Theism

Part Two

$$W$$e shall continue our examination of the principal doctrines of process theology with a critique of point 13.

(13) "Whatever is experienced is included, in its particularity, within the experience of it." That is to say, the essence of experience is to possess data. If x is a unit event, then subject y will have x as its object (although x will have no relation to y because of asymmetry in time). Societies will have symmetrical relationships, although only God has unqualified inclusion of all data. The point Charles Hartshorne wants to make here is that experience is composed of other experiences (e.g., John's love for his wife is his sharing her feelings, her life, her particularity).

But is this possible even for God in the Hartshornean system? Both the doctrine of asymmetry and the doctrine of symmetry disallow the sharing of contemporaneous experiences, since every emergent occasion is on the front line of creativity all alone and absolutely elsewhere in relation to other emergent occasions. If that is true (although I deny it) then not even God can experience x and y in their immediacy, but only as perished data. And since x and y as objective data are no longer subjects experiencing their own immediacy, the very quality of their living subjective immediacy can never be experienced by a, b, c, or God. Not even the experience itself, x or y, can have itself as datum. There is irreparable loss even for God, since he no more than we can experience the immediacy of an emergent occasion. Hartshorne denies this, but only illogically.

Accordingly, since there is enormous loss of immediacy in the process model, it is incorrect to say that "whatever is experienced is included, in its particularity, within the experience of it," or "that relation to x includes x, though x does not thereby include the relation." For relation to x does not include x's subjective immediacy, but only x as perished. All relations, therefore, including God's, are of perished data, not of living immediacy. The process doctrine of radical temporalism makes this a logical necessity. Time lag is the tyrant that makes it impossible for anything or anyone to experience another's present. Hence John's love for his wife is really his sharing the feelings, life, and particularity of some past "person" now perished. The subtle metaphysics of a naturalist theology wedded to time has taken us to the absurdity of marriage to the dead and to past wives and husbands. Because John and his wife can never share their contemporaneity (otherwise they would lose their freedom), they can never have each other except as perished. The loss of substantial identity in process theism has taken us so far that even monogamous marriage itself is under attack, polygyny or polyandry being the only possibility!

Classical Christian thought transcends the limitations and tyranny of spacetime and contends that God genuinely participates in the world's immediacy while upholding its relative freedom to choose. This is biblical mystery or merismus, the logically odd way God speaks through the Scriptures. Scriptural language about God and created persons is genuinely bipolar and does not reject the mystery by absorbing the pole of transcendence and identity into the pole of process. Moreover, since persons are created in the image of God, they can experience derivatively this bipolarity and come so close to God in faith, and to genuine friends and lovers in moments of oneness, that they share the immediate present without objectification. Note the mystery and bipolarity in Paul's use of the personal pronoun *I* and his separateness yet unity with Christ: "I have been crucified with Christ; it is no longer I who live, but Christ who lives in me; and the life I now live in the flesh I live by faith in the Son of God, who loved me and gave himself for me" (Gal. 2:20).

Of course this is roundly denied by process thought, but the price of denial is a heavy one. When philosophical theology cuts itself off from biblical revelation and decides to make spacetime an ultimate, there comes a moment (it happened to me) when one stares down a gaping hole and sees only the darkness of perished data as the essence of what is taken to be reality, and then the words of judgment in Genesis 3:14-19 come home with a vengeance: The tempter's query, "Hath God said?"(KJV) and his promise "You will not die" (vv. 1-4) end with God's speaking a curse on the rebellious serpent, pain for the woman, sweat for the man, and above all, an inevitable entropy and return to the dust of earth. With the most brilliant and ingenious speculations of the human mind (and process theology *is* ingenious and fascinating), its final word is that all data are dead: all experience of other things and other persons is of perished data, with the irreparable loss of immediacy. Hartshorne denies that anything is lost to God in his own everlasting self-surpassing procession, but he is certainly wrong in this regard, as Eugene Peters himself has made clear in his criticism of Hartshorne's illogic, given the doctrine that no one, including God, has any contemporaries with whom he can interact with living immediacy.[1] It is an awful fact in the logic of process theology that the greatest loser of all is God, for precisely what is lost to God universally and everlastingly is the subjective immediacy of every emergent occasion or experience-event, except his own. He, with the rest of us, has only dead data to work with and to remember forever. All the rest escapes him; that is, all the free, living, and choosing occasions that are parallel and independent along the front line of time. God is therefore truly finite in the process system. If God is limited to timespace, he has no present but his own, for reality is comprised of myriads of emergent monads, jumping unrelated into the future-become-present with windows only on the perished past.

(14) "God, then, is unsurpassable passivity." That is not to say that God is merely passive, but that he is not sheer immutability. God has an unlimited capacity to receive. But has Judaism or Christianity ever said that God is *sheer* immutability? Thomas Aquinas perhaps comes closest to it, but a fair reading of his writings makes it clear that in Christ's creative and redemptive work and in the work of the Holy Spirit God is supremely active in the world. The only prominent figures in the Western tradition who might be accused of proffering a God of sheer immutability would be Parmenides, Aristotle, and Plotinus. Surely the Old and New Testaments evince a high regard for God's activity in nature and history and his concern for what his people do. One half of the biblical mystery is that God is unsurpassably affected by the response of his people. By minimizing or rejecting the biblical drama, process thought has fashioned a straw man out of Christianity and proceeded to attack it for a one-sided doctrine of which it is not guilty. It would be difficult to find a more unsurpassably passive and loving God than Christ upon the cross. I recall that in conversation following one of Hartshorne's lectures during his visit to my former campus one person remarked to me, "But process theology has a God who really *cares!*" the implication being that biblical Christianity does not. That God cares for us, even to the unimagined extent of

---

1. Eugene Peters, *Hartshorne and Neoclassical Metaphysics: An Interpretation* (Lincoln: University of Nebraska Press, 1970), pp. 113-27.

passively bearing our sins in his own incarnate body on the tree, is the central proclamation of good news in Christian faith. And he continues to care for us and to nourish us in our present immediacy.

That is what the process deity cannot do, and therefore cannot care for us as the Christian God can. In process theism God is actually not unsurpassably passive, for if he were he would be able, like the biblical God, to be affected by our living immediacy. The process deity is surpassably passive because he is eminently surpassed by the living God of the Scriptures. Moreover, the god of process thought cannot be the ground of truth, if truth is agreement with reality, for reality is not the past by itself, but the past as it is ingested by immediate emergent occasions. Even the entire past is not the only truth about God and reality, for truth is what God *is* in himself and what he views as real, including present actualities and (for us) future possibilities.

Biblical faith has historically held together the two polarities of the mystery that God is beyond timespace as the infinite sovereign Lord and Creator, *and* the Redeemer of timespace as the incarnate and personal Lord of history. God *is* unsurpassable passivity because of the miracle of his incarnation and his unlimited capacity to receive. But he is able to do this because of his sovereign power, not, as process metaphysics would have it, because of his finitude and utter dependence on the universe for the content of his existence. Hence the biblical God is genuinely bipolar in his relations, whereas process thought is really monopolar (although it claims to be bipolar); for, as we have already observed, Alfred North Whitehead's attempt to satisfy the requirements of the pole of timeless infinity by reference to some peculiar primordial nature of God and Hartshorne's claim that God's absolute pole is an abstraction from his processing concrete pole are both failures because they give pride of place to time and space. The real problem with process thought, as I see it, is how God can possibly be *active* in the world, since his primordial or abstract nature has no personal actuality except as "it" passively receives concrete actuality *from* the world. Process theism tries, in other words, to conceive of God's actuality as consequent upon the world. But, as I have noted earlier, the velocity of light and the relativity of space make it impossible for God to experience unqualified inclusion of all data, unless he also transcends all limitations of velocity and spatial position. The two polarities of transcendence and immanence must be credibly held together, as biblical Christianity has long insisted. Process theism has sacrificed genuine talk of God's transcendence and activity to the one polarity of his immanence; and in that one polarity there are inseparable problems for the process school because a god who is bound to time cannot even be *perfectly* and unsurpassably passive.

(15) "Existence and actuality represent logically distinguishable levels

of reality." Actuality precedes existence, where existence connotes the abstract defining traits of actual states. Since, however, process theism assumes that God does not have his own actuality prior to and independent of the created universe, as biblical theology has claimed, it is caught in a logical error. Accordingly, the process model of God is in serious difficulty, for it must hold that God's existence—that is, his abstract character—depends upon actual states in the temporal world that give concretion to those personal, defining traits. This doctrine accords priority to the world of spacetime, making God's existence derivative from or dependent upon an independent world. God has no actuality prior to the world, according to process thought. Such a notion, I have argued, not only raises serious logical problems (how can God independently affect the world, since he is actually consequent to it?), but also is fundamentally at odds with classical Christian trinitarian belief in which God's revealed existence (whatever he says about himself in self-revelation, whatever is said about him in Scripture and Christian doctrine) is derived from his own self-contained actuality prior to the world, and from his self-initiated redemptive work in the history of his own created world.

(16) "Ideas express contrasts and one pole of a contrast cannot stand without the other as its logical mate." So far I would agree. When the process metaphysician goes on to argue, however, that one pole denotes what is the inclusive whole while the other denotes its constituent (examples are possibility-actuality, necessity-contingency, infinite-finite, abstract-concrete, permanence-change, where the first pole denotes the included element) I would find some cause for cavil. What, for instance, is the sense of saying that the finite includes the infinite? Surely that is irrational and logically impossible. Or that contingency includes necessity? Or that change encompasses permanence? I would agree that actuality includes possibility but would posit that actuality in God's own eternal and noncontingent triunity, which is ultimate sociality beyond created timespace. In biblical theology, the universe is a possibility become actuality only because of God's prior actuality and decision to create and sustain it. Process theism illogically locates actuality in the finite universe, making God its eternal consequent possibility-becoming-actual; God is eternal only because it is assumed that some finite universe or other will everlastingly afford him spatiotemporal actuality. This is logically irrational because it cannot then account for God's own non-contingent creative contribution to the process as total simultaneity. The pole of finitude (the relativity of time and space) cannot possibly account for the pole of infinity and simultaneity, whereas biblical Christian trinitarianism can account for infinity encompassing finitude. God the definite and richer includes the indefinite and poorer realm of spacetime

nature, not the other way round. The possibility of man's landing on another planet, including man's ability to land on that planet, is entailed in God's actual presence on that planet as Creator and Sustainer of the universe. But an earthling's finite accomplishment of actually landing on that planet (at present, the moon) does not entail the possibility of landing on every planet in the universe. Finite actuality (landing on the moon) cannot possibly entail infinite possibility. Only infinite actuality (God) can entail finite possibility. That is a mystery, but it is logically explorable if not exhaustible, whereas process metaphysics ends in a logical absurdity.

Moreover, to return to point 16 ("Ideas express contrasts, and one pole of a contrast cannot stand without the other as its logical mate"), it should be noted that it would be a mistake to take that as a law to which God is subject, in the sense that infinity *requires* the polarity of finitude. Logic does not dictate to God that he *must* bring a spacetime world into being, else the law would be greater than the God who is the source and sustainer of logic. According to the biblical Story, God creates the world out of the fullness of his actuality by some interior logic of love. Whatever necessity lies behind the coming into being of the world is, says Scripture, purely within the divine volition, not external to it, as in Whitehead's abstract notion of "creativity" which stands logically prior to everything, including God's abstract primordial nature.

(17) "Being actual, God is finite, but not fragmentary." It is the process view of God that "any of his experiences is a definite, actual reality, and as such it is a selection from possibility, hence, finite."[2] Here, I think, lies the principal error of process theology: it assumes that creativity and possibility are entirely dependent on the world of finite spacetime for actuality. Accordingly, if God is to be conceived as other than unmovable and frozen actuality and simultaneity, he must be incomplete in terms of moving linearly through timespace as he processes toward ever-increasing but never completed actuality. Such is the logic that makes timespace necessary to God's concrete experience. When this model is assumed, all the derivative logical difficulties follow suit.

There is no question for me, having been a process thinker myself for many years and now reconverted to classical Christian theology, that it is far superior logically to accept the God of historic Christian thought whose eternal transtemporal and transspatial actuality includes a boundless, everlasting, and inexhaustible love within his own triunity at an infinite "speed" incomprehensible in spatiotemporal categories. The biblical God is not static but inexhaustibly dynamic, *on his own terms, not ours*. There lies the difference between biblical theology and speculative

2. Eugene Peters, "Philosophic Insights of Charles Hartshorne," *The Southwestern Journal of Philosophy*, vol. 8 (February 1977): 168.

philosophical theology. The first allows God to be who he says he is; the second insists on defining him in human terms, that is, insists on human freedom at the expense of God's sovereignty: "The incomparable beauty of God can only be understood as restrictive of possibility, hence, as finite and contingent."[3]

The problem then arises for process theism that if God is contingent upon the world for his actuality, why is he not simply fragmentary, the abstract sum of all spacetime atomicity? This is unacceptable to the process school; thus it argues that God somehow transcends the universe both spatially and temporally so as to possess and incorporate all creatures. Here the organic model is brought to bear by Hartshorne, namely, that as a person's body is to himself, so the actual world is to God.[4] The universe is God's body. But surely this is unsatisfactory. The process-Buddhist view of the relation of mind to body in the human realm cannot serve as a valid model for God's relationship to the world because the model does not begin to explain how the atomicity of the body, or in Buddhist thought how the network of skandhas in bodily existence, accounts for a conscious mind and will that is then able to encompass and direct the whole. This is the root illogicality in the process model, and when it is enlarged to account for God's relation to the world the difficulties are compounded.

How *does* a unitary mind arise from fragmentary, spatiotemporal atomicity? Just saying that it does does not make it so. Process thought cannot argue that God's metaphysically unique being which encompasses all creatures is an actuality apart from the spacetime world, any more than it can argue that the soul distinguishes human experience. Whence and how this nonfragmentary and unique mind of God? My criticism of statement 17 is that not only is it unbiblical to say that God is finite, but also it flies in the face of logic and the law of excluded middle (point 19 which is to follow) to say that God is finite but not fragmentary. One cannot have both. If God is finite and ineluctably dependent on the atomicity of the universe for his actual concrete experience, there is no accounting for his unifying and encompassing transtemporal and transspatial mind. If there is something substantial and actual about his encompassing mind, then he is transcendent over the fragmentary atomicity of the universe, hence not necessarily finite and contingent.

In the latter case, which I take to be true, it would be specious to argue that God has to have the finite world to be conscious *of.* There is no logical necessity about that. If one allows that God's mind is nonfragmentary and all-encompassing, that is tantamount to saying that he is

3. Ibid.
4. Ibid.

temporally and spatially independent of the limitations of atomicity. Thus one can just as well say that God's principal consciousness is of himself in his eternal and inexhaustible fellowship of love within his Triune Self. Process theism cannot account for any unity in or out of the world because it begins with a monopolar prejudice in favor of finite timespace and atomicity, and cannot logically derive unified, transatomic experience from irreducible atomicity. It is a serious problem and the real fallacy, as I see it, in process metaphysics. It begins with the monopolarity of becoming and atomicity and can never really explain being and unity. It is Heraclitean, a modern version of the old "many" school in the long-standing one-many controversy first articulated by the pre-Socratics.

Biblical trinitarianism, on the other hand, can satisfactorily explain the intimate relation of One and Many, Being and Becoming as self-contained in the ultimate Fact, the Triune God himself, who is infinite, eternal, and unchangeable in his being, wisdom, power, holiness, justice, goodness, and truth, and dynamically inexhaustible in his ontological love as ultimate Family of Father, Son, and Holy Spirit. As Creator, God has derivatively placed his indelible stamp upon the created world. If we could see the world with believing and unidolatrous eyes we would clearly perceive something of his eternal power and deity (Rom. 1:20). But as regards the process metaphor of organism (the universe is God's body), it simply does not work, either logically or empirically. While the speed of light is sufficient to account for the nearly instantaneous and unified experiences of the human self, it is far too slow to account for God's simultaneous experience of the vast universe. If one follows the organic analogy, then God could have a unified experience of the universe perhaps once in an entire universal cycle, but he could hardly be the God who cares for every atomic occasion everywhere and at once. Two insuperable problems appear here to militate against the process organismic metaphor. First, as I have intimated, the speed of light at 186,000 miles per second, while fast for us, is woefully slow for God if his brain cells are comprised of creaturely entities. The interchange of information that would enable God to make effective decisions for the universe would not occur in time for him to do anything creative for this vast finitude called the universe. Even in our own galaxy, millions of light years are required for light to reach us from a distant star, now calculated to be elsewhere in its course. What complications of delayed information would be entailed for God over the immense universe simply boggles the mind. The cost of opting for a temporally finite deity has to be paid for at this counter.

Secondly, process thought, aware of the problem, then becomes quite irrational and claims that God has simultaneous experience of the entire process of the universe just behind its creative advancing edge, as well as

Figure 8

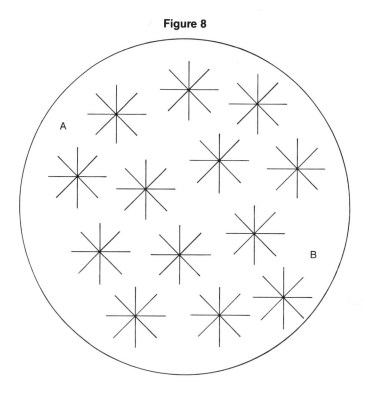

of its cumulative finished past. But two problems arise here. The first, of course, is that such a notion discards God's subordination to time and borrows from biblical Christianity the doctrine of God's omnipresence. That is illogical if one still holds that God is finite and subject to space-time. The second difficulty is the very notion of simultaneity itself. Physicists appear agreed that due to the relativity of multifarious events in spacetime, it is simply not conceivable that anyone could have a simultaneous experience of the whole if limited to the system, for there is no one temporal pattern within the universe that could comprehend simultaneously all other relative systems. The illustration (Fig. 8) of a cluster of star systems emitting light at a uniform rate of C would include such a complication of atomic events occuring at relative temporal frequencies that it would be impossible for any being limited to the process of the system to comprehend its multiplicity simultaneously from A to B. There is no uniform "front" of creativity moving neatly and simply forward from left to right (Fig. 9). Instead it is probably more like an expanding football that started blowing up from the center in all directions at the initial "big bang" and is still expanding, although at decreasing speeds, in all directions. (See Fig. 10.) But meantime all along the spectrums of expanding

Figure 9   **Figure 10**

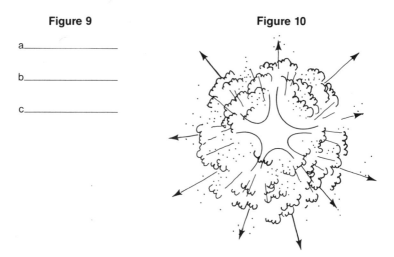

a_____

b_____

c_____

light are myriad worlds of atomic events occurring at various velocities, many of them adjacent and intersecting in all directions, but most not within a sphere of interaction at all because of impossibly large distances which exceed the life-tenure of events themselves. Thus it is inconceivable that there could be a simultaneous, unified, and unfragmented experience of all atomicity by a finite deity, itself limited to the process of time and space.

This impresses upon me the complete failure of a finitist theology. If God is ontologically finite *necessarily* in his concrete experience, he is necessarily fragmentary—unless the finitist wants to say that eventually, moving at the speed of light, he has a single unified and nonfragmentary experience of the universe perhaps once in the history of any particular universal system, if even that is possible. But even if it were, such a relatively slow-moving deity would be irrelevant, for then he would be merely passive and unable to affect the whole cosmic body in any immediate way until it was too late. A finite and fragmentary deity might affect that part of the universe he could handle with some temporal proximity, but never the whole universal body, so as to make any difference to the finite creatures inhabiting the various world systems.

Biblical faith would agree that God is a metaphysically unique Being who incorporates all creatures in his covenant creativity, but he can do this, where the process deity cannot, because he is transtemporal and transspatial. Only the biblical God is unfragmented.

(18) "God had a role in causing all events that preceded me, and He will be influenced by all events that follow me." This statement is acceptable only if one qualifies it by saying that the sovereign God freely gives his creatures limited freedom by sheer grace and makes himself available to

their needs through his gracious love. Thus he graciously allows finite creatures to participate in the making of this world and in the choosing of their own destinies. As such he is the God who cares and who responds to our needs. But the intention of statement 18 is to summarize the finitist doctrines of process theology, in this case to say that while God has a role in causing all events that preceded me, he does not have a sovereign role because he is *of necessity* limited by the independent power, however small, that I and other creatures hold over against him. God does not bring the cosmos into being (according to this theory), although he determines the cosmic order through the laws of nature. There is a virtual contradiction here as to the extent of God's power, a matter I discussed in chapter 1. If God determines the cosmic order, in what sense does he not have power to bring the cosmos into being, to what degree does it have independent autonomy, and how did it get that autonomy? Biblical theology is much more satisfactory, for it avoids the serious difficulties of such a neo-Manichean dualism by disclosing that God brought the universe into being by the fiat of his divine Word, and has graciously endowed humankind with the ability to think his thoughts after him and to make relatively free choices. God remains absolutely sovereign. Creaturely freedom is not a metaphysical right, but a bestowed gift of God.

As for the second part of statement 18, biblical faith would not agree that God is "influenced" by cosmic events as though he were processing in time and were surprised at the unfolding of possibilities as actualities. In the biblical Story, God is indeed a participant in our sufferings and struggles as incarnate and risen Lord, as the writer to the Hebrews makes clear: "For because he himself has suffered and been tempted, he is able to help those who are tempted" (2:18; cf. 4:15). God does participate in time because he has a privileged access to the time that he has created and that he continually sustains. But if he is necessarily limited to time, statement 18 could not be true, for God could not possibly be influenced by all events everywhere. As we have seen, the basis of the notion of simultaneity has collapsed with the radical views of modern relativity physics. There is no one direction, no one velocity, no single framework in the vast relativities of the universe that would allow any finite creature, including a finite God, to comprehend or be influenced by the whole.

Process theology is accordingly naïve, for it wants to hold on to the classical biblical notion of God's omnipresence in the universe while defining his experience in time in terms of its own reason rather than the divine disclosures of God in the Scriptures. Unaided "reason" leads inevitably to the Kantian antinomies, and process theism is no exception. It is caught in an impossible logical dilemma. Far better, I think, to be faithful to the biblical view that God is both sovereign over timespace *and* engaged redemptively in our created cosmos:

> For thus says the high and lofty One
>   who inhabits eternity, whose name is Holy:
> "I dwell in the high and holy place,
>   and also with him who is of a contrite and humble spirit,
> to revive the spirit of the humble
>   and to revive the heart of the contrite." [Isa. 57:15]

That God performs these dual roles is a fact of biblical revelation. *How* he does is probably forever beyond our ken. But surely biblical mystery is far preferable to logical contradiction. This brings us to statement 19.

(19) "The law of the excluded middle is the criterion of the actual; it does not apply to possibility." That is to say, if p is possible, not-p is also possible; but if p is actual, it is false that not-p is actual. This is the heart of process theology and takes us back to chapter 1 on anthropodicy. The law of excluded middle does not operate on future possibilities; therefore I am free to make my own choices as long as God does not know the future as actual. The statement is a defense of human freedom.

Yet observe how arbitrarily the law of excluded middle is applied by process thinkers to God. In theory their principal reason for conceiving of God as finite is to make him relevant to our becoming in time. Hence what is past and actual for God conforms to the law of excluded middle—it cannot be other than it is. But the future is open to God because he does not know in detail what his relatively free world is going to do. It may rain this afternoon or it may not. So, existence ("standing out" into the future of possibility) is as true of God as it is of us and is radically different from actuality. Needless to say, process theologians are not Calvinists!

Now logically, following the law of excluded middle, the process finitist ought to argue as follows:

I. God moves and experiences at a finite velocity as subject to the finite velocities of time.

　1. Whatever moves at a finite velocity cannot be everywhere at once.

　∴ God cannot be everywhere at once, is not omnipresent, and is therefore not omniscient or omnipotent, since he cannot know and experience all actualities simultaneously.

Process finitism holds that God is omnipotent, omniscient, and omnipresent in the sense that he has all the power he could possibly have in a social universe where the power is shared; he is omniscient in the sense that he knows all actuality as past (but not future possibility as actuality); and he is omnipresent simultaneously with all the events of the universe, but not in their living immediacy. But this redefinition of omnipotence, omniscience, and omnipresence begs the question and defies the law of excluded middle. Observe the following passage:

Nonetheless, because existence is not identical with actuality, existence may in some exceptional case be co-extensive with possibility—in which case the law of excluded middle is inapplicable. God, in His unlimited capacity for experience, is alternativeness itself and, hence, is existentially noncontingent.[5]

Now the question is, how, apart from divine revelation, does process theism know that God has unlimited capacity for experience? Certainly that doctrine does not come from a rigorous application of logic, for if God is by definition finite and subject to time he cannot, by the law of excluded middle, have unlimited capacity for experience. He must, logically, be fragmented and incomplete within the cosmos of the actual, for he could not possibly experience simultaneously the entire universe, moving as he must at the speed of light. Nor could he nonsimultaneously experience the entire universe, since many actual occasions would have perished beyond recall before he could reach them at his finite velocity.

If, however, Hartshorne would object that this is an ad hominem argument and that God is always coextensive with all actuality, then I would argue that God is no longer subject to time and space but transcends them both. Thus the whole foundation of process theism collapses, and we were better off to stay with biblical theology to begin with. But what of the argument that God is alternativeness itself, the one who has unlimited capacity for experience? The same rebuttal applies. If God cannot, because finite, be coextensive with all actuality, no more can he be coextensive with all possibility, and only one who experiences all actuality could have unlimited capacity for experiencing possibility as it becomes actual.

What, then, of the final argument of process theism that if God is sovereign over created timespace then we are not free because what we choose could not have been otherwise, God having known all things eternally as actual? The reply to this simple way of putting the question may take several forms, among them the insights of relativity theory that future and present may vary depending on one's frame of reference and hence that the even-line model of time which process theology seems to work with is naïve and must not be used to dictate to God what he can and cannot do. But the answer goes deeper. The prosaic logic of process theism has already been seen to break down at numerous crucial intersections, and in light of the higher logic of biblical mystery must be considered inadequate to deal with such tremendous issues. If logic fails the process metaphysician at crucial points, then it cannot be used to demand of God that he give up his sovereignty necessarily in order that

5. Ibid., p. 169.

human beings might be free in the sense that they demand to be free. Hartshorne cannot bring himself to allow that God is *really* finite, incomplete, and fragmented even though the doctrine of God ontologically in process within timespace demands it. He cannot make the dionysiac plunge to a genuinely finite deity but illogically holds to the remnants of classical Christian theology regarding God's omnipresence and omniscience in respect to all actuality and possibility.

It is far better, and certainly more obedient to God's self-disclosure in the Old and New Testaments, to accept the biblical view that God is both sovereign over creation and above timespace as its creator, and yet intimately involved with the process of redemption within the world; sovereign in power, while gifting individuals with limited freedom of choice. This is biblical merismus and reflects the repeated theme of the unexpected in God's redemptive activity. Who would have anticipated that God would so love his fallen creatures that he would send his Son as incarnate gift and sacrifice for their redemption? Certainly a humanly employed logic would never have dreamed of such a thing; hence Christianity was rejected by the frozen legalism of Pharisaic logic and by the rationalistic humanism of Greek tradition. Yet it is even more true of God than it is of us that until a person reveals himself to another there is no knowing what he is like. Only when God the infinite Person reveals himself to his creatures can they, in their fallen state, have any adequate clue as to the nature of God, in spite of God's revelation of his power and deity in nature. The Holy Scriptures claim to give trustworthy evidence of God's justice and love which is confirmed by the believing head and heart of the experiencing creature. What God reveals about himself is that he is both infinite as the Creator of spacetime and incarnate in Jesus Christ for the redemption of the world. *That* he is both is a fact of scriptural revelation. *How* he does it is not within the capacity of the finite mind, and especially the fallen finite mind, to divine.

Accordingly, the insistence of the finitist that God must be limited in his knowledge of the future, else we creatures are wholly determined and "could not be otherwise," strains the question. Precisely because God is sovereign human beings are endowed with relative freedom as a gift from him. Each person has special responsibility for the destiny of his or her soul, according to the choices he or she makes. God's knowledge of what x will choose to do is not in spite of but precisely through what x will in fact freely choose to do. That God does know the future as actual is a fact of Christian faith and of biblical teaching; how he does is no more comprehensible than the modern theory of relativity which says in "meaningful" language that the universe as a whole is incomprehensible.

Thus if the law of excluded middle is taken as the final criterion of truth, it must be used consistently throughout the system. If p cannot be

p and not-p at the same time (that is, if there is no middle ground), then God cannot be both bound to process and simultaneous with all process. The law of excluded middle can be used to show the illogicality of process theology and its final recourse to logically odd paradoxes. The notion that a *finite* deity could be coextensive with all actuality and possibility itself defies the law of excluded middle. As regards the realm of possibility, it should be noted that there are two levels: the larger and incomprehensible is God's inexhaustibility within his own triunity as everlasting fellowship and love; the created and therefore finite continuum of possibility to which the creature, but not God, is subject. Only by a grand miracle of grace could God subject himself voluntarily through the incarnation to the finite realm of possibility, and only through the mystery of divine logic (from our point of view "the logically odd") does he remain sovereign over timespace while acting redemptively within it.

(20) "The principles of aesthetics are basic and pervasive in reality. Hartshorne holds that the scope of aesthetics is greater than that of ethics." This, the last point in Peters's summary of Hartshorne's process theology, draws our attention to the doctrine that reality is principally feeling, from the ground up so to speak.

But this raises a serious problem and confronts process aesthetics with the same dilemma one finds in Buddhist theory, to which it bears striking similarity. If each unit event is an aesthetic creation, why not allow everything to be what it is and not superimpose any ethical principle of discrimination upon it? A fundamental tenet of Buddhism, at least in theory if not in practice, is that one should superimpose no ethical judgment on the "suchness" or "thatness" of the processing world, but should let each occurrence be exactly what it is, whether health or disease, life or death, simplicity or complexity. From the more original Therevada teachings to Zen Buddhism the underlying doctrine is that attachment to one thing more than to another, or ethical discrimination of any kind, leads to craving attachment to passing forms, and thus attachment to pain, which is the fundamental human problem. Moreover, in Zen, which comes by way of Mahayana teaching, every unit event contains within it all spacetime, past, present, and future, and therefore is perfect and complete in itself. Accordingly, no ethical judgment is needed to discriminate between good and bad. Everything can be aesthetically enjoyed for just what it is in itself.

Process theism does not accept either the Buddhist doctrine that attachment is pain or that each unit event contains the perfect actuality of all past, present, and future timespace. But it does agree that aesthetic feeling is more basic than ethical judgment. Notice, however, the logical contradiction in the following two sentences which explain point 20: "Thus, an animal or a human infant, to which ethical categories are inapplicable, may nonetheless be understood aesthetically. The animal, for example, may be subject to monotony, an aesthetic evil."[6]

Now surely use of the term *aesthetic evil* constitutes an ethical judgment. Otherwise why would monotony be an aesthetic evil? It would be just what it is as far as feeling is concerned, or aesthetically, as the Buddhist would argue. Process doctrine has already determined on ethical grounds, however, that organic complexity and reflective consciousness are superior to simpler forms of feeling. How does one come to that conclusion except ethically; indeed, without drawing on biblical tradition? For there is nothing in nature itself that would necessarily accord superiority to more complex organisms; and in Eastern ethics the doctrine of ahimsa requires the same compassion be shown to the insect as to the human.

But if, as process theology would have it, love is sharing the feelings of another, and if "this sharing is aesthetic in nature, involving such factors as contrast, balance, richness, unity, harmony, etc.,"[7] then it is clear that the scope of ethics is greater than that of aesthetics. Otherwise it would not be possible to discriminate superior feelings that exhibit contrast, balance, richness, unity, or harmony from pain, sorrow, and dying. Biblical Christianity, embracing as it does the rich tradition of the Old and New Testaments, is ethical and aesthetic to the core. All creation exists primarily to give glory to God, and derivatively to provide enjoyment for the highest of the creatures, man and woman. Indeed, eschatologically all creation is to participate in the aesthetic joy of redemption when Christ completes his saving work in history and nature. It too will obtain the glorious liberty of the children of God (Rom. 8:18-24). Aesthetics derives from the ethical work of Christ. Thus no unit event has intrinsic aesthetic value, since many feelings in nature, from the simplest to the highest, are bent and evil and stand under divine condemnation.

Process theism tacitly admits this whenever it employs a vague language of discrimination between feelings. But it is caught in the logical contradiction of atomism. Beginning ontologically from the ground up, it ought to allow things to be just what they are; but since this is impossible, it then superimposes human values epistemologically upon the whole from the top down. It were better to begin from the top down in terms of biblical theology, where God is seen to create with ethical and aesthetic intent from the beginning. The redemption of a rebellious and fallen world is necessarily, in view of the righteousness of God, an ethical matter of rooting out rebellion against God by the one sacrifice that satisfies God's justice, namely, the sacrifice of his Son on the cross. The ethical

6. Ibid., p. 170.
7. Ibid.

problem must be dealt with first in order that the truly aesthetic might flourish and be universally enjoyed. Otherwise, would the process theist want to say that the unit event of a cancerous cell, which makes its contribution of aesthetic feeling to the cancerous tissue in the human host, is summed up in majesty and beauty in the life of God?[8] Or the murderer or the purveyor of falsehood? Yet the Hartshornean system has the naïve view that God somehow continually reaps the beautiful harvest of aesthetic values that are intrinsic to this independent world. How can the mean and the ugly, of which there is so much in this world, be finally summed up with the whole in majesty and beauty? Majesty and beauty would then have no meaning, for they are ethical, discriminating terms which perforce reject the mean and the ugly.

Two further epistemological problems arise for the process finitist at this point. The first is, how does one know by autonomous human reason (scriptural revelation having been rejected) that God is actually the "self-surpassing surpasser of all others who guarantees that life is essentially affirmation and hope, the reaping of intrinsic values and the expectation of future harvest"?[9] Has not this eschatological hope been borrowed from biblical capital? A second problem is related to the first: how does one know what to choose in life if each unit event achieves intrinsic value? Does this not lead to self-defeating relativism? Buddhist acceptance of all as it is would seem the logical path to follow, except that it too is incapable of following through logically with its doctrine of nondiscrimination, for it requires its adherents to *love* everything as it is, rather than hate everything as it is, thus discriminating between the crucial attitudes of love and hate. A study of Buddhism of every variety reveals that it is really in practice ethical to the core and exacts extremely demanding disciplines from its serious adherents (as witness the ethical precepts of the Eightfold Path: *right* knowledge, *right* aspiration, *right* speech, *right* behavior, *right* livelihood, *right* effort, *right* mindfulness, *right* absorption).

What then of process finitist theology? Our observation has been that in attempting to guarantee human autonomy by conceiving of the future as open even for God, it has opened more than the future, indeed a veritable Pandora's box. Like liberal theology in general it wants to retain the classical Christian doctrine of God's omnipresence but cannot manage to accept the equally biblical doctrines of his omnipotence and omniscience as the one who has created and sustains time and space. A finite deity that is limited to timespace is of necessity fragmented and contingent. Adopting the Whiteheadian doctrine that reality is incurably

8. See ibid.
9. Ibid.

atomic, process finitism has rendered the identity of creatures and of God impossible as creative agents. Process metaphysics is unable to explain how either the creature or God himself has personal identity and how such an identifiable agent is able to affect a cause if he himself is the continually changing effect of prior causes. If the cosmos comprises the brain of God, how does he as an independent agent affect those finite causes? And how can he affect them comprehensively and simultaneously if he is limited by time and space?

Finally, by viewing reality from the bottom up through irreducible atomic unit events rather than from the top down through the creative mind of God, process theism is faced with the problem of meaning. Logically, the system says, feeling must be fundamental to all reality. But then it qualifies this doctrine with a warning that discrimination is needed to distinguish good feelings from bad feelings. God is the source of this discrimination, but he has no independent consciousness until he is made concrete by emerging atomic events. The system is circular. My conclusion is that if one starts from the bottom he cannot get to the top, to God; but if he starts at the top with God as he has revealed himself in the Scriptures, he can account for the bottom.

PART THREE

Biblical Revelation and Human Speculation

A Critique of Neville, Ogden, Cobb, and Ford

7

Process Theism
As a Hermeneutic
for Biblical Interpretation

A Critique

In his excellent summary critique of process theology Bruce A. Demarest isolates the central issue as doctrinal, for the god of process theology is not the God of the Bible.[1] This has consistently been my point in our examination of process theism. I will illustrate it further by considering two prominent authors, one of whom attempts to apply a process hermeneutic to interpret Christian doctrine and the Bible. The second makes cogent criticisms of process theism but turns its fundamentally man-centered focus toward what I consider to be the natural object of its logic, namely, a complete relativizing of the claims of Christianity and the location of theology not in the believing community but in the university, where other religions and even antireligious secular traditions may be viewed "objectively" as genuine alternatives to Christianity.

---

1. "Process Trinitarianism," in Kenneth S. Kantzer and Stanley N. Gundry, eds., *Perspectives on Evangelical Theology* (Grand Rapids: Baker, 1979), pp. 15–35, especially p. 33. See also Norman L. Geisler's critique of process theism in Stanley N. Gundry and Alan F. Johnson, eds., *Tensions in Contemporary Theology* (Chicago: Moody, 1976), pp. 237–84.

The Locus of Authority

This latter view I would like to take up first in the form in which Robert C. Neville addresses it.[2] Neville writes from a relativist perspective and as a proponent of the university setting for doing theology. Notice how his adoption of John B. Cobb's relativism regarding a firm commitment to Christianity[3] leads to the concept of the university as a substitute for the church:

> A practical result of this recognition of the world-cultural context for theology is that the best institutions for theology are universities in which the world's religions are presented with as much philological and hermeneutical objectivity as possible. *Particular religious institutions are no longer the home of theology.* Theology with a traditional institutional label, for instance "Methodist theology," or even "Christian theology," is less public, more partial, tentative and incomplete than theology needs to be. This is a revolutionary consquence both for universities and for church institutions.[4]

Neville's proposal is indeed a revolutionary but natural consequence of employing an anthropocentric hermeneutic such as process thought. His locus of authority has become predominantly humanistic, hence the shift from the worshiping community and the theological seminary to the secular university where all competing positions can be subjected to critical scrutiny under the supposedly objective canons of scientific inquiry. I have argued for just the opposite point of view because I am convinced, after many years of teaching on a secular college campus, that the one place where the lived coherence and viability of historic biblical Christian faith will not enjoy a truly phenomenological openness of spirit is in the secular setting. Cobb, Neville, Lewis S. Ford, Charles Hartshorne, Alfred North Whitehead, and others who subscribe to a process model in some degree concur that in the last analysis it is the human mind that has the right to decide what is true and authoritative. Accordingly they are already committed to a certain view of truth that is inimical to biblical faith, for historic Christianity holds that truth about the actual condition of the world and humanity, namely, that it is bent by rebellion and is in need of redemption through God's reconciling gift in Jesus Christ, can be

2. *Creativity and God: A Challenge to Process Theology* (New York: Seabury, 1980).

3. See *John Cobb's Theology in Process*, David R. Griffin and Thomas J. J. Altizer, eds. (Philadelphia: Westminster, 1977), p. 168, where Cobb, although claiming Christian faith, writes, "To commit myself unqualifiedly to Christianity would be inconsistent with a full recognition of the inadequacy, unclarity, and distortion of the beliefs through which I identify myself as a Christian."

4. Neville, *Creativity and God*, p. 145. My italics.

known and appropriated only by the self-disclosure of the personal infinite God himself. No neutral, objective ground is possible in answering the question as to where religious truth resides.

In a recent study in New Testament hermeneutics I have argued that the secular university seldom provides a setting in which historic Christianity and sympathetic biblical exegesis are given pride of place because of a secular philosophic commitment to the model that truth is in process and is relative.[5] Following Michael Polanyi's model of faith seeking understanding which is essentially fiduciary and heuristic, I would point out that the university ideal of doing theology objectively is an illusion. Polanyi informs the reader in his epistemological study, *Personal Knowledge*, that his purpose "is to show that complete objectivity as usually attributed to the exact sciences is a delusion and is in fact a false ideal."[6] No methodology is free of the scientist's or the critic's heuristic commitments; hence all knowledge is personally accredited knowledge which functions within the framework of personal presuppositions. One indwells a certain set of commitments just as he indwells his body.[7] Moreover, learning how to do biblical exegesis and theology must be learned, as with anything else, in the environment appropriate to it. Polanyi speaks eloquently and convincingly of acquiring skills and of practicing the art of those skills. Such connoisseurship is learned by the apprentice from the master connoisseur.[8] I have argued and will continue to hold that the skill and art of doing biblical exegesis and Christian theology must be learned within the worshiping Christian community and the confessional seminary where theology is lived with deep commitment. In the area of gospel criticism, for instance, I have discovered that the more the gospel material is analyzed without a sympathetic personal commitment, the more abstract and secular the theories used to explain the phenomena of the Gospels. This also has been my experience with process thought. The more I threw myself into metaphysical speculations about God and the world, the more I found myself falling away from and deprecating the traditional worshiping Christian community. Even the theological seminary became suspect because of its assumed lack of objectivity. What I now have come to see is that I was substituting one fiduciary commitment for another, in my case a new and

5. See my *New Approaches to Jesus and the Gospels: A Phenomenological and Exegetical Study of Synoptic Christology* (Grand Rapids: Baker, 1982), chapter 8.

6. Michael Polanyi, *Personal Knowledge: Towards a Post-Critical Philosophy* (New York: Harper and Row, 1964), p. 18.

7. Ibid., p. 60. This approach is similar to that of Cornelius Van Til, who is also a presuppositionalist. See his introduction, pp. 3-68, in B. B. Warfield, *The Inspiration and Authority of the Bible* (Philadelphia: Presbyterian and Reformed, 1948).

8. Polanyi, *Personal Knowledge*, p. 53.

momentarily heady and emancipating faith in what I thought was a truly academic, objective perspective of God and the world for an outmoded biblical view. I had actually substituted one faith for another—a modern secularist faith in human authority for the authority of God's self-revelation in the Judeo-Christian Scriptures.

Consequently, Neville's agreement with process thought that Christian theology belongs to the analytic discipline of philosophical theology within the university, rather than to biblical exegesis within the seminary as an extension of the worshiping church, constitutes a central attack on biblical faith. With Polanyi I would agree that Christian faith discloses itself only to the attentive and obedient disciple who approaches it in heuristic expectation. In other words, Christian theology can be done authentically only by believing Christians in a setting of Christian "conviviality."[9] Since the reigning attitude in most centers of academe today is secular and positivistic, the kind of conviviality provided by the secular university is characteristically hostile to the supernatural character of biblical theology. In the final analysis it is apprenticeship within the worshiping community that affords the apprentice, journeyman, and master himself (or herself) the proper context for interpreting Christian theology with fidelity to its biblical origins and historic past; otherwise the locus of authority will simply shift from the authority of the Scriptures to the authority of the secular interpreter. As Polanyi says,

> Only a Christian who stands in the service of his faith can understand Christian theology and only he can enter into the religious meaning of the Bible.[10]

And,

> Any inquiry into our ultimate beliefs can be consistent only if it presupposes its own conclusions. It must be intentionally circular.[11]

The suggestion that the subjection of biblical theology to the secular norms of philosophy or philosophical theology will really get to the truth of the matter is therefore a fundamental shift of priorities and represents a countercommitment of faith to anthropocentric authority. Process theism ostensibly aims to formulate a more rational, coherent, and relevant theology to meet the needs of the contemporary person who has been brought up on the heavy fare of science and empiricism and who has been taught to do his or her own thinking apart from other authoritative

9. See ibid., pp. 203–45.
10. Ibid., p. 281.
11. Ibid., p. 299.

systems. The assumption is that older models of God, such as that of the Bible and of patristic Christian thought, are arcane and unsuitable for the modern mind. "We can do better," I remember Hartshorne once saying at a soirée during one of his visits to our college campus. On the other hand, what I have tried to do in the preceding critical chapters is to show that the autonomous modern mind does not really honor its promises when it tries to fashion a better theology than historic biblical Christianity. On the level of rational debate itself the process school is deficient at a number of levels that are crucial if one is to abandon classical Christianity for a modernized version.

In this chapter, I would like to continue the rational debate with process representatives in order to show further oddities and illogicalities in the system; and while we are considering Neville's hard-hitting critique in *Creativity and God* (although in the last analysis he is in their camp rather than mine), to bring to the attention of the reader the more difficult doctrines of process and the problems that arise within the school itself.

The Relevance of Genetic Division to God

Neville brings up the nettling question of Whitehead's coming-to-be, or genetic division as he calls it, and its relevance to God. Ford, with whom we will spend some additional time in chapter 8 concerning biblical hermeneutics, tries to solve the problem primarily in terms of the primordial nature of God, arguing that God in relation to the world has a single everlasting concrescence with successive phases; that is, God's "process" is only genetically temporal, not physically temporal. In the difficult scholastic language of the school Ford explains: "Now there is only one act of self-actualization, but this one act is genetically (not actually) analyzable into successive decisions having within their particular phases the same properties Whitehead ascribes to the occasion as a whole with respect to decisions."[12]

Neville's critique of Ford follows the line that he is misconstruing Whitehead's doctrine of genetic division, for "incomplete phases of an occasion are themselves abstractions from satisfied occasions. They have no existence in themselves so as to be able to exist earlier than the satisfaction phase."[13] Moreover, Ford does not do justice to the distinction between becoming and being, between appearance and reality. What

12. See Lewis S. Ford, "On Genetic Successiveness: A Third Alternative," in *Southern Journal of Philosophy*, vol. 7, no. 4 (Winter 1969): 422.

13. Neville, *Creativity and God*, p. 25.

successiveness does God really experience? Ford holds that God's concrescence is never complete because it is an everlasting genetically (not physically) temporal process. Accordingly, says Neville, the weakness of Ford's hypothesis is "its inability to allow God's concrescence any opening to the world." Neville continues with an absolutely devastating critique of the irrelevance of Ford's deity to our temporal process. His argument is tight and tough and begs our careful scrutiny:

> The very meaning of genetic successiveness in contrast to physical time is that after the initial phase the concrescence is closed off from the outside influence until it reaches satisfaction; this is necessary to preserve the discontinuity of becoming. If no phase of the divine concrescence is completely determinant as a physical satisfaction, there can be no hybrid physical prehension of God by finite occasions, and hence God cannot contribute subjective aims to the temporal finite process. On the other hand, if the divine concrescence is everlasting, as if data from physically antecedent occasions enter the concrescence only in its initial phase, then God can comprehend nothing of the world; God's only data could be the divine primordial nature. God could never pick up *initial* data about a finite occasion because the divine *initial* phase would always have preceded it. If God can neither concresce to satisfaction before any finite occasion nor begin a concrescing experience after one God is strictly speaking contemporary with everything else and therefore absolutely isolated. This is Whiteheadian deism.[14]

The outcome of this critique is highly ironic. The advantage of process theism is supposedly to interpret God as supremely relevant to our needs in a way that is superior to the God of classical theology. And yet on close analysis not only is the language of the new theism barely comprehensible, but also the deity that it proposes is quite irrelevant to our needs; not only is he not "the God who cares," but also he *cannot* be the God who cares as does the God of the Old and New Testaments. Moreover, such a God cannot be prehended by us because he is never sufficiently determinate. We are left not knowing very much about God. While Neville's own theology is hardly biblically oriented, he is correct in what he suggests about knowing God:

> If God is known, it is through creating revelations of the divine creative character; God at least can be known as creator of this particular world. Because God is not separate from the creative act, God is not separate from the creature, so as to have a problem knowing them.[15]

14. Ibid., p. 29. His italics.
15. Ibid., p. 34.

Of course I agree, but I would ask Neville how he knew this to be true apart from God's self-disclosure in Holy Scripture. Does philosophical theology guarantee this kind of knowledge?

Neville touches critically and correctly on a related theological issue that has to do with God's prehending us in our immediacy—something that is denied by Whitehead and Hartshorne and most process thinkers: "Furthermore, the creator does not have to prehend only the objective character of occasions as finished facts; as creator, God is at the heart of their coming-to-be."[16] This avoids God's isolation from the world, which is one unhappy consequence of Ford's genetic interpretation. It also avoids the unfortunate implication of Hartshornean metaphysics that God (as well as we) experiences only perished data and never the coming-to-be immediacy of other persons and occasions.

Neville's attention now focuses on a further weakness in Whitehead, namely, that his category of the ultimate is not sufficient to account for ontological unity. The ontological principle (really the cosmological principle) in Whitehead's system claims that for every particular factor in the process of becoming there is a decision somewhere, whether prior to it or during its own concrescence, that accounts for it. The category of the ultimate attempts to account for ontological unity in terms of one, many, and creativity. The process of unifying many into one is viewed as creativity, where many become one and are increased by one in primordial togetherness. Whitehead separates this activity of creative unification from God in order to allow each actual entity to be free and self-creative in relative independence of other actual entities, including God. Neville specifies the difference between this doctrine and biblical theology:

> In the more usual view of creative unification, God in some sense is the source of both ontological and cosmological unity, with created entities being the cause of the latter in some different but complementary sense. But, along with the more usual view goes a commitment to the thesis that God is intimately present as creator to every creature even in the subjectivity of the creature's free self-constitution. In the usual view, people are not free from God's creativity, whereas in Whitehead's view God's creative influence is limited to the provision of data for the finite actual occasions to objectify. . . .[17]

16. Ibid. See also Neville's "Metaphysical Argument for a Wholly Empirical Theology" in *God Knowable and Unknowable*, Robert J. Roth, S. J., ed. (New York: Fordham University Press, 1972); "Can God Create Men and Address Them Too?" *Harvard Theological Review* 61 (1968): 603–23; *Cosmology of Freedom* (New Haven: Yale University Press, 1974), chapters 4–6; and *Soldier, Sage, Saint* (New York: Fordham University Press, 1978), chapter 5.
17. *Creativity and God*, p. 40.

In the biblical view, God is the ultimate, personal source of all creation and creativity. But in process thought there is a strange and modern penchant for reducing personal activity to impersonal principles. Ford does this with rigor in his restatement of trinitarianism as he reduces the personal triunity of God to three impersonal principles.[18] Cobb evinces the same sort of abstract reductionism in his attempt to bring Buddhist and Christian thought together.[19] But do principles ever do anything? Are they not rather descriptive abstractions from living occasions, and on the human level abstractions from personal centers of consciousness who choose to act? Whitehead takes for granted that there is primordial creative unification but then assigns this to an abstraction. It is far more logical and biblical to assign creativity not to some abstract principle but to the transcendent Creator who shows himself to be Creator in his act of creating. One of the positive contributions Neville makes to the debate on process metaphysics is his appreciation for the classical biblical view of God as the Creator who is immediately present in the being of his creatures.[20] Although unfortunately he does not return to a truly biblical theology, his critique on these two points is largely what I have been saying in my criticism of Whitehead and Hartshorne, namely, that Whitehead cannot really solve the problem of how the many become one with a bare principle of creativity.[21] Nor does Hartshorne escape difficulty with his notion of God's existence as the bare abstractions contained, in Aristotelian fashion, within the concrete occasions of process. Moreover, as I have pointed out in my earlier criticism of Hartshorne, his doctrine that God is subject like the rest of us to asymmetrical temporality means that he cannot interact with us in our immediacy. This much Neville seems to agree with, and to this extent he is right.[22] Although he agrees with a number of Hartshorne's principles which I have rejected in the last chapter, he has difficulty with Hartshorne's failure to offer a substantial argument for continuity, his virtual denial of the self, and his softening of the problem of evil.

The Concept of God in Neoclassical Theism

Neville's critique of Schubert M. Ogden is even more severe, as he catches him on a number of serious logical errors,[23] especially Ogden's

18. Lewis S. Ford, "Process Trinitarianism," *Journal of the American Academy of Religion* 43 (1975): 199–213.

19. John B. Cobb, Jr., "Buddhist Emptiness and the Christian God," *Journal of the American Academy of Religion* 45 (March 1977): 11–25.

20. *Creativity and God;* for example, pp. 46, 63, 74, 82f., 86f.

21. See ibid., chapter 3, "Ontology of the One and the Many," pp. 36–47, for a trenchant criticism on this point.

22. See his critique of Hartshorne, ibid., chapter 4, "God as Social," pp. 48–76.

23. See ibid., chapter 5, "God as Neoclassical," pp. 77–97. See also Schubert M. Ogden's

criticism of classical theology for what he misconstrues as its static and therefore irrelevant concept of God. Neville correctly reminds Ogden that in classical theology God is related to the world in a Creator-created way, since God's relation to the world as Creator, Redeemer, and Lover is a matter of grace, not of necessity. Ogden, following Hartshorne, wants to make God necessarily dependent on the world, and this is where biblical theology parts company with modern process theism. The necessity of the world derives from the divine cause, not from something external to God. The world is contingent upon God, not God upon the world. Neville expresses this interestingly, if not entirely correctly. Nature and will are inseparable in God as Person; nothing is necessarily external to God:

> The Christian motive for holding to free creation has chiefly been to account for the belief that creation is a matter of voluntary grace; this requires that God could do otherwise than create, just as God could do otherwise than redeem. The *classical* question of the priority of will and nature in God deals with just this issue: If God's nature is prior and determined to create, then the will is necessary, and so is creation: if God's will is prior, then nature is derivative from willing and creating, and the divine creation is not necessary.[24]

A larger issue is at stake here. God is not determined by anything external to his living concrete willing—his very nature as Person is one with his willing, choosing, and acting. God is not one who wills and acts because of some arbitrary impersonal principle of power external to his being. He is what he is in willing and acting as the infinite and personal God. God does not obey an external impersonal principle called justice; what he wills and does by nature is just. Moreover, Ogden's complaint that the supposedly static and complete God of classical *actus purus* must be indifferent to our praise of him is answered deftly by Neville when he remarks that "people serve God by glorifying God. This does not improve God, it only gives the divine glory. God is not better off with more glory than less; it is just better to glorify God than not, since that is what human betterment is in classical Christian conceptions."[25] When we add to this observation the fact that in Ogden's neoclassical theism, as in Hartshorne's, God cannot prehend the plurality of particulars as subjec-

primary work, *The Reality of God* (New York: Harper and Row, 1966), and his earlier work, *Christ Without Myth: A Study Based on the Theology of Rudolf Bultmann* (New York: Harper and Row, 1961). See also David Tracy, *Blessed Rage for Order: The New Pluralism in Theology*, Library of Contemporary Theology series (New York: Seabury, 1979) for a Roman Catholic appropriation of process thought in the Ogden vein.

24. Neville, *Creativity and God*, p. 86. His italics.

25. Ibid., p. 87.

tive realities in process of concrescence but only as finished data, then the case for the neoclassical substitute pales, for the world as it is and God as he is are mutually external to each other and mutually unknowable. Surely this is no improvement on biblical theology which speaks of the intimate covenantal relationships of God, nature, and humankind. Neville's critique of neoclassical theism, similar to the one I have made earlier, is devastating:

> If all relations are subjectively external, then neoclassical metaphysics has not accounted for the unity of things; certainly God cannot unify the world, since God can prehend the things in it only after their subjective reality or process had ceased to be.
>
> This is a disastrous consequence for the religious applicability of the neoclassical concept of God since it means, in effect, that God knows only the objective reality of things, not the things themselves as subjects. This consequence might be avoided if the process understanding of the subjective reality of finite occasions were abjured. But if that were done all the cheers about temporality and creativity would be hollow, and the whole theory about God's sympathy would collapse. Accepting the consequence, it might be well to look again at those classical theories that, by reference to creation, account for how God is present to the subjective reality of things, "closer to them than they are to themselves" as their creative ground. There is no contradiction in the claim that God creates a procession of processing actual occasions.
>
> The fact that the neoclassical concept of God can include neither the normative universal principles that make God necessarily what he is relative to the world nor the world considered in itself, makes the theory "radically incoherent," to throw back Ogden's description of classical theories. The attempt to combine abstract and universal necessity with concrete relatedness by the notion of dipolarity has difficulties just as grave as Ogden imputes to classical theology.[26]

In considering three fundamental teachings of biblical faith—God's action in history, the lordship of Christ, and the eschaton—Neville correctly charges that Ogden's neoclassical process theism fails to better the classical position. Concerning the first (God's action in history) Ogden wants to say that God prehends every event exactly as it is and redeems it by combining it in the best possible way with other divine prehensions. Thus God's "redemptive activity" in history is symbolic and universal. Neville raises my now familiar criticism that in process thought there is not enough substantiality and continuity of occasions for there to be serious talk of historical responsibility. But more specifically, Ogden's theology necessitates that God redeem everyone and everything. Neville replies:

26. Ibid., pp. 90f.

It is not that there is a universal goal that God works to bring about by special symbolic events, but rather that God has a special goal that has meaning only in terms of its historical context. So Christians claim that salvation consists in participation in Jesus of Nazareth, the risen Christ, not that participation in Jesus is historically symbolic of a historically universal salvation.[27]

I detect in Ogden the same tendency as in other process theologians to give pride of place to speculative metaphysics rather than to the revealed will of God in the Scriptures. In classical biblical theology, God's free and sovereign will is prior to nature, creation, and redemption; hence these are matters of grace and revelation, not of necessity and of reason. Neville observes:

In classical Christianity, people thank God for gratuitous creation and salvation; for neoclassical Christianity, God cannot help but always do the best, and no thanks need be given. The chief wonder in the Christian experience is the divine grace which constitutes God as Saviour by bringing the world to participate in Christ when there is no antecedent necessity that God do so. Neoclassical metaphysics cannot escape necessitarianism.[28]

In regard to Christology, Ogden wants to say that Jesus Christ is a representation of what God universally is everywhere and always to everyone.[29] Ogden uses an economic trinitarianism to argue that "Jesus Christ" is the equivalent symbol of "God our Father," the God of Old Testament history. But both are seen to be subordinate to the real God. Like the process christology of Norman Pittenger[30] (although differing from it in

27. Ibid., p. 92.
28. Ibid., p. 93.
29. See "What Does It Mean to Affirm 'Jesus Christ as Lord'?" in *The Reality of God*, pp. 188–205.
30. See Norman Pittenger, *Christology Reconsidered* (London: SCM, 1970); *The Divine Triunity* (Philadelphia: United Church Press, 1977). I vividly recall Pittenger's visit (at his own invitation) to my former campus in the midseventies and his ardent defense of homosexuality, the authority of the Mass (he is Anglican) over Scripture, and his notable remark in one of his lectures, in support of the nonsubstantiality of the self, "I look within myself and find no substantial thing called 'I'"; to which I remarked, "Who is making the statement?" Although some readers may wish that I had given more attention to Pittenger in this book, I consider him more a popularizer of process theology than a seminal thinker. He does attempt, perhaps more than others like Cobb, to relate process thought to traditional doctrines, such as Christology. He writes well and persuasively, and to the uninitiated may appear to flow within the mainstream of orthodoxy. When one looks carefully at what he is saying in view of his process presuppositions, however, he appears in a rather different light. The following passage from *Christology Reconsidered*, p. 141, locates him clearly in the Whiteheadian school: "as the chief causative element in all causes and

many regards), Ogden's loyalty to process categories does not allow him to interpret Jesus Christ biblically as coequal with God the Father and the Holy Spirit in ontological triunity. The meaning of Jesus Christ is wholly economic or symbolic. (Neville does not make this point, since he does not subscribe to Christian orthodoxy.) As far as biblical eschatology is concerned, Ogden completely reinterprets its meaning in existentialist terms. God is affected by all things and "resurrects" them everlastingly in his own life, by his love of all, overcoming the threat of perishing, of death, and of sin.[31]

But of course the inaccessibility of the present in process metaphysics compels one to redefine what "unbounded" love God can actually have for the world, since God cannot prehend or love things in their subjective immediacy. Hence, as I have noted in my critique of Hartshorne, what actually slips away from God and is eternally lost to him as well as to the creaturely subject is precisely the subjective immediacy of the individual. This problem of genuine loss and irreversible tragedy is built into the process system and goes back to Whitehead's doctrine that only objective experience of others is possible; that is, God can remember us only as perished data, not as living concrescing subjects. This is surely a Faustian victory, for the price of freedom in the process system is then to be understood as freedom *from* God's interfering or determining presence in the subject's own immediacy, hence the everlasting loss of that immediacy when it peaks and perishes. Eschatologically it is a tragic vision. As Neville remarks, God's memory of objective events is not what Scripture means when it describes resurrection as the gift of personal subjective immediacy beyond death. Instead of eschatological participation in God, Ogden's neoclassical eschatology offers only everlasting separation from God.[32]

Moreover, there is no eschatological hope that the losses and perishings of a fallen world will ever be overcome by God, as Scripture attests, for in Ogden's process theism God necessarily must always have a world to be relative to. With biting sarcasm Neville questions Ogden's motives and audience: "To give up the integrity of the world with its own

---

the chief affected element in all affects (notice I write here 'affects', not 'effects', since I am talking about God as the ultimate recipient of what goes on in the world), God is present and God is active in every cause and in every effect. But he is there, not by dominating those causes and affects so that they lose their integrity by losing their freedom; he is there as the omnipresent lure, the omnipresent aim, the omnipresent agency for effecting good in the world. Thus every occasion, in its own quality and in its own degree, is an incarnation of the divine dynamic which we call by the name of God. Whitehead was entirely correct in saying, at the end of his life, that 'God is in the world or he is nowhere'."

31. Ogden, *The Reality of God*, p. 226.
32. Neville, *Creativity and God*, p. 95.

inalienable subjective process would be to give up its autonomy and the ultimate significance that Ogden thinks secular people would like."[33] This is a hard criticism and challenges the motives of process theists; but I include myself in the indictment and see rather more clearly now how intimidated I was by secular norms and the desire for acceptance in the humanistic setting of the college-university; more seriously, how rebellious I was against the sovereign grace of God. The pattern of process theology vis-à-vis Scripture is the pattern of the rebel, and its motivating question the same as that of Genesis 3:1 (KJV): "Hath God said?" The price of this rebellion is expulsion from the logic of Paradise.

Neoclassical theism terminates in the rejection of all the essential self-disclosures of God in Scripture. Most serious is that God is no longer conceived of as the final redeemer of a fallen world but as a finite deity who is at the mercy of a perverse universe that forever frustrates his attempts to redeem it. When we look at process theism circumspectly we find a theistic system which, although initially attractive, turns out to be as illogical and irrelevant as a theology could possibly be. Ostensibly designed to confront the world with a "God who cares," neoclassical theism offers a God who has no transcendent experience or consciousness prior to the world, cannot fellowship with anything or anyone in its or his present immediacy, and cannot eschatologically overcome the sin and evil of the world.

The Attempt to Synthesize Major Religions

Cobb's attempt to build bridges between Asian and Western cultures comes under sympathetic examination by Neville, especially in terms of Cobb's important study, *The Structure of Christian Existence*.[34] Cobb makes use of Karl Jaspers's interpretation of the major world religions in China, India, Persia, Israel, and Greece during the "axial period" of the eighth to sixth centuries B.C.[35] I myself used Jaspers's essay on the axial period extensively in teaching during my process years and find it still a fascinating study with, however, questionable conclusions. His approach to a phenomenology of world religions has the effect of pressing the data toward a pluralism of viable positions. It had that effect on me and it has had a similar effect on Cobb. His analysis of the developments of lines of reflective thought in India, Greece, and Israel is in many ways valid as a descriptive study, but placing Judaism and Christianity under the same

---

33. Ibid., p. 96.
34. (Philadelphia: Westminster Press, 1967).
35. See Karl Jaspers's *The Origin and Goal of History* (New Haven: Yale University Press, 1953).

microscope of analysis with other religions has the subtle effect of leveling and relativizing all the plural approaches to reality. I know as a reconverted classical Christian (and I am sure this is true of practicing adherents in other religious traditions as well) that such a "descriptive" approach tends to sidestep the normative claims of faith as it attempts to analyze all religions from some higher contemporary authority of dispassionate scientific objectivity.

Nevertheless, one can (and Neville does) appreciate Cobb's description of the articulated structure of existence by the ancient Hebrews as a prophetic mentality in which the person is responsible for his actions in covenant relationship with God. This is contrasted with the Indian view of the self as ultimately unreal and the Greek view of reality as aesthetic and rationalistic. The Greek way, Cobb argues, has been incorporated into the Hebraic-Christian structure, forming the Western tradition. Hence today, the major options are Christianity and Buddhism, says Cobb, and they appear to be irreconcilable.[36] Cobb does feel that Christianity has the edge pragmatically; in view of the expanding world of technology and ecological problems, it has more to say about covenantal responsibility.

Neville criticizes Cobb, however, for opting rather too strongly for the survival of Christianity and suggests that a genuinely Whiteheadian approach would be rather to integrate resources in a new way by selecting compatible elements from available options. This, he points out, is what Whitehead sees as the general synthesis of process (hybrid, physical prehensions), and is what most of the people in the contemporary changing world are trying to come to terms with. Neville appeals for a new created structure of existence that will adapt the richer contributions of the past to the higher human values. Whether or not his earlier criticism prompted Cobb to attempt a creative synthesis between Christianity and Buddhism, it is surprising that Neville makes no mention in his chapter of Cobb's rather extensive attempt in the 1970s to do exactly that,[37] although he has remarked approvingly in chapter 8 that Cobb has expressed clearly and courageously the need for a "relative" Christian commitment.[38]

Neville lays out his own program in line with Cobb's position but goes beyond him in pressing for a truly synthetic approach to world religions:

> . . . Christians, Buddhists, and all other contenders ought to be looking for agreement on what structures of existence are appropriate for the various

---

36. *The Structure of Christian Existence*, p. 148.

37. See Cobb's article, already referred to: "Buddhist Emptiness and the Christian God," *Journal of the American Academy of Religion* 45 (March 1977): 11-25.

38. See Neville, *Creativity and God*, p. 144, where he quotes from *John Cobb's Theology in Process*, p. 168.

interested parties. This is not to say the same structure must be agreed upon for all, only that they all agree on the just distribution. I am not at all sure that, in proposing his options, Cobb needs to suggest that Buddhism is right for some people, Christianity for others, but that would be a logically tenable position.[39]

Hence, in spite of Neville's sometimes astute defense of classical Christian theology against process alternatives, he is not really biblically oriented at all but evinces the same confidence in the autonomy of human reason to establish the norms of religious needs and to describe the relative truth about reality. Of course he qualifies this as perhaps an unrealizable ideal, but nevertheless one that we as cultural leaders ought to aspire to as pacesetters in the modern world with all its horrendous problems: "the impetus to solve these problems fosters, and may indeed require, the development of the delicate but intense sensitiveness of a new structure of existence."[40]

Neville offers a relativistic view of the rise of the major world religions (factors of environment, geography, climate, cultural artifacts and the like figure prominently). As a radical empiricist,[41] he holds that an empirical analysis of the structures of existence represented by the world's religions discloses basic conditions inherited by all cultures—for example, suffering is universal; language is universal; the symbolic interpretation of suffering is universal; the conflict between those symbols and shattering intrusions is universal; sacred ceremonies associated with suffering, birth, death, maturation, and ecstasy are universal. Neville proceeds to develop a radical process model according to three aspects of personal life[42] as Plato describes them in the *Republic*—the appetitive, the rational, and the spirited.

> Plato's three ideals for the soul illustrate three aspects of personal life that can be developed according to the abstract categories of the process model. Desires correspond to the many data providing value and energy to the process, seeking new objectification. Reason corresponds to the function of mentality, providing conceptual propositions, including new ones for subjective harmony. And spirit corresponds to the drive for unification restricted by the "categorial obligations," to use Whitehead's term, and perfected by the degree to which the richest desires (most valuable data) are incorporated in the wisest way for mutual enriching objectification.[43]

39. *Creativity and God*, p. 122. See also p. 123.
40. Ibid., p. 124.
41. See Neville's "Metaphysical Argument for Wholly Empirical Theology" in *God Knowable and Unknowable*.
42. For a closer examination of these three aspects, refer to Neville's *Soldier, Sage, Saint.*
43. Neville, *Creativity and God*, p. 126.

The soldier is like Arjuna in the Bhaghavad Gita who perceives and acts without ego and in so doing reflects the pure essence of things. The sage who gains enlightenment takes his place as a religious type alongside the warrior. And "all religions have their saints, the lovers whose divine love has salvific power."[44] Different structures in the world religions emphasize one paradigm above the others, although all three are present in some form. Neville's process model now poses the question of finding appropriate new forms of the soldier, sage, and saint, "so as to minimize the loss of old traditions and to maximize the intensity of cultural life in the context of the current environment."[45] We can see very clearly here an evolutionary empirical model that informs process thought fundamentally.

Neville has a definite agenda that already precludes the essential teachings of most world religions. This is the weakness of all liberal eclecticism. Christianity's distinctive offer of salvation in Christ alone and by grace alone is discarded; "and particularly," Neville says of his program, "it is insensitive to the Buddhist 'quest for the cessation of all cravings.'"[46] But of course! Even an eclectic creative synthesis of the old lays down the norm of what is and what is not acceptable in the evolutionary process, and in this case the Buddhist is required to give up his absolutely fundamental quest, without which there would be no Buddhism. As I remarked earlier in describing Cobb and his attempt to synthesize Christianity and Buddhism through process hermeneutics, process thought takes the individual and future empirical experience very seriously, whereas Buddhism holds that process is the essential problem and lies at the core of suffering.

Nevertheless, Neville genuinely believes that the basic religious structures and ethical patterns are so similar in the world's religions that it is pointless to press any essential differences between being in Christ for the Christian and having the Buddha nature for the Buddhist, between the Christian's loving and the bodhisattva's loving. However—and here Neville shows himself to be a radical reconstructionist and evolutionist in theology—he claims that "the particular mixes in each case are inadequate to our times."[47] I take this to mean that Christianity has no special claim to truth. Indeed, Neville faults Cobb's *Structure of Christian Existence* for not being radical enough. Cobb, he says, has been "seriously remiss in suggesting that Christianity, Buddhism, or, indeed, any of the great axial cultural traditions have clearly identifiable natures."

44. Ibid., p. 128.
45. Ibid., p. 129.
46. Ibid.
47. Ibid., p. 132.

There is no such thing as "the Christian" or "the Buddhist"; and it is very difficult to make generalizations about "Christians" or "Buddhists." There are many different kinds of each. I agree with Cobb in his recent statements that there is not even such a thing as "essence" to a tradition unifying the historical variations.[48]

That is about as strong a statement from the relativist standpoint as we would hope to find. No tradition is essential or authoritative, and the desire to find such, Neville says, is probably only for the purpose of identifying an opposing tradition and trying to refute it. Would the same caveat apply to Neville's own authoritative defense of relativism and his desire to refute all traditionalists? (It is an old argument—Plato used it against Protagoras.)

The really frightening prospect of Neville's radical process program is that he is now willing to let the case for relativism lie with individual lifestyles; but since he is committed to Whitehead's and John Dewey's concept of reality as social and public, he wants a creative synthesis, a new unifying structure beyond arcane and obsolete religious structures of tradition. Thus in one fell swoop the sensitive descriptive phenomenologist has now become the dogmatist who prescribes what the contemporary world needs. It does not need the message that Christ died for a sinful world, nor the Buddhist counterpart:

If hereditary Christians interact with hereditary Buddhists, then neither can find full meaning for that interaction solely from their own inherited traditions without treating the other as uncultured ciphers in the interaction. Moral as well as practical pressures send us scurrying to find cultural resources from many worlds.[49]

What Neville fails to see, however, is that he now has not one but two uncultured ciphers angry at him for rejecting their views of reality as normative—both evangelical Christians and traditional Buddhists. The synthetic relativist transfers the center of authority away from scriptures held to be sacred to a human view of the nature of reality. Neville is not willing to settle for some homogenized technocracy to bring our cultures together, but wants a daring new creative synthesis on the order of Augustine's blend of Hebrew and Greek cultures. While respecting the existential aliveness of much personal religious experience, Neville nevertheless calls for the analysis of the situation in terms of the abstract

48. Ibid., p. 133. The reference is to *John Cobb's Theology in Process*, pp. 169f.
49. Ibid., p. 134.

categories of metaphysics, as in process thought, for these alone can provide common ground for understanding diversity.[50]

The controversy with Cobb, then, is intramural. Moreover, it is with an earlier Cobb, for we have noted that Cobb has engaged himself more latterly with these very questions of a new creative synthesis among human cultural traditions. Neville does fault Cobb for dealing largely with those aspects of process thought that concern natural cosmology, causation, and individual existence in social environments rather than exploring the categories that define process theism. Cobb in fact feels that the concept of God that is defined by process theism is incompatible with the Buddhist view since Buddhists are ultimately concerned with the elimination of craving and with emptiness, where Christians stress things that have to do with God. Neville observes that in view of the fundamental incompatibility of process theism and Buddhist emptiness "perhaps that Catholic argument lacks force," and it were better and more neutral to hold to a conception of God the creator as "indeterminate apart from creation" and "immanent in the determinate being of things within creation."[51] That, of course, comes closer to biblical faith and the historical confessions of classical Christianity, although Neville remains firmly tied to the basic tenet of evolutionary theology and to the theory of new emergent forms of religious structure.

Neville's Concept of God, Creativity, and Human Freedom

This radically processive posture comes out forcefully in a concluding brief chapter in which Neville sums up his own position. There is great need to address our common problems of social life and to create an intellectual milieu through the deployment of abstract categories of speculative process philosophy, he argues. But as he noted in his critique of Cobb, the process conception of God is not one of the process categories that may prove useful in the discussion. The process concept of God has few if any advantages over more classical conceptions of God in its dialogue with Buddhism, or as an interpretation of Western experience itself. There are a number of serious problems in the process view of God, such as Whitehead's separation of God and creativity, Hartshorne's difficulty in explaining the role of abstract necessity if God is a society, and Ford's view of God as a unitary actual entity unrelated to this world.

The separation of God and creativity should be abandoned, Neville

50. Ibid., p. 135.
51. Ibid., p. 136. See also "Metaphysical Argument for a Wholly Empirical Theology" in *God Knowable and Unknowable.*

argues, and I agree, although on more orthodox grounds. Whitehead's category of the ultimate is ontologically too abstract. Neville is correct when he argues that "the ontological question can be answered only by conceiving every determinate complexity to be the product of a kind of ontological creativity not contained with the system of the world or explained by creative categories." But he is much too cautious and perhaps fearful of being too closely identified with biblical faith when he adds the unhelpful comment, "Whether ontological creativity can be related to a conception of God is, of course, another matter."[52] It is, certainly, another matter that lies beyond speculative metaphysics, but the "whether" troubles me, for one would hope that a Midwestern Methodist by confession would have more certainty that biblical theology does describe the intricate ontological relation of God and creativity; indeed on the first page of Scripture: "And God said, ... and there was ..." (Gen. 1:3). Creativity cannot be a function of an abstract principle that has no ability to discriminate between what is positive (creativity) and what is negative (destructivity). Only the personal and infinite God who consciously wills, speaks, and acts can give genuine content to a word (namely, "creativity") that in ordinary language usage is applied by persons to personal activity. Only an infinite and personal God beyond timespace who is the actual source of creativity can underwrite its derivative function in the created world. Otherwise there will be only chaos and no cognizant person to recognize the aesthetic power and beauty of creativity itself.

Neville also detects a flaw in Whiteheadian and Fordian logic with respect to God's being a single actual entity, for if so, then God cannot in any finite time objectify an occasion's hybrid physical prehension of the divine ideal, for the process of a finite occasion and its antecedents are always simultaneous with the everlasting divine concrescence. Not only is the vocabulary awful, but the logical paradoxes are even more awesome!

If one then adopts a Hartshornean model as a society of occasions in order to avoid the dilemma of Whiteheadian theism, he has to face another logical difficulty. What does God's nature consist of in such a case? Is there an actual enduring Individual, an infinite Person, or only an abstract normative principle that guides the society of occasions? And if so, how do principles do anything? Then there are the other related questions, which I have raised in my own critique of Hartshorne in regard to simultaneity and velocity of experience, that Neville does not mention.

On one very important issue he does again attack the process school, and this concerns the question of human freedom. I said in chapter 1 that my own understanding of the motivation behind process theism is

52. *Creativity and God*, pp. 139f.

that it is a defense of human autonomy and freedom (anthropodicy). Neville cogently points out that process theism guarantees nothing of the sort:

> But with regard to freedom, a person is less free from God's lures than from anything else among given data; the ability to alter subjective aim within the process of concrescence is trivial, less by far than the ability to reject or alter more ordinary initial data.[53]

This is precisely my point in chapter 1. Hartshorne, for example, really has to admit that God's influential power is very great indeed, yet he wants to hold on to the subjective aim of the finite occasion as some right of independence that the creature has over against the Creator. Neville remarks:

> Rather than regard God's presence in the world as sufficiently limited so that people can be free over against God, the better strategy would seem to be to conceive God's presence as coincident with people's freedom and characterize freedom as a function of relations within the world.[54]

While that does not say all that needs to be said on the subject, it certainly is a distinct improvement on the process view which conceives of the world as *necessarily* independent of God and therefore supposedly free. But that is a high price to pay for freedom, for not only does it not make the creature as free as he thinks, but also it renders God impersonal, inconceivable, and irrelevant.

Another criticism of Neville's with which I concur is that in the process system God can prehend only the objectified satisfaction of the finite occasions, not their subjective comings-to-be. We have spent a good deal of time on this deficiency and have noted that its appeal to human freedom is again purchased at the price of God's not being able to know us as we are in our inmost being. God has us only as memory, for "precisely what cannot be remembered is the present immediacy that constitutes the heart of our inmost reality."[55] I do not agree, however, with Neville's pantheistic solution: "It may be preferable to say that our own spontaneous immediacy, as well as our prehended pasts, are products of an ontological creativity that has no character except that of its products; in this case our immediacy would *be* the divine character."[56] This would make us God and would go further in the wrong direction of

53. Ibid., p. 141.
54. Ibid.
55. Ibid.
56. Ibid., pp. 141f. His italics.

speculative metaphysics and impersonal abstraction, rather than return (as Neville occasionally hints he might be going to do) to the greater consistency, coherence, applicability, and adequacy of scriptural faith. At least Neville agrees that process theism does not provide such coherence: "If theism is true, it is not true in the process form."[57]

But Neville's radical alternative of impersonal and abstract ontological creativity suffers from the same category mistake as process theism in according creativity to the whole process without a conscious and willing God who creates. This cannot be. Nature discloses not only creative but also destructive elements in its process. The word *creativity* is a value-laden term that connotes what builds up, is ethically correct and aesthetically pleasing. Conscious, willing, and acting persons speak of creativity, detect creative activity in nature, and aspire themselves to be creative on the human level. It is illegitimate to retroject creativity onto reality as an ontological principle and consider it the surround, indeed the sum, of all that is; principles do nothing (like stone images that do not hear, speak, or act). Further, if one adopts a pantheistic position he must take the whole as it is, undifferentiated into good/bad, beautiful/ugly, creative/ destructive. To call the ultimate ontological principle "creativity," whether it is Whitehead or Neville who is naming the whirlwind, is already to have made a decision on other grounds (the legacy of Christianity) that creativity is preferable to destructivity. Nature, however, seems to make little distinction between building up and tearing down, evolution and entropy, creativity and dyscatastrophe.

Neville's view, then, is as open to criticism as is process theism, for both are Western evolutionary models that build on the optimistic aspects of nature, with structural support from a naturalized Christian eschatology. Neville's semitheism is drifting Eastward, however, and poses real problems:

> Perhaps then one might inquire into whether the conception of ontological creativity I have been urging as an alternative to process theism is closely enough connected to the Western religious traditions to be adequate to their important intuitions and to warrant the name God. Although there is justification for connecting this to certain Western mystical traditions, it must be admitted that this hypothesis also has close affinities to Eastern traditions not often regarded as theistic. Perhaps this is a quasitheism, and is warranted. Perhaps it is as unwarranted as the hypothesis of process theism. Perhaps some other theistic traditions are simply wrongheaded. As far as proof goes, the situation is very open.[58]

57. Ibid., p. 142.
58. Ibid.

Neville's concluding remarks leave us straining to hear something definite, but all we hear are the uncertain sounds of a trumpet. He agrees with process thought that the formulation of God as an abstract hypothesis under the auspices of speculative theology is a great gain for Western thought. One must enter into debate with such abstract alternatives to biblical theology, but I must confess that I find little that is solidly logical, coherent, or adequate in either the process view or in Neville's neopantheism. From a biblical point of view, the best the human mind can imagine is not good enough, for man always seems to triumph, with God reduced in size or eliminated altogether. At least for Neville the situation is very open, although I think his mind is closed to biblical orthodoxy. Biblical theology is no longer God's disclosure, authoritative and infallible, but is a hypothesis along with other hypotheses to be weighed by a "new logic for theology"—namely, "assaying the conceptual viability of traditional, experiential claims. . . . Inquiry thus is free."[59]

But is it? Is the creature really free when he assumes that his own power to weigh, accept, reject, or modify is normative? Then the context for theology is no longer revealed Scripture and the gracious proclamation of God's unmerited grace in Jesus Christ toward a bent world. Rather, the context becomes world-cultural and humanistic. The Story of the gospel is rejected in favor of a relativism that is in reality a substitute absolutism, for now theology must serve the pragmatic purpose of bringing the Christian, the Buddhist, and the nontheist together through new structures of existence on human terms, not those of Scripture.

Neville sees all this as a promising sign. I could not agree less, although I once shared his evolutionary optimism. It signals the erosion of the Christian proclamation of the Good News; and insofar as it has been put into practice, it has witnessed the diminution of those church bodies that have subscribed to its pluralism. What is emerging in the place of classical biblical theology is a new humanism which ostensibly has high goals and will try to realize them through cultural transmogrification and political liberation. What new gods lie in the speculative imaginations of process and creativity theologians we can hardly guess, but I wonder whether any will address human beings with the power of a gospel that proclaims good news to Jew and Greek, slave and free, male and female, for whom Christ died and rose again.

In the final chapter we will look at the work of Ford and his attempt to apply process hermeneutics to the interpretation of Scripture itself. It is there, I think, that the really anthropocentric nature of the enterprise becomes fully visible.

59. Ibid., p. 144.

8

Process Theism
As a Biblical Hermeneutic

A Critique of Ford's *Lure of God*

A process hermeneutic has not been widely adopted as an exegetical method in biblical circles, owing partly to its very speculative and often abstruse vocabulary, partly to its relative newness and unfamiliarity among biblical scholars, but largely to its tendency to be metaphysical and deductive where most exegesis is historical, literary, and inductive and works from the Scripture texts themselves. Even radically liberal biblical criticism, although motivated by historicist presuppositions which are often inimical to the supernatural storyline of the text, still retains a relatively high respect for Scripture, at least for a canon within the canon.

Process theism has little regard for revealed Scripture, and it is rare when one finds a process theologian who is very interested in seriously exploring the relation of biblical studies to process presuppositions. Lewis S. Ford's *Lure of God: A Biblical Background for Process Theism*[1] attempts to do just that, although Ford is a philosopher rather than a biblical scholar by training and one detects at once in the book the deductive posture the author assumes as he interprets Scripture in process terms. In fact the subtitle indicates that the author's purpose is to use the Bible to support process theism rather than to show specifically how process theism can function as a method for doing biblical exegesis. My

1. (Philadelphia: Fortress, 1978).

purpose in this chapter is to show that a basically humanist approach to biblical interpretation, which Ford's is, is not really positioned to listen to the biblical texts sympathetically, but will consistently accord to human autonomy the right to reinterpret Scripture through the canons of speculative metaphysics. This is what has impressed me in my first and subsequent readings of the book. Ford's fundamental theme is divine persuasion rather than divine sovereignty, for in his view God does not have sovereign power over the world but being finite and limited by the world seeks to lure and persuade it to creativity. The one biblical doctrine that is most unacceptable to process theism is the sovereignty of God, for this logically seems to undercut the right of human beings to be free. Hence my first chapter on anthropodicy is a clue to the primary agenda of process thought to defend human freedom over against any notion of God being sovereign. The process deity by definition must be limited in such a way that he can no longer pose a threat to the freedom of the creature.

This rather strident and antibiblical tone is struck by Ford on the very first page of the book where he takes undisguised pleasure in the collapse of neoorthodoxy and in the growing recognition by contemporary theologians of the need for "a wider conceptuality which frees theology from the ghetto of sacred history and places it within the whole sweep of human and natural history." This attempt to find an ecological balance between both nature and God "challenges many of the presuppositions of classical theism by overcoming their felt conflicts and contradictions."[2] That this modest hermeneutic will fail will be apparent to the reader who has stayed with my argument thus far and has been introduced to the conflicts and contradictions of process logic. It will be my purpose to take Ford to task in his stated purpose, first as a theistic philosopher advancing a theory that "must be both consistent and coherent in itself, and adequate and applicable to human experience"; and secondly as a biblical interpreter who will try to do justice to "the biblical witness to Israel and to Jesus, his role as the Christ, the meaning of the death and resurrection, and the implications of the Christian proclamation of the Trinity."[3]

It is important to note at the outset that Ford's basic presupposition which will control his hermeneutical approach to Scripture is Whiteheadian; hence the book is less an open exegetical study of the internal claims of Scripture than an attempt to interpret the Bible by a hermeneutic drawn from speculative philosophy. It is, as Ford admits, "properly an essay in Christian theology." He makes no apology for his approach, charging that theology is often insufficiently rigorous philosophically and

2. Ibid., p. ix.
3. Ibid., p. x.

that the two extremes of philosophy and biblical studies ought to be fruitfully married in the theological enterprise.[4] Let us see how fruitful the marriage may be and whether the biblical side of the matrimonial alliance is to be allowed a voice in the managing of the household. To be truthful, I as a New Testament interpreter am skeptical whether the importation of philosophical speculations as guides to biblical exegesis can ever succeed, since they force Scripture to conform to conceptualities prejudicial to the natural storyline of the Bible itself. A Bultmannian hermeneutic has not succeeded because it has employed the secular ontology of Martin Heidegger; and now the suggestion is that biblical exegesis should adopt another nonbiblical model which aims to explain how God's omnipotence may be qualified in terms of divine persuasion in order that the problem of evil in the world may be dealt with and human freedom defended.

The Basis of a Process Hermeneutic

Setting the scene for a process hermeneutic, Ford describes the pilgrimage of Alfred North Whitehead from an early evangelical pietism, through agnosticism, to his speculative reconstruction of reality in terms of basic atomicity and the principle of God as lure to creativity and as the ultimate recipient of the world's process. Ford briefly sketches how Whitehead modified the classical biblical doctrines concerning God's omnipresence (he needs a world and therefore is not sovereign and independent as absolutely omniscient Lord); his omniscience (he does not know the future in detail, hence we are to that extent free); and his omnipotence (God is not all-powerful but functions as the persuasive lure to creativity).[5] As we have already seen, this is a rather tall order and entails a complete redoing of biblical theology as it begs pride of place over Scripture in determining the nature of God. Ford comments that at first glance such modifications of God's foreknowledge and power may seem quite foreign to the biblical tradition, but defends his revisionist hermeneutic because he feels it may help us to understand and appropriate that message in a new way.

The Old Testament and a Process Hermeneutic: Sovereignty or Persuasion?

The problem of approaching the Bible with preconceived doctrines that are already bent on radically modifying the text is evident in Ford's first attempt to apply a process hermeneutic to the Old Testament. In

4. Ibid., p. xi.
5. Ibid., pp. 1–12.

chapter 2, "Divine Persuasion in the Old Testament," he begins with the admission that Whitehead felt little affinity for that section of the Bible (a historian would see the reflection of Marcion gnosticism here). For the Old Testament to be acceptable on Whiteheadian terms God must be conceived, Ford feels, to be a persuasive agency, not a coercive despot. But he dismisses the one key to a proper interpretation of a biblical story, and that is the necessity of accepting biblical bipolarity on its own terms, that is, the scriptural declaration that God is all-powerful (e.g., "Does evil befall a city, unless the LORD has done it?" [Amos 3:6b]) and divine appeal to human responsibility ("Seek good, and not evil, that you may live" [Amos 5:14]). This is biblical merismus, a part here and a part there, and is enormously important in understanding the biblical paradox of polarities. God is sovereign *and* we are responsible secondary agents. Equivocating on either point does not do justice to genuine biblical bipolarity. The attempt to highlight human freedom by dismissing the doctrine of the sovereignty of God gets the philosopher into all kinds of trouble, as we have seen in our study to this point. But Ford, as a rationalist, will not accept the seemingly logically odd nature of biblical rhetoric, nor the conviction of the biblical writers that God's power is often experienced as the expression of divine will in interaction with his people. He writes:

> That context, however, is no longer our context. The history of God's dealing with Israel can no longer serve as the all-embracing horizon for our understanding of God, which must now be correlated with a greatly expanded world history, a scientific understanding of nature and man, and a drastically altered social and ethical situation. It would appear that only a philosophical structure can provide a sufficiently inclusive context suitable to our needs. Therefore the hermeneutical task calls for the translation of Israel's experience into a contemporary systematic and conceptual framework, one that can do justice to its historical concerns.[6]

Whitehead's strong antipathy for Old Testament theology as "a barbaric conception of God"[7] and, in its Christian form, as "the deeper idolatry"[8] betrays his own rejection of biblical authority and his decision to make human freedom as he conceived it the primary issue. Whitehead and Ford caricature the Old Testament when they attack its teaching of God's sovereignty as a denial of human freedom and responsibility, for they miss the point that only an infinite and personal God can guarantee the ethical correctness of covenant responsibilities, hold human beings

6. Ibid., p. 16.
7. Alfred North Whitehead, *Religion in the Making* (New York: Macmillan, 1926), p. 55.
8. Alfred North Whitehead, *Process and Reality: An Essay in Cosmology* (New York: Harper and Row, 1957), p. 520.

responsible for keeping covenant relationships inviolate, and assure that they are in a position to be freely responsible. Whitehead's attack on the Old Testament is really an unwillingness to accept God as sovereign, focusing instead on how God could make those guarantees; and not finding a rational answer to that question then assuming that God *cannot* do that, since the given is that we creatures are free and must be free at all costs. Ford curiously but understandably spends most of his time in his second chapter dealing with the question of coercion, arguing for a limited, finite God who acts primarily in terms of persuasion. The tone of the chapter, which purports to be an exegesis of Old Testament theology, is philosophic and speculative rather than exegetical. Ford simply cannot get past a theoretical formulation of the problem to see the biblical answer. For him the integrity of the Old Testament resides in the argument that "insofar as God controls the world, he is responsible for evil: directly in terms of the natural order, and indirectly in the case of man."[9] But responsible to whom or what? The sovereign Lord of the Old Testament is the one who *defines* evil: he is not the one who must himself be obedient to some higher good which is sovereign over him. Good and evil in the Old Testament are defined by God in view of what Israel and the nations do in keeping or violating the covenantal relationships that God sets as the parameters of human existence. Catastrophes in human events and nature are never viewed as surds somehow outside the context of God's sovereign judgment, but as the means whereby his righteousness and justice are articulated in a world that is fallen and bent. Evil is defined in the Old Testament and in the New as that which is contrary to God's revealed will for his creatures. He himself cannot do evil, nor does he give answer to anyone or anything as though he were responsible to something higher than himself. What he does is good by definition, since he is absolute righteousness. Evil is what creatures do in removing themselves from a loving and obedient relationship to him. Evil in the Old and New Testaments is defined as that which originates in the abuse of the creaturely will as it poses the rebellious question, "Hath God said?" (Gen. 3:1, KJV).

In the biblical view of divine sovereignty and human responsibility, God creates and sustains the conditions in which his creatures elect to do good or evil by either keeping or forsaking their responsible relationships with him and with one another. That is, God works through valid secondary agents. The paradox is that he sustains the life of the evildoer in his very act of doing evil, as he sustains the obedient in their choice to do good, thereby sovereignly integrating all nature and human activity in his decretive will, even though it is not his preceptive will in terms of the

9. Ford, *The Lure of God*, p. 20.

welfare of his creation and human souls that evil be pursued. This language is of course charged with merismus, but it is the language of Scripture and is genuinely bipolar. Ford, following Whitehead, does not want logically odd biblical language to hold pride of place, however, and opts to think in monopolar fashion, forcing the biblical doctrine of the sovereignty of God and God's gift of human freedom to be redefined as freedom *from* God, God necessarily paying the cost of that redefinition by becoming limited and finite. The result of this radical reinterpretation of biblical revelation is a far more serious logical problem theologically, not to mention the exegetical violence done to the biblical concepts themselves.

The problem with process theism as a hermeneutic for biblical exegesis is that it is not sufficiently phenomenological. It is not open enough to the texture of Scripture itself to be able to listen to its themes and rhythms, but must impose a foreign genre upon the text, an evolutionary model that assumes (contradictorily) no beginning or end to an everlasting process. Hence Ford must reinterpret the Genesis creation account and reject the disclosure that God is the sovereign author of all creation.[10] He also is forced to reject biblical eschatology and God's final control over the future because the ambiguities of history and the independence of the world from God's sovereign power comprise the fundamental commitment of process metaphysics to defend the freedom of the creature, at whatever cost.[11] Salvation for Ford ultimately is self-salvation. Even God depends upon us to fulfill his lure to aesthetic creativity. How we fulfill it is relative to our cultural settings, which will vary, for the Word addressed to Abraham was not the same as the Word addressed to Akhenaton or Gautama or Lao-tse.[12]

Ford's view of biblical authority is accordingly a rather low one. His locus of authority resides in human autonomous reason: "any limitation placed upon philosophical reason ultimately appears to be arbitrary. . . . It is no accident that leading exponents of process theism have shied away from revelatory or kerygmatic theology."[13] The assumption is that biblical theology is suspect because it is insufficiently rigorous logically; but as I have pointed out, it is process theism itself that I have come to view (reluctantly at first) as most open to the criticism of philosophic illogicality and therefore insufficiently rigorous by the criterion of lived coherence. Yet biblical theology is also in need, says Ford, of the insights of process philosophy which provides a description of the necessary conditions that make contingent divine activity possible. This historical development of God in conjunction with the world is completely open-ended,

10. Ibid., p. 21.
11. Ibid., pp. 23f.
12. Ibid., p. 24.
13. Ibid., pp. 25f.

according to process metaphysics, but is supported by the necessary conditions of creativity and divine lure (an even deeper paradox, I would observe).[14]

Ford admits that process theism appears to be an alien hermeneutic for doing biblical exegesis, since the understanding of divine power is quite different in each setting, and with that I would agree. But his rationale for continuing with the project is his conviction that the Bible needs process interpretation in order to be made relevant to new and changing conditions and that it may be retold in terms acceptable and appropriate to our own age.[15] I know what Ford is speaking of, having gone through a similar phase myself. In fact there sits on my shelf an unpublished manuscript of book length from the early seventies, written just prior to my reconversion to biblical faith, my last will and testament on Old Testament themes seen through the eyes of process theism. I entitled it "Love and Hate in the Old Testament" and my thesis was the same as Whitehead's and Ford's, namely, that the Old Testament God is acceptable only when seen in terms of *ḥesed* and *ahab* love, but not in terms of *mishpat* and *ḥerem* judgment, capital punishment, and holy war. It was a pious manuscript, mistaken only on the second point—I did not want justice or judgment, not on Old Testament terms. Hence I sat in judgment on the only source that can normatively disclose the awesome and awful justice of God, which continues unabated into the New Testament and is satisfied only by God's gracious gift of love and righteousness in Jesus Christ.

No one sees the power of God's bipolarity as it is revealed in Scripture, however, until he or she is willing to leave off claiming the right to judge and define God apart from his self-revelation in Scripture and submits in gratitude to his grace and glory in Jesus Christ. To continue to hold fast to one's "right" to define the nature of God and his creation is, on biblical grounds, to recapitulate the role of rebel in Genesis 3:1 by asking the perennial question of the rebel, "Hath God said?"

The New Testament and a Process Hermeneutic: Inaugurated Eschatology versus Apparent Determinism

That Ford is principally concerned with the threat to human freedom posed by God's sovereignty in classical biblical theology is apparent; in his third chapter the kingdom of God becomes his focus of attention as he deals with the New Testament concept of "Divine Sovereignty." Again the process theme of persuasion is brought to bear, this time on Jesus'

14. See ibid., p. 27.
15. Ibid., p. 28.

attitude toward kingship. Ford admits that "this image of God as king poses serious difficulties for process theism," for "the inner dynamic of Israel's experience of God's sovereignty over history leads inexorably to the view that he exercises absolute control over the future."[16] But he takes consolation in the fact that Jesus' proclamation of the kingdom seems to introduce a radically new way of experiencing God's sovereignty as the power of the future. It is important to observe what Ford proceeds to do with Jesus' proclamation in view of a process hermeneutic that has already entered the interpretive circle earlier and described the size of the circle and what will be allowed into it. He correctly agrees with Joachim Jeremias's widely shared view that Jesus proclaims an inaugurated eschatology that confronts the hearer with persuasive appeal, not coercion, in the here and now. Yet it would appear that the primary reason Ford adopts this interpretation is to set Jesus' radical view over against the apparent determinism of apocalypticism which assures the consummation of God's kingly rule in the future, the latter being the eschatology within which most of the New Testament is articulated.[17] What controls Ford's exegesis is not an open phenomenological approach to the New Testament texts themselves but a search for that strain of material which may be construed to fit into the concept of a finite God who cannot control the future (else we would lose our freedom). Hence, Ford has centered on Jesus' partially realized eschatology and dismissed the apparent determinism of the remainder of the New Testament material.

How does Ford interpret Jesus' inaugurated eschatology in view of a process hermeneutic? Since, according to process ontology, our freedom lies in our present power to select and organize what we inherit from the past and to select from future possibilities, Ford interprets Jesus to mean that the reign of God is realized always only partially and ambiguously in the vicissitudes of this life. He has to eliminate, however, the clear teaching of Jesus (and the rest of the New Testament) that what has been inaugurated will reach fulfillment at the close of the age, for a process hermeneutic sees no termination to the everlasting historical flux. God's reign is partially actualized in the present, but as an abstract ideal of future possibility it remains forever future:

> The power of the future is effective only insofar as it is responded to by the power of the present, and that response is usually highly fragmentary, since it is also colored by the power of the past. None of these three powers actualizes anything independently of the others. This means that God as the power of the future is necessarily effective in all things, but it also means that nowhere is he the sole agent.[18]

16. Ibid., pp. 30f.
17. Ibid., p. 35.
18. Ibid., p. 38.

Accordingly, while the reign of God can be partially realized in the here and now as long as we respond effectively to his lure to creativity, it "is forever future, never capable of surrendering its futurity to present realization."[19] The rejection of God's sovereignty and his ultimate control over the plan of salvation as attested by Scripture, Old and New, compels Ford to limit God dramatically and to opt for an eternal dialectical dualism between God and the world (or some world or other):

> Because God's judgment is always for the sake of some further ideal, it can never be final in any absolute sense. He is always the power of the future, and therefore cannot motivate absolute termination beyond which there is no future. . . . For that reason [the final consummation] cannot be a future event, as every event in this temporal world requires the conjoint activity of both God and creatures. Our irreducible freedom, moreover, means that we finally determine, through our own present power, how effective God's future power will be.[20]

There we have the fundamental dualism of process eschatology stated baldly. The price of holding tenaciously to what is considered one's right of freedom is that there never can be a final answer to the problem of pain and evil. That is why I said earlier in this study that process theism is essentially a neo-Zoroastrianism or neo-Manicheism, since it opts for an everlasting duality between the abstract and pure ideals of God in the primordial and eternal sense, and the hybrid and never certain mix of the world and God in the consequent and temporal sense. There is no final resolution of sin and evil, as Scripture clearly attests; hence the system Ford represents, although he wants to call it "Christianity made relevant for modern man," is fundamentally unchristian in light of the Scriptures and what Christians have always held to be the Bible's teaching until the recent dethronement of biblical authority and the enthronement of autonomous human authority in the modern post-Enlightenment era.

But even if Ford's interpretation of God's eschatological reign is accepted at face value, is this deity really more relevant, coherent, and acceptable to the needs of reasonable and struggling human beings in our contemporary setting than the God of the Bible? In the preceding chapter I referred to Robert C. Neville's devastating critique of the Whiteheadian-Fordian concept of God, and it would be well to repeat it here in view of the following passage from *The Lure of God* which reveals a very serious dualism in the process system:

19. Ibid.
20. Ibid., p. 40.

Apart from the world God has neither past nor future, but is pure presence. Nontemporal, he creates himself as the envisagement of the infinitude of all pure possibilities. Just as the world acquires a future from God, so God acquires a past from the world. Each individual creature receives its past from the other creatures of the world, and its future ultimately from God, and out of these creates a new present. God's presence is internal to himself, derived from his nontemporality, but out of that and the past which he receives from the world he creates a new future, as he transforms his pure possibilities into real possibilities, that is, realizable possibilities under the conditions of the world. Thus we do not say that God is a future reality which does not yet exist. Most properly, he is a nontemporal actuality who influences us by the future he now creates; by means of the real possibilities he persuades the world to actualize.[21]

This is hard going logically; can the modern skeptic say that God is a nontemporal actuality who nonetheless sets goals for a changing world, is influenced by the world, in fact can only actualize possibilities under the conditions of the world, yet apart from the world is pure presence with neither past nor future? Classical biblical theology can assert this, although the God of the Scripture is a very different God because the paradox is couched in God's personal if paradoxical self-disclosure in the authoritative story of salvation. But a speculative system like Ford's cannot convince because of its logical improprieties. Take, for example, Neville's criticism of one of these serious inconsistencies:

The fundamental objection to Ford's hypothesis seems to me its inability to allow God's concrescence any opening to the world. The very meaning of genetic successiveness in contrast to physical time is that after the initial phase the concrescence is closed off from outside influence until it reaches satisfaction; this is necessary to preserve the discontinuity of becoming. If no phase of the divine concrescence is completely determinate as a physical satisfaction, there can be no hybrid physical prehension of God by finite occasions, and hence God cannot contribute subjective aims to the finite temporal process. On the other hand, if the divine concrescence is everlasting, and if data from physically antecedent occasions enter the concrescence only in its initial phase, then God can prehend nothing of the world; God's only data could be the divine primordial nature. God could never pick up *initial* data about a finite occasion because the divine *initial* phase would always have preceded it. If God can neither concresce to satisfaction before any finite occasion nor begin a concrescing experience after one, God is strictly speaking contemporary with everything else and therefore absolutely isolated. This is Whiteheadian deism.[22]

21. Ibid.
22. Robert C. Neville, *Creativity and God: A Challenge to Process Theology* (New York: Seabury, 1980), p. 29. His italics.

Hence Ford has backed himself into a corner. The irony of rejecting the biblical God for a supposedly more adequate concept of deity is once again apparent. Now God cannot even provide subjective aims to the finite temporal order, much less experience our own feelings in the way the writer to the Hebrews says God in Christ experiences with us ("For we have not a high priest who is unable to sympathize with our weaknesses, but one who in every respect has been tempted as we are, yet without sinning" [Heb. 4:15]). The Whiteheadian-Fordian concept of the reign of God, far from doing justice exegetically to Scripture, is on rational grounds alone unacceptable and incomprehensible.

The Difficulties in Process Christology

Substantiality and Unity

As we would expect, the problems in Ford's theology continue into his speculations on Christology, the subject of his fourth chapter. Criticizing the church fathers for identifying too quickly Christ and the second member of the Trinity, and dismissing the classical concept of a social Trinity, Ford denies that it is possible for the divine subjectivity to become actualized in some way within the man Jesus. Rejecting the New Testament teaching of the miracle of the incarnation and the humanity and deity of Jesus Christ, he attacks the possibility of the social Trinity on Whiteheadian grounds. Whitehead equates person with substance in the sense that "the unity of an actual entity in its process of coming to be is precisely its unification or growth together (concrescence), which is its subjectivity as experienced from within. Subjectivity and substantial unity cannot be displaced from one another."[23]

Now curiously Ford should not be talking about personal substantiality and unity, for that is exactly what Whitehead and his school cannot account for, and it is especially specious to equate processive subjectivity in the process sense with the word *substance*, since the process school rejects the category of substance in the classical sense. It is strange therefore to find Ford claiming the term and then turning it upon the "time honored formula, *una substantia in tres personae*," and rejecting the formula except in a modal sense, where "persona" is understood rather as an abstract aspect or mode of activity of a single concrete subjectivity.[24]

What process ontology fails to see is that the two polarities of change-less substance and dynamic experience must be held together dialectically in a genuine bipolarity—precisely what biblical theology is seen to

23. Ford, *The Lure of God*, p. 49.
24. Ibid.

reveal of God. In biblical merismus, God is transcendent, changeless, omnipotent, omniscient, omnipresent ("substance itself," to use classical terminology), and at the same time reveals himself as inexhaustibly dynamic, but not in the sense that he is dependent on the world for that dynamic experience. God creates the world, sustains the world, loves the world, redeems the world, judges the world, but the world is always seen as derived from his sovereign grace. The world is ectypal and depends for its existence on the sheer grace of God. It reflects the archetypal one-and-manyness, and the changelessness and dynamism of the First Family, the inexhaustible and dynamic and changeless triunity of Father, Son, and Holy Spirit, ectypically disclosed in the burning bush of Exodus 3:2 ("The bush was burning, yet it was not consumed"), and in Jesus' declaration (radical critics to the contrary, an authentic saying), "Before Abraham was, I am" (John 8:58). In Scripture, God reveals himself as both changeless and dynamic, but on his own ontological terms. Created timespace is not necessary to him, nor will he be limited by the speculative and tentative definitions of the autonomous finite mind.

Accordingly, I am arguing that it is illegitimate to take a term (*substance*) that has no place in the vocabulary of process thought, equate it with a process definition of persons, and then proceed to dismiss the classical formulation of the Trinity which has its roots in God's self-disclosure in Scripture. What transpires in Ford's christological reformulation is what we would expect, for it is typical of modern nonevangelical attempts to redefine the incarnation— "*every* creaturely activity is also a divine activity, incarnating God's purposes in the world, to greater or lesser degree"; this is so because "without the world, God's aims for the world would never be realized, since God acts solely by the power of persuasion, which can be effective only so far as it elicits concrete response."[25] Of course Jesus has to be held as special in some sense, although it can be only in degree since he was only a man, it having already been ruled impossible that the Second Person of the Divine Triunity (itself denied) could be incarnate in Jesus of Nazareth. Hence, some superlative word needs to be found to describe Jesus' unique embodiment of the creative lure of God.

But before he does that, Ford takes us on an excursion of nine pages to other possible worlds through the lens of theistic evolution (very like Teilhard de Chardin's *Phenomenon of Man*) in order to make his point that God is gracious and "incarnate" in whatever worlds he influences; therefore the symbol *Christ* as applied to Jesus is historically conditioned and relative. Indeed, our forefathers were naïve in assuming the uniqueness and exalted status of man. Hence the Logos of John 1 refers to the

25. Ibid., p. 50. His italics.

totality of God's creative aims throughout the universe of possible worlds and must not be identified solely with Jesus as the Christ in Christianity, although *for us* "the Word appropriate to our condition becomes incarnate by becoming fully actualized in the word, deeds, and suffering of Jesus."[26] Jesus is not the only incarnation possible in the universe, however, nor is he the only incarnation for mankind. Agreeing with John B. Cobb's incarnational relativism in *Christ in a Pluralistic Age*, Ford remarks that perhaps it is better to speak of incarnation as embodiment rather than actualization:

> In this sense God is incarnated in every religious tradition through every image and symbol which effectively expresses its deepest response to God's leading, although the Christian can confess that for him Christ, the incarnation of God, is supremely exemplified in Jesus.[27]

I know this position well and held to it with pride and confidence for a dozen years. But it is not convincing exegetically or logically, as I came to see. It is what we want to hear and believe in this pluralistic age, because God's revealed remedy for sin through the sacrificial gift of his own Son incarnate in human flesh, the satisfaction of divine righteousness in his life, death, and resurrection—God's way of justice, reconciliation, and salvation—makes claims upon human autonomy that we do not want to face, until we are humbled by the awesomeness of evil and by the greater awesomeness of God's grace in Jesus Christ. The erosion of belief in the authority of Scripture, combined with an epistemological agnosticism in general, compels Ford to question whether Jesus possessed the unique authority Scripture accords him, for "how could we possibly *know* the inner psychic experience of another to ascertain uniquely differing features of his structure?"[28] I would refer Ford to the phenomenology-of-persons school (represented by Ludwig Wittgenstein, G. E. M. Anscombe, and Michael Polanyi, which I have employed in a recent study) that follows the dictum "Look and see!"[29] Jesus' unique and astounding authority is clearly to be read in the words and acts that reveal his intentionality; he claims correlativity with God in his declaration of the arrival of the saving reign of God in terms of his own person as he forgives sinners and invites them to open table-fellowship. His use of the personal pronoun *I* is extraordinary. But the recognition of this unique authority

26. Ibid., p. 64.
27. Ibid., p. 65.
28. Ibid., p. 67. His italics.
29. Refer to Royce Gordon Gruenler, *New Approaches to Jesus and the Gospels: An Exegetical and Phenomenological Study of Synoptic Christology* (Grand Rapids: Baker, 1982).

of Jesus requires sensitivity to the exegetical method, and of that there is hardly any hint in Ford's entire chapter on Christology. This further confirms my earlier criticism of process thought: that it is not a viable hermeneutic for biblical exegesis. It has already made prejudgments on so many crucial issues before coming to the text that there is little interest in any genuine listening to or being challenged by what Scripture is saying.

The Resurrection

We now know what Ford will say on each of the basic doctrines of biblical faith. What interpretation does he lend to the biblical witness to Jesus' resurrection? In his fifth chapter, "The Resurrection as the Emergence of the Body of Christ," he takes I Corinthians 15 as a starting point but interprets it to mean that the appearances of the risen Jesus to the disciples do not rest on literally valid testimony but are the encounter of the Spirit of Christ through hallucinations. Since Ford takes the christological aim of God in Christ to be the next stage in the emergent evolution of the world, "the creative emergence of a new organic unity incorporating man,"[30] it is not surprising that for him the resurrection of Christ is not the dramatic reversal of death in the rising of Jesus Christ as person from the tomb, but the emergence of the church, the body of Christ, and the furtherance of the evolutionary advance.[31] The process theists' use of some of the same vocabulary and Scripture as that employed in classical orthodoxy discloses to the discerning eye how misleading all of this can be to the lay person who is unaware of the total reconstruction of biblical faith that is going on in the process hermeneutic. The centrality of Christ's personal resurrection from the dead as the new Adam that he might establish a remnant community is completely bypassed in Ford's identification of the "risen Christ" with the church. Such eisegesis is an example of what happens when a humanly conceived speculative system approaches Scripture with hardened presuppositions. From the New Testament interpreter's point of view, such a hermeneutic lacks exegetical integrity.

The Cross and Reconciliation

What then, working backward, does Ford make of the cross of Christ? In his next chapter he tries to answer the question by reflecting on "Reconciliation through the Cross" (chap. 6). Philosophical speculation rather than sound biblical exegesis of the relevant texts once again dominates the discussion, as Ford asserts that classical theism has mixed Greek ideals of the impassibility of God with biblical patterns. Yet he

30. *The Lure of God*, p. 75.
31. Ibid., pp. 78–79.

himself relies upon Whitehead, a Platonist, and would impose neo-Platonist metaphysics upon the Judeo-Christian Scriptures! Complaining that classical Christian theology decreed two natures in Christ, one human and one divine, the human nature being the one in which Christ suffered and was crucified, Ford suggests the opposite, namely, that in Christ God's own suffering is truly demonstrated. Aside from the patri-passionist argument employed here, the striking fact is that Ford's process ontology does not allow God to suffer in his primordial nature any more than does the eternal nature of God in classical theology, since the primordial aspect of God is

> the nontemporal dimension of God's being, for it is God conceived of as divorced from time, wholly independent of the world, timelessly envisioning the entire multiplicity of pure possibilities. It is Aristotle's God thinking on thinking.[32]

Alternatively, he says, it is the God of the Old Testament in his role as creator, lawmaker, and judge.

Of course the latter comparison is not correct, for the Old Testament God who creates, gives laws, and judges is the active and dynamic God who interacts with Israel in history, and this contact with the world is not possible for Ford's Aristotelian deity. He wants to say that this unconscious primordial deity employs the realm of pure possibility, the Word, to command and to create; but to command and to create is to impinge on objects that God commands and creates, and the primordial God cannot do that. Notice the impossible contradictions in logic that are to be found on a single page:[33]

1. This realm of pure possibility, the primordial nature of God, "provides all the pure forms of value, in terms of which each effort of the finite world is evoked, and in terms of which its final achievement is judged."
2. But "in himself, God is independent of time. . . ."
3. Yet if God is nontemporal thought about thought independent of the world, he cannot impinge upon its process primordially as lure at the initiation of concrescence, then judge it at the conclusion of concresence, since
4. the only sense in which God impinges upon the world is as consequent, that is, as passive and receptive, not as initiative and active.

Aware of the problem, Ford addresses three possible answers. The first is Aristotle's radical distinction between God and the world (God is not

32. Ibid., p. 83.
33. See ibid., p. 83.

aware of the world). The second is classical theism, in which God knows the world, but the world's temporality is only apparent. This is not the biblical view, of course, and Ford is mistaken if he thinks it is. It is also not the view of classical Christian theology, for which the world is temporal and real because God has created it so; and he is able, while remaining transcendent, to enter immanently into the world and redeem it. Ford is here demolishing a straw argument which perhaps fits better into a Hindu model of deity. The third option is his own preferred solution in which

> God's eternal nature is supplemented by a temporal nature, itself directly dependent upon the world's finite actualization for its concrete content of experience. In himself God knows only pure, unbroken, nontemporal unity, but this knowledge is further enriched by the temporal experience of the world's plurality.[34]

I may sound repetitive in my query, but perhaps it could be explained how Ford's concept of the two natures of God makes more sense than the biblical merismus of God's transcendence and immanence, when the very logic by which Ford wants his theology to be judged superior to classical Christian theology ought to forbid his making the category mistake of pure, unbroken, nontemporal unity influencing and being influenced by temporal diversity. If God says he is transcendent and immanent by self-revelation in his infallibly inspired Scripture, that may be logically odd from a human point of view, but it is certainly to be listened to with respect, for who else would know who God is and what he can do but God himself? Epistemologically God's self-revelation in Scripture is far superior to autonomous human speculation on the nature of God. At least God's self-disclosure in Scripture is explorable exegetically, if it is not exhaustible. But for a naturalist and rationalist to say that it makes more sense for a temporal consequence to affect primordial nontemporality is illogical. The problem with the Whiteheadian-Fordian system is that it short-circuits itself by definition. The nontemporal nature cannot act as responsive lure to the processive world, for it would have to be conscious of all the contours of the world and universe to provide it appropriate and relevant lures, and it would therefore have to be temporal; but by definition it is locked away from temporality. Likewise a consequent nature that passively experiences the process of the world could not affect the primordial nature because, again, the primordial nature is atemporal. If God is one long eternal concrescence, as Ford holds, he cannot experience the epochal discontinuity that is supposed to be at the core of Whiteheadian process.

34. Ibid., p. 84.

On the surface the system seems sound, but on examination it collapses. One reason why process metaphysics gets into difficulty is because of its insistence that what is really important in a system is how much it discerns the abstract, invariant structures of existence that are to be discerned by human reason alone. Ford's objection to the Judeo-Christian Scriptures as inerrantly authoritative is his belief that anything historical is contingent and therefore relative, in this case relative to Israel and to Jesus of Nazareth. To these historical contingencies philosophic generalization will not bow. I think the crux of the matter lies in the epistemological presuppositions of the two approaches. Scripture is empirical in that God makes his absolute claims and disclosures in normative historical events (e.g., the exodus; the cross and the resurrection). This is the way God has chosen to disclose himself, and what he says he can do, he can do. Our responsibility is to be receptive to his gracious speaking and acting. Philosophical reflection can be creative and credible only when it builds upon the historical disclosure of God as the infinite and personal Lord. It is this personal, dynamically inexhaustible God who reveals himself as transcendent and immanent, never as unconscious and impersonal generic abstraction, on the one hand, or conscious and consequent and personal on the other. By insisting on investigating primarily the generic and invariant structures of existence through human reason,[35] rather than the self-disclosure of God in Scripture (which also discloses that human reason is bent and unreliable), Whitehead and Ford have committed themselves to a rejection of the foundation of Christian faith, and to a fruitless enterprise. The results are not impressive, even by the canons of logic.

Accordingly, we can expect that process metaphysics will not take very seriously sin or the radical measures (the sacrificial system in the Old Testament, the sacrifice of Christ in the New) God has provided for the defeat of sin, evil, death, and entropy in the world. Rather, the cross is symbolic of a universal salvation that depends upon our own appropriation of God's creative lures: "It is God's consequent experience of our lives which calls forth his dynamic provision of new aims for our lives, by which we have redemption." The new birth of John 3:3 means that "in terms of the perishing occasions of our temporal life, we are being born anew and from above as we receive novel initial aims from God originating our subjectivity from moment to moment."[36] Not only is that what the new birth and the cross do not mean exegetically (they entail a radical change in our nature and motivation), but also God cannot really provide

35. Ibid., pp. 84f.
36. Ibid., p. 86.

those aims either as consequent, because passive, or as primordial, because nontemporal.

Sin is understood by Ford not to be disobedience to God on the part of the covenant-breaking creature but "the mutual obstruction of things; their conflict and disharmony engender suffering and loss."[37] Consequently, the cross is a symbol that in Jesus God has brought peace by assuring us that evil is transformed by him into harmonious good. But sometimes God fails, as in the case of Jesus. At this crucial point in his interpretation of the meaning of the cross and Jesus' rejection by the Father, Ford shows how a process hermeneutic completely misses the profound meaning of what God is doing for our salvation in laying upon his Son all the sins of the world. Ford cannot accept this intratrinitarian separation of the Father from the Son because of Whitehead's dictum that a distinct subjectivity is a distinct actuality, which Ford thinks leads to tritheism. It is a pity that such a set definition in an already logically contradictory speculative system should be the primary determinant in Ford's rejection of Nicean and Chalcedonian doctrines, which represent the wise decisions of the church fathers in light of revealed Scripture against the earlier threats of unbiblical speculations by those who would have diminished the beauty and power of the social triunity of God and the divine-human incarnation of Jesus Christ. After comparison with process alternatives, the biblical classical doctrines look better than ever to me.

Observe, for example, the travesty Ford makes of the cross and the Father's rejection of the Son, which in biblical theology evinces the paradox of God's power in his weakness, his wisdom in his foolishness. In Ford's reconstruction, God at a most critical moment cannot provide the necessary creative aims to assure Jesus of the peace that is supposed to come of the divine desire to transform evil into harmonious good:

> In the hour of Jesus' deepest need, he could not feel the presence of God, because there were no redemptive possibilities that God could provide, no aims which could vouchsafe to him the infinite resourcefulness of the divine life in clothing his actions with resplendent meaning, sending him forth with renewed courage. For Jesus, there was only the cross and death. In his cross the weakness of God is revealed, as he stood by powerless to comfort his beloved. The worst of it was that God intimately experienced Jesus' awareness that this sustaining grace had suddenly been taken from him. God did not abandon Jesus, but he knew this abandonment, as Jesus knew it, in the depth of his being.[38]

37. Ibid., p. 93.
38. Ibid., p. 94.

Certainly this has to be one of the worst examples of exegesis in theological annals in light of what the Scripture actually says about the dynamic power of God in the cross. Paul declaims that "Christ did not send me to baptize but to preach the gospel, and not with eloquent wisdom, lest the cross of Christ be emptied of its power. . . . But to us who are being saved it is the power of God. . . . We preach Christ crucified, a stumbling block to Jews and folly to Gentiles, but to those who are called, both Jews and Greeks, Christ the power of God and the wisdom of God. For the foolishness of God is wiser than men, and the weakness of God is stronger than men" (I Cor. 1:17–25). Surely anything less than this divinely attested interpretation of the cross invites a soteriology without hope. For if God fails to provide the proper redemptive lures and assurances for one such as Jesus, what failures must await us? This passive "ruthlessness of God" does, Ford promises, evoke new intensities of being in the emergence of the lure of resurrection in the near future; that is, the emergence of the body of Christ, the church. But for Jesus as person, the occasion of the cross is the moment of his perishing without hope in the everlastingness of a past datum. Ford believes this gives us hope for new emergents, but I do not see this. I do not see how he can state that "Jesus underwent the abandonment of God, so necessary for the emergence of the resurrected body, in order that we might be spared this experience."[39]

But how? What does Jesus accomplish in his death that guarantees we will be spared the anguish of the absence of God at our own death? Indeed, process theism offers so limited a deity that we are at death forever cut off from his presence as conscious ongoing persons, since death is the final termination of consciousness for all of us. God remembers us only as perished data, but data that necessarily exclude our present immediacies while we have lived, for that would make him contemporaneous with us and would usurp our freedom to choose apart from his control. In the process system God cannot influence us primordially as a conscious and loving God because he is unconscious, nontemporal, and wholly abstract; and he cannot help us as consequent, since he is only passive when he is actual and has us as dead data. The entire theological system is a shambles, and since, on Ford's own admission, he is an Arian and a Patripassionist,[40] we can only be grateful that the church fathers were led of the Spirit to draw out the teachings and implications of Scripture correctly. Christianity would probably have ceased to be a viable religion if such heretical options to orthodoxy had triumphed in the early centuries of its life.

At all costs Ford denies the identification of the risen Christ with the

39. Ibid., p. 95.
40. Ibid., pp. 92, 95.

preexistent Logos because he cannot accept the biblical disclosure that God the transcendent is capable of entering into time. I quote the following passage at length because it summarizes where a speculative process christology makes its turn away from normative biblical faith and the tradition of the church fathers, adopting instead a hybrid Arianism which is thought to be superior to orthodoxy:

> . . . Christ is temporally created, not begotten. On the other hand, we also agree with Athanasius that the Logos, the second member of the Trinity, is nontemporally begotten "before all worlds." We can be both Arian and Athanasian by denying the one point they share in common, namely, the identification of the risen Christ with the preexistent Logos. Here Arius errs philosophically in supposing this preexistent Logos could be created in time and errs religiously in worshiping that which is other than God. The living subjectivity of Christ is temporally emergent, but not "in the beginning," nor even in the birth or baptism of Jesus. Jesus died so that Christ might be born. But Christ is not to be worshiped in himself, but serves only as a mediator, magnifying the availability of God to us. In him the divine aims for our lives can be intensified in a way not possible without him. Yet the very fact that he is our privileged means of access to God, such that only in Christ do we encounter the fullness of God, should not blind us to the createdness and relativity of even the risen Christ. There may be other transhuman societies, in the future or even now, just as there may be other living societies embracing intelligent life on other worlds, or even emergent forms capable of incorporating the fullness of Christ within an unimaginable intensity and richness of being. The possibilities which the divine creative Word holds for the future are inexhaustible, and any restriction of the Word to the risen Christ bespeaks a parochial anthropocentrism we should eschew.[41]

According to this process christology, therefore, Christ and the cross are of only relative importance.

A Process Concept of the Trinity

What does Ford make, then, of the Trinity? We know that it will not be a social Trinity, and we more than suspect that the components of this triadic model will be abstractions, following Whitehead's penchant for abstract principles as components of the primordial antecedents to actuality. In his seventh chapter, "A Process Trinitarianism,"[42] Ford adduces precisely what we might have anticipated—a thoroughly abstract and impersonal model of the Trinity, based on three Whiteheadian prin-

41. Ibid., p. 95.
42. For a more detailed version of the argument see Ford's "Process Trinitarianism," *Journal of the American Academy of Religion*, vol. 43, no. 2 (June 1975): 199–213.

ciples. The fourth Gospel (e.g., John 17:1-5) is rejected as incorrect in its disclosure that the preexistent subjectivity of Jesus is to be identified with the second member of the Trinity, for according to Whitehead there cannot be distinct subjectivities within the Godhead since this would lead to tritheism. I earlier objected to the substitution of Whiteheadian speculation for scriptural revelation and again register a logical objection to Whitehead's and Ford's notion that whatever has actual unity enjoys its own subjectivity in pure privacy and therefore is a totally separate actuality. This is illegitimate, since it is not possible on the process model to speak of subjective *unity*. This is a deep problem in process metaphysics. Having opted for basic atomicity and epochal occasions at the heart of actuality, process metaphysics allows no place for a continuous and unified substratum of personal identity and subjectivity; there is only a series of discrete occasions that are supposed to have unity and subjectivity through memory and anticipation, but there is no accountable continuous subject to remember and anticipate. Hence it is hardly legitimate for such an inadequate ontology to legislate what can and cannot obtain in God's own inner being.

In addition, I would point out that no philosophical system has been able to explain how oneness and manyness, being and becoming are related, although most would recognize the reality of these two polarities at various levels of actuality. God's self-disclosure in the New Testament indicates that he himself is the ultimate and infinite unity in society and society in unity as the intimate Family of Father, Son, and Holy Spirit. The beauty of biblical classical trinitarianism is that it not only is faithful to God's own self-revelation in Scripture, but also provides the ultimate archetypal explanation of unity and plurality and of being and becoming in the ectypal created world, for as God is unity in plurality and is changeless yet dynamically inexhaustible in his ontological triunity, so as Creator he has left his indelible signature on all of creation. The ultimate ontological "principle" is demonstrated by the ultimate infinite personal God who is three Persons in one substantial unity, comprising the consummate ontological Family. The revealed correlativity of the personal Triunity is made clear by Jesus who promises that abiding peace will come through "the Counselor, the Holy Spirit, whom the Father will send in my name," and that he "will pray the Father, and he will give you another Counselor, to be with you for ever, even the Spirit of truth, whom the world cannot receive, because it neither sees him nor knows him; you know him, for he dwells with you, and will be in you" (John 14:26; 14:16-17). It is through the restitutive work of Christ and the ensuing gift of the Holy Spirit that the believer is able to see what a fallen and bent humanity can no longer see. As Paul says in Romans 1:19-20: "For what can be known about God is plain to them, because God has shown it to them. Ever since the creation of the world his invisible nature, namely, his eternal power and deity, has been clearly perceived in the things that have been made." But unaided, autonomous reason distorts this disclosure of God in the oneness and manyness, being and becoming of nature, absolutizing one aspect or another of creation rather than worshiping the true Creator (Rom. 1:21ff.). My criticism of process thought, apart from its logical inconsistencies, has been its idolatrous absolutizing of time and space and of the human mind to construct absolute truth about the nature of reality without reference to God's self-revelation in Scripture. Yet we have seen that process metaphysics itself has to appeal to what is generically beyond time and space to keep the tyranny of time from degenerating into sheer chaos.

The question that faces Ford in his modern restatement of trinitarianism is whether the ultimately generic is personal or impersonal principle. Rejecting the first he opts for the second. Here process theism pays an enormous price. I would remind the reader that I find this wholly unacceptable, for a phenomenology of persons (which includes our use of language and our accrediting language with meaning) makes clear that principles do not do anything: they are simply abstractions from the functions of living actualities and are ascribed to things and people as generic descriptions by conscious persons who have the power of abstraction. In my critique of Ford's abstract trinitarianism, I want to underscore how many personal attributes are assigned to impersonal principles by those who unthinkingly make abstractions absolute (and thus commit the fallacy of misplaced concreteness), the point being that these "principles," in order to exercise such personal attributes, must be personal not impersonal.

The Logos

First, Ford discusses the Logos, which is the totality of the divine aims. This is equivalent to Whitehead's primordial nature of God which is unconscious and impersonal. Observe how Ford describes the hierarchical emanation of more personal aspects from the impersonal Logos, almost in Plotinian fashion:

> Those aims capable of addressing an entire species by infusing in them a novel order bringing about the emergence of a more advanced species constitute that part of the Logos which we call the *creative Word*. That creative Word which is specifically addressed to humankind is the *Christ*. Christians find this creative Word most fully actualized in the life, death, and resurrection of Jesus as they participate in that body whose living mind they discern to be the risen Christ.[43]

43. *The Lure of God*, p. 100. His italics.

In this passage the vector is from impersonality to personality, from the abstract generic to the contingent and personal. That is why Ford cannot identify the incarnate Christ with the second member of the Trinity. The generically abstract is higher than and prior to the personal. The New Testament has it the other way round. Principles, laws, and morals are abstractions from the person or persons who proclaim them, underwrite them, and stand in back of them. Whatever generic principles are discernible in the world are underwritten by God who has spoken through his Son, the Cocreator and Sustainer of all things. The writer to the Hebrews makes the identification of the historical Jesus with the second person of the Trinity when he says, "In these last days [God] has spoken to us by a Son, whom he appointed the heir of all things, through whom also he created the world. He reflects the glory of God and bears the very stamp of his nature (*character tēs hypostaseōs autou*), upholding the universe by his word of power (*pherōn te ta panta tōi rhēmati tēs dynameōs autou*)" (Heb. 1:2-3). The *rhēma*, or word, of Christ is not a self-subsistent principle any more than the Logos of John 1:1 is an abstraction, but is identified with Christ the living, speaking, acting Jesus of Nazareth. Here I part company epistemologically with Ford, Whitehead, and all philosophers whose approaches to reality accord the impersonal and the abstract pride of place over persons who disclose themselves in word and act and story. Biblical epistemology resides in the spoken and acted story of the personal God who manifests his nature, will, and love consummately in the empirical incarnation of his Son, Jesus Christ. Hence Jesus can say, "Truly, truly, I say to you, before Abraham was, I am" (John 8:58). This is not a redactional creation of the Johannine circle, but a genuine and logical consequence of the miracle of the incarnation of the Second Person of the Trinity in the empirical setting of historical contingency. This is the grand miracle, logically odd, to be sure, but profoundly significant both theologically and philosophically. Jesus is the God-man, as the New Testament and classical orthodoxy have always held, and these demonstrate their superiority in logical debate over the impersonal abstractions of modern restatements like Ford's.

God As Father

When he comes to the question of God as Father, Ford introduces a rather novel and difficult definition:

> The one nontemporal concrescence is God's innermost subjectivity by which he radically transcends the world. In Plotinus's terms, it is the unknowable "One" which is the source of the eternal generation. We can only know of it insofar as it is expressed in the primordial nature, for in

itself it is God in his hiddenness, in the inexhaustible mystery of his being.[44]

The rational mind boggles at the logical contradiction of applying the word *concrescence* to a nontemporal abstraction (how can something nontemporal concresce, especially in light of the process definition of nontemporality?); and the phenomenologist wonders at the illegitimate use of the noun *Father* and the personal pronouns *he* and *his* to refer to an impersonal deity; while the nonspecialist asks innocently how so much can be known about a deity that is locked into transcendent hiddenness. Ford tries to define the Trinity and the Father's role in the following manner:

> In Whiteheadian terms, we may interpret God in his full unified actuality as a transcendent subjectivity, which is manifest in two natures, one primordial and the other consequent. There is no need to introduce a third distinct nature on a par with these two. "God the Father" is simply God, not another member within the Godhead.[45]

Hence God as simply God (i.e., "Father") is impersonal, and God as primordial Logos (the "Son") is also impersonal.

The Spirit

When Ford comes to the question of what to do with the "Spirit" and the consequent nature of God he finds more problems, for he does not want to say that the "Spirit" is simply what makes it possible for the world to be immanent in God, but that the Spirit also makes it possible for God to be immanent in the world in the guise of ordinary divine aims. This is interesting, since one of the signal difficulties in the Whiteheadian model is how to get the nontemporal primordial aims related to the temporal world. The Logos is concerned with *what* is provided, the Spirit with *how* the aims are given, he says.[46]

However, Ford cannot explain *how* the Spirit does this; he slips, rather, into an experiential description of the evidence *that* the Spirit functions through normal and religious "intuitions." This is a strange move for a rationalist, to posit a radical reconstruction of biblical classical trinitarianism because the classical doctrine does not meet certain logical requirements, then appeal to an awareness of God that is, in his own words, "highly indirect" and intuitive! Surely one must do better than that. When I analyze Ford's subjective evidence for the working of the

44. Ibid., p. 102.
45. Ibid., p. 103.
46. Ibid., pp. 103f.

Spirit I find really serious problems. His model for sensing the presence of other feeling subjects is described in terms of knowing the higher animals, especially persons:

> Here all our experiential evidence is indirect, but reliable. We feel the presence of another person in his actions, for we experience those actions as living responses to ourselves and our actions. There can be an exchange of feeling, because I can experience his action *as* his responsive experience of me. So it is with the Spirit, which can bear witness to God's responsive experience of his creatures.[47]

But since the Whiteheadian-Fordian deity is not personal in its nontemporal innermost subjective concrescence, nor is the primordial Logos, and since the personal consequent nature of God works only upon past data, how does God convey his presence to us? Who or what is the Spirit and what is it relating and relating to? It would seem that on the analogy of sensing the presence of other persons we can have intimations of God's presence only if he is personal. But the only personal aspect of God in process metaphysics arises from his consequent nature which cannot touch us in our process of concrescing. And surely Ford must realize that he cannot introduce a new tertium quid, the active Spirit, which somehow applies the initial aims of the nontemporal, primordial Logos to the processing world ("So it is with the Spirit, which can bear witness to God's responsive experience of his creatures").[48] The Spirit principle seems to be introduced to bridge logical gaps in the system. As though he were anticipating such questions Ford insists that we must not think of the primordial and consequent natures as separate divine actualities. Since the two are aspects of the one unknowable God, the third principle indicated by the Spirit does not have the primary function of uniting them. This Ford assigns to the aboriginal nontemporal act from which all aspects of God are generated, and to their mutual coherence.[49] But it is hard to understand how we can talk intelligently about some amorphous nontemporal and impersonal act and of some unexplained coherence of principles that is supposed to explain the relevance of the process deity to our temporal needs and experiences. A further problem with the Whiteheadian model on the temporal level is that its insistence on atomicity as absolutely basic locks God and all of reality into windowless subjectivity. God as consequent cannot function in any unifying way because, as Ford argues, quoting Whitehead, "the transcendence of God is not peculiar to him. Every actual entity, in virtue of its novelty, transcends

47. Ibid., p. 104. His italics.
48. Ibid., p. 104.
49. Ibid., p. 105.

its universe, God included."[50] "Every actual entity, including God, is something individual for its own sake; and thereby transcends the rest of actuality."[51] This doctrine denies the fundamental biblical teaching that God is with us and substitutes the notion that God is, in his concrete and processive actuality, necessarily *after* us in point of experiencing us as data. In the Scriptures, however, the Spirit is the personal Presence who in our very immediacy of praying "helps us in our weakness; for we do not know how to pray as we ought, but the Spirit himself intercedes for us with sighs too deep for words" (Rom. 8:26). Here is no impersonal principle, but a personal and immediate intercessor who is profoundly with us. Hence, whatever freedom from God the creature enjoys is a sheer gift of God, who alone is noncontingent.

Creativity and Divinity

In the ultimate sense of God's unsurpassed sovereignty, biblical faith makes it clear that God is not metaphysically banished from any aspect of his creation. The contingent creature can claim independence of God only at his or her own peril, for God is the one who sees and knows in secret our innermost thoughts, and blesses or judges accordingly (Matt. 6:1–18). Whiteheadian atomicity is a doctrine foreign to Christian faith, for it accords the creature the right to be individual "for its own sake." This is misplaced concreteness in the worst sense because it is, on biblical terms, the ultimate idolatry, according the creaturely realm an ultimacy in terms of independent creativity. Creativity as a principle requires that God, with all other actual entities, advance independently into novelty; creativity transcends even God, who is subject to the open novelty of the future.[52] In process thought an abstraction, namely, creativity, rather than the personal and sovereign God of the Scriptures, is ultimate. God is assigned the role of explaining *how* the many become one, where creativity antecedently requires *that* they become one.[53] But in this system, God is only an accident of creativity, the one who is supposed to give some particular character to creativity through primordial envisagement.

The extreme difficulties of this suggested process trinitarianism, which is based on abstract and impersonal principles rather than on the self-revealed Triune God, become desperately clear when Ford argues that "sheer creativity is utterly formless, essentially indifferent to all its instantiations, whether good or evil."[54] Thus we should worship only that which

---

50. Alfred North Whitehead, *Process and Reality: An Essay in Cosmology* (New York: Harper and Row, 1957), p. 143. Quoted in Ford, *The Lure of God*, p. 105.

51. Whitehead, *Process and Reality*, p. 135. Quoted in Ford, *The Lure of God*, p. 105.

52. Whitehead, *Process and Reality*, pp. 130, 134–45, 339–40. See Ford, *The Lure of God*, p. 106.

53. Whitehead, *Process and Reality*, pp. 10–11.

54. *The Lure of God*, p. 107.

is the ultimate source of human good—God. But this will not do. First, to say that creativity is utterly formless and indifferent to its instantiations is to speak illogically, for the word *creativity* is already a value-laden noun that connotes the positive sense of bringing disparate things into unity. It is fraught with evolutionary presuppositions, the assumption being that creativity is somehow the positive backdrop for everlasting creative advance. But as I have noted before, if creativity is utterly indifferent to all its instantiations, then in fairness it ought to be called by some other name, since that which produces evil as well as good is not only creative but also destructive. Destructivity should have equal claim alongside creativity as the surround of reality. It were better to call it the ground of being, as Paul Tillich does, or the abyss, or simply power. Then the finite deity that valuates the abyss of power would be termed the primordial Logos, and the consequent, Spirit.[55] With Tillich, the impersonal ground of being is the Godhead which resists nonbeing and gives the power of being to all that is. For Whitehead, God is a portion of impersonal creativity which shares creativity with finite atomic occasions. Both agree that the starting point is dynamic, impersonal being itself, the difference being that Whitehead opts for a model in which God is only the chief exemplar of self-creation, necessarily sharing this power with the rest of us, whereas Tillich establishes a traditional dichotomy between uncreated creator and created creatures.

Ford chooses Whitehead because he believes his system protects God's goodness (theodicy) and ensures human freedom (anthropodicy), and redeems the first principle of creativity from being sheer chaos and burning fire.[56] Divinity cannot be simply identified with creativity, says Ford; otherwise we have "the divine-demonic power that the prophets of Israel struggled against in declaring Yahweh to be a God of Justice." Rather, he argues, hoping to avoid the biblical doctrine of God's sovereignty, "God cannot be sheer creativity, but only that creative act which supremely exemplifies the metaphysical principles."[57] This argument takes us back to chapter 1 and the process defense of human freedom independent of God's sovereignty. In the Whiteheadian-Fordian system, creativity is really larger than God, for it is not exhausted in producing the Logos; there is some creativity left over for us so that we can be self-determining and therefore free. The creature enjoys its own intrinsic creativity distinct from and over against the divine creativity. Creativity is therefore conceived to be pluralistic rather than monistic, a theme that is certainly

55. Paul Tillich, *Systematic Theology*, 3 vols. (Chicago: University of Chicago Press, 1951), vol. 1, pp. 250-51.
56. Ford, *The Lure of God*, pp. 107-8.
57. Ibid.

characteristic of the modern age. In the process system God does not preside over all creaturely activity, but he does embrace it as consequent; he is more the supreme effect than the supreme cause of what is, for he is effected by everything (except the immediacy of everything), whereas he does not efficiently affect everything.[58] The consequence is that we create God as much as if not more than he creates us, since the whole creaturely universe transcends God in some degree of power or other (although Ford does not spell out the relative distribution of power to the point of our inquiry in chapter 1—any more than does Hartshorne).

Just how far distant this process model lies from the claims of biblical faith is apparent in Ford's radical dismissal of God's sovereignty, which is the central doctrine in both Old and New Testaments. Following the general opacity of process theologians in appreciating biblical merismus (God is sovereign, and creatures are genuinely responsible for their volitional acts), Ford rejects the traditonal biblical teaching that creation derives all of its power and being from God, and argues instead for the independence of the creature from God:

> The creature can only transcend God if it can become something in and for itself independently of God, in the privacy of its own subjective becoming. The world transcends God on its own, but its subsequent immanence within God requires an additional element of receptive dependence within God. For God is dependent upon the independent transcendent activity of the creature for knowledge and experience of it.[59]

Ford concludes that a final threefold abstract distinction in the Trinity is necessary:

> Thus in the final analysis we must assent to an ultimate triunity of principles defining the divine life: the divine creative act nontemporally generating the primordial nature, from which proceeds the consequent nature as implicated in the Whiteheadian "categorial conditions" established by the primordial envisagement.[60]

If such language is seriously meant to replace biblical trinitarianism, it must be deemed to be decidedly inferior. A triunity of principles is no substitute for a triunity of persons who, according to the New Testament, sovereignly and transcendently comprise the ultimate Family of God, both Many in One and One in Many. Principles, as I have repeatedly insisted, do not do anything; persons do. How can an impersonal principle,

58. Ibid., p. 108.
59. Ibid., p. 109.
60. Ibid., p. 110.

however divine, perform a creative act? This is person language that is drawn from the activity of persons and illegitimately assigned to the nonpersonal. Next, how can an impersonal act generate nontemporally the primordial nature? How can that which has no nature act so as to produce its own nature, and do that without any sequence of time, without any before or after? Here, in the generation of Ford's second principle, temporal language is illegitimately applied to what is supposed to be nontemporal. If something is generated—in this case the primordial nature—something comes into being that was not present before, and that is logically inadmissible. (Only the eternal generation of the Son by the Father in the inexhaustible dynamism of God himself, as classical orthodoxy affirms, can such logically odd language be admitted, because it has the backing of God's own disclosure of his nature through scriptural revelation.)

Finally, if the consequent nature proceeds from the primordial as it envisages possibilities (another illegitimate use of temporal language), and comes into being as personal when it works upon the data of the world, it must be subject to the limitations of the speed of light, must therefore be radically finite, and since it is forever limited to consequent effects, never capable of participating in the living immediacy of finite creatures or of simultaneously integrating the total data of the universe. Ford's process trinitarianism of principles is therefore not only logically unacceptable, but also irrelevant. It bears no likeness to the trinitarian God of the Bible who both loves and judges the world, and who in the disclosure of the Son's suffering without sin is seen to be the God who consummately cares for and redeems his people (Heb. 2:14). The process deity can neither know us as we are nor be known as he is. That is the price to be paid for rejecting the self-revelation of God in the Scriptures and demanding the absolute right to be independent of God. It is the ironic judgment upon every system of thought that adopts what the Bible describes as the posture of covenant-breaking; that is, fashioning God after the likeness of creation.

A Process Eschatology

Two short chapters conclude Ford's attempt to reformulate biblical faith for our times. In "The Sources of Christian Hope" (chap. 8) he denies that God can effect any final eschatological victory over evil. We could have anticipated this denial from the logic of a system that limits the power of God in order to guarantee the freedom of the creature, which process theism assumes is absolutely dependent on an open future. But an open future, even for God, means that the biblical teaching about the absoluteness of God and his ability to bring about a final renewal of the cosmos and victory over sin, entropy, and death (Rom. 8:18–39; I Cor. 15:20–57) must be rejected. Ford, not really appreciating the logically odd and paradoxical grammar of Scripture, assumes that if God is sovereign over the outcome of the future then its coming is inevitable and we need neither strive to bring it about nor take it seriously, for there is no ultimate risk.[61]

Biblical eschatology, however, takes into account our human response to God's appeal, for the future does not come to pass in spite of what we do (fatalism) but precisely in terms of what we do. God predetermines the pattern of the future through responsible secondary agents, not in spite of them. Hence it is absolutely necessary for the Christian who believes in God's sovereignty to fulfill his calling ethically, for there can be no indolence in view of what it means to have the mind of Christ and to bear witness to him in this fallen world (Rom. 12; Phil. 2:1–18). It is truly impressive to see how intimately biblical eschatology is tied together with responsible ethical action. The two are inseparable, and Ford has badly missed the mark, not only exegetically but also practically, when he assumes that those of Pauline and Reformed persuasion lose all serious sense of responsibility and ultimate risk with their biblical doctrine of God's sovereignty. This simply is not so, either logically or historically. There is, however, the danger on the other side that an absence of belief in the certainty of the triumph of good and the judgment of evil will encourage irresponsible behavior, as has been amply attested by the enormous destruction of human life in the twentieth century as a result of world views that have denied the certainty of God's eschatological triumph and judgment of evil.

We need, Ford says, both hope and freedom. But he seeks the answers through speculative philosophy, not through revealed Scripture. Where New Testament revelation is definite about the resurrection of believers (I Cor. 15), Ford speculates that the soul is too tied to the body to survive; he thus misses the point that the New Testament teaching about resurrection is in terms of the embodied self on a higher level of experience, on analogy of the seed and the full-grown flower (I Cor. 15:35–50). He proceeds to reject the biblical promise of subjective immortality in favor of a speculative suggestion that God, holding us in objective immortality, transforms this memory of our earthly life into tragic beauty.[62] He avers that "the quest for subjective immortality may simply be a disguised affirmation of the substantial, enduring self of traditional thought," and plumps instead for the notion of the insubstantial self:

61. Ibid., p. 113.
62. Ibid., pp. 116f.

It might just be barely possible to insist upon this precept that each should suffer for the evil he inflicts, if the self endured to experience the result of its own actions and decisions. But within a Whiteheadian cosmology built upon momentary occasions, this is not possible. No occasion ever experiences the outcome of its own actions. What it experiences is bequeathed to it by others, for good or ill, and the results of its decision affect subsequent occasions, never itself. What we as momentary selves experience can never be that which we have done.[63]

This is truly an incredible argument, especially in view of Ford's earlier complaint that biblical theology undermines personal responsibility with its doctrine of God's sovereignty and definite eschatology. In process anthropology, a person with a name can be responsible neither for his personal future nor for his past, since he will not survive into the future and has not enacted his own past. We are dealing here with the dilemma of the discontinuous self which comes of Whitehead's notions on the primacy of atomicity. Of the dilemma Ford sees between God's sovereignty (then why does he not overcome evil?) and God's finitude (there is no guarantee that he will ever overcome evil), he chooses the latter in accordance with the doctrines of process theism. I would note, however, that he is relying for his authority not on revealed Scripture but on autonomous human speculation and the secularity of contemporary experience that renounces otherworldly answers as wishful thinking. This certainly is no way to do biblical exegesis, but it does reveal how profoundly presuppositions affect the interpretation of biblical texts. In view of the following commitment, it is clear that process theism cannot serve as a valid hermeneutic for doing biblical exegesis:

God cannot guarantee that evil will be overcome simply because he is not the sole agent determining the outcome of the world. It is a joint enterprise involving a vast multiplicity of actualities responding to his cosmic purposes. Since all these actualities are free to respond as they will, it is conceivable that most may all elect to frustrate the divine aim. The world could possibly generate into near chaos. There can be no metaphysical guarantee against such a catastrophe.[64]

Yet if that is the case, are there really pragmatic grounds for hoping in God's evolutionary advance in the world? Yes, says Ford, in light of the past eighteen billion years of rich evolution. But he admits the possibility of the extinction of the human race. In spite of this, he feels we can find renewed confidence in the hopeful symbol of Jesus' death and

63. Ibid., p. 118.
64. Ibid., p. 119.

resurrection. Even though God suffered loss and was defeated at the cross by the forces of evil, he emerged victorious in the body of his disciples.[65]

I find this radical reinterpretation of traditional biblical language difficult, because Ford does not mean the same thing by the death and resurrection of Jesus as did the original believers and as do Christians down to modern times. He is employing a model of evolutionary emergence and describing it symbolically as the risen Christ. The risen body of Christ is his disciples, and therein perhaps lies, he feels, the hope of mankind. But he is making an uncertain sound on his instrument, certainly not such that will rally the troops to do battle against the forces of evil. The very notion of evolutionary emergence is itself a whistling in the dark when one considers the inexorable law of entropy that propels everything finally to death in the collapse of the vast cosmos. Inconsistently Ford and other process theists want to hold a secular eschatology of creative evolutionary advance. But the guarantee of that eschatological optimism has been removed by discarding its only support, namely , the sovereign God of the Scriptures who overcomes evil in his own logically odd but marvelously gracious way through Christ's death and resurrection and return at the end of the age.

With his radical substitute for a rejected biblical eschatology and his denial of every basic Christian doctrine by the authority of secular tastes and speculation, Ford leaves the reader with pragmatic maybes and a stoical confident despair. The whole approach simply lacks exegetical integrity and rational consistency, and will not carry the day for any who, like Paul, know whom they have believed and are persuaded that he is able to guard until that day what has been entrusted to them (II Tim. 1:12).

The Failure of a Process Hermeneutic

The epilogue of *The Lure of God* reiterates its author's plea that philosophical abstractions and Scripture should interact. But Ford makes it clear that speculative philosophy demands pride of place, mainly because philosophical metaphysics analyzes God's necessary abstract aspects, while the Scriptures have to do with contingent or historically relative examples of those necessary truths.[66] Hence, while it is important in our rich Western heritage, biblical faith does not afford absolutely normative propositions about God's nature. Process metaphysics has already determined presuppositionally what the nature of God is. God's power is the

65. Ibid., pp. 119-20.
66. Ibid., p. 123.

limited power of persuasion, not the omnipotence of divine sovereignty. Therefore God does not control the future. Jesus is not to be identified with the Logos, the second abstract member of the Trinity. The "Son" of God is an abstraction; there is no preexistent Christ in the biblical sense; there is no blood atonement by which God graciously satisfies his own righteousness by laying our sins upon his Son on the cross; there is no personally risen Jesus Christ. The "consciousness" of the risen Christ came into being at the "resurrection" and is somehow analogous to the mind as it arises from the atomic parts of the living human organism. The coordinationism of Father-Son-Spirit expressed in Scripture and at Nicea is rejected for subordinationism (God-Christ-Spirit), and the Trinity is redefined in terms of abstract metaphysical principles, in spite of an attempt to view God through the first person singular pronoun of Exodus 3:14. That passage is interpreted by Ford not only as "I am who I am," but also as "I will be what I will be" in the sense that God provides "that sort of ultimate stability later sought in metaphysics."[67] But in no case does this God of Exodus 3:14 or of later Scripture afford an absolute revelation that is valid once for all, for new needs demand new evaluations, and we must have the courage to tear down and reshape our structure of values according to a deeper integrity, of which the Bible is only a partial record.

Behind this appeal for a radical reconstruction of theology is the curious process notion of a nontemporal and changeless primordial envisagement of all pure possibilities by which God determines himself to be what he is. Ford speculates on this transaction:

> It is thereby God's act of self-creation. Or, to express it in classical terms, it is the way the Father (= the originating power) generates the Son(= the Logos, the order of all possibility) "before all worlds" (= nontemporally). This basically nontemporal ordering is then temporally emergent in God's interaction with the world. It is never fully given in any temporal moment.[68]

In this passage not only is a personal relationship between Father and Son rejected, since both are reduced to principles, but any possibility of an absolute and infallible revelation by God in history is also dismissed. The only seemingly infallible absolutes are to be arrived at by philosophical examination into the underlying metaphysical structures of God's character. The Bible is too full of logically contradictory images of God (e.g., God of judgment/God of love) to be accepted today in and of itself.[69] We must find its deeper significance through philosophy. The paradigm of historical revelation has outlived its usefulness. We now see that Job's

67. Ibid., p. 126.
68. Ibid., p. 128.
69. Ibid., p. 129.

preoccupation with the problem of evil undercuts the easy assumption of the wisdom school, the Deuteronomic historian, and the whole prophetic interpretation of history. We now must see that God is limited in his power to persuade, and that the narrow perspectives of the biblical writers must be widened to include the value of every culture and people in our pluralistic age. Apocalyptic writings, with their reliance upon angels to accomplish the divine purpose, lack creative freedom and accordingly destroy the doctrine of divine persuasion.

Dismissing the apocalyptic, eschatological, prophetic control of history by the sovereign God, Ford settles for the uncertainty of the future. It is impossible to discern God's providential hand in history with the confidence of the biblical writers simply because, he believes, God cannot know the future in detail in a world where we all have a share in creative power. Accordingly he feels that "theology today must be articulated by means of philosophical criteria of consistency, coherence, adequacy, and applicability."[70]

Accepting the challenge, I have written this book; and if my arguments are at all valid then by the criteria of rational coherence process theism must be rejected as a viable option. Its internal logical inconsistencies are simply too many to sustain one for very long, as I can personally attest. As for Ford's claim that process theism is the natural ally of biblical history because it can provide the contemporary conceptuality by which we can appropriate this ancient literature,[71] I can only reply that from a biblical exegete's point of view, process presuppositions so distort biblical faith that it becomes simply unrecognizable. Process hermeneutics is essentially narcissistic; it sees only its own face reflected in the pool of reality. Hence, philosophically on the level of rational cogency as well as exegetically on the level of legitimate biblical interpretation, process theism is not what it promises to be. It is, as I argued in the first chapter, primarily an essay in defense of human freedom, an anthropodicy, the ever recurrent attempt of *homo curvus* to claim independence of the sovereign God who has revealed himself in Scripture as both Savior and Judge of the cosmic order. As a hermeneutic for biblical exegesis it imposes too many alien philosophical doctrines on the Bible to be of value, and as a rational system for unlocking the mysteries of existence it employs logic too illogically to sustain its own argument.

My analysis demonstrates, I think, that the rejection of God's personal self-disclosure in sacred Scripture may appear at first blush to be a rational demolition of the God of traditional Christian faith, but on deeper reflection will be seen to be an irrationalism posing as rationalism

70. Ibid., p. 135.
71. Ibid.

because it is controlled by the presupposition that the human mind is self-sufficient to reconstruct God in its own image. Any biblical exegete worth his salt (who is faithful to the Word of God) can predict where that commitment to the speculations of the autonomous human mind will lead. It will lead to an irrational exaltation of finitude, in the case of process theism to the exaltation of creativity above the sovereign God of Scripture. It is not a move that is either new or promising. It is not a rational move, and certainly not one that is exegetically faithful to the God who speaks and has spoken in his infallible Word.

An Agenda for Biblical Faith and the Challenge of Process Theism

W e have examined the claims and projects of process theism and found them exegetically and philosophically wanting. We have studied fundamental issues a number of times from different angles in order to make the case that the school of process is unimpressive in its logic and exegesis of Scripture, in its understanding of God, and in its view of persons. Alfred North Whitehead was correct at least in one respect when he remarked that all philosophy is only a series of footnotes to Plato. That is true of non-Christian thinkers who reject God's self-disclosure in Scripture, and for whom there are only three possible explanations of God, process, and reality: God is timeless and impersonal being; God is to be identified with the process of timespace itself; or God is a combination of these two. Process theism opts for the last and argues that God provides the ideals of possibility for timespace process only as impersonal and unconscious abstraction, while the world of already perished data supplies him with the content of his personal and conscious experience. It is a curious, mind-boggling, and ultimately unsuccessful attempt to combine the Absolute and the Relative into a workable AR system.

Still, we need to ask what there is about process theism that is so attractive to so many intellectuals today. I have already indicated that from a biblical point of view the natural mind is in rebellion against the sovereign Lord of creation and will at any cost avoid standing under his judgment or acknowledging his radical grace in Jesus Christ as revealed in authoritative Scripture. That is the negative, and larger, side of it. But there is yet common grace and the revelation of general truths in nature that need to be considered, no matter how distorted they may be by the bentness of the human mind.

Part of the attractiveness of process theism is that it appeals to a fundamental truth already deeply invested in creation and in Scripture and used as borrowed currency by process thought, namely, that God and the world are dynamically social. The Old and New Testaments speak in terms of God's covenants with his creation, but the idea is the same. While process theism misconstrues God's social nature and his dynamic activity in terms of his necessary dependence on the world, there is a biblical truth here that needs to be explored, exegeted, and articulated by evangelical scholars in new and captivating ways.

For example, I have entitled this book *The Inexhaustible God*, implying that God is inexhaustibly dynamic in his ontological triunal relationship as Father, Son, and Holy Spirit. Again and again process theists attack historic Christianity as adhering to a static doctrine of God. Although that charge is overused and rests on a false understanding of what classical Christianity has meant by the impassibility and aseity of God, it is nevertheless necessary for us as biblical interpreters to anticipate that charge by taking a chapter out of the book of process and applying the concept of AR to the Triune God, as he is ontologically, quite apart from the created universe. That is to say, we ought to do more with the fact that God exemplifies consummately and infinitely not only the characteristics of changelessness, infinity, eternality, and absoluteness in being, wisdom, power, holiness, justice, goodness, and truth (= A for Absolute), but exemplifies as well, within the sociality of his own Family, the dynamic inexhaustibility of love between Father, Son, and Holy Spirit (= R for Relational). God is within himself both Unity in Plurality and Plurality in Unity; he is both changeless in character and inexhaustibly loving as the Family of God (AR).

One of the most important disclosures of God's inner dynamic love as archetypal Family is through the dialogue of Son, Father, and Spirit in the Gospels, and through the nuances of that relationship evidenced in Acts, the Epistles, and the Book of Revelation. Viewed in light of the New Testament, the Old Testament also bears witness to the intimate dimensions of an inexhaustible dynamism within the Godhead. Taken together, these texts afford a portrait of God as both unchangeable and social as the sovereign First Family.

Exegetical and systematic exposition of the biblical basis for belief in the Trinity is therefore of prime importance in offering a thoroughly Christian alternative to the speculative theism of process thought. Both biblical faith and process theism agree that God and the world are social. The crucial difference is that biblical faith insists on God's sociality as self-contained and independent of the finite universe of timespace, while process theism associates God's consciousness and concrete experience with finite timespace necessarily and everlastingly. Biblical faith takes seriously the Genesis account that God brought the universe into being and exercises sovereign control over it, while process theism is essentially dualistic and holds to the necessary everlastingness of some universe or other and God's dependence upon it.

This brief excursus invites me to suggest two agendas for evangelical scholarship.

The first agenda is that evangelical theologians (meaning all who subscribe to historic Christian orthodoxy) need to pay careful attention to the biblical grounds for trinitarian theology, making clear that in his own personal and infinite being God supremely exemplifies both unity and plurality as First Family and at the same time supremely exemplifies steadfastness of character and inexhaustible, dynamic love as Father, Son, and Holy Spirit. In addition to being faithful to Scripture, biblical trinitarianism avoids the logical improprieties that arise in process theism when it attempts to refashion God as abstract principle metaphysically and therefore ties him to a finite and changing universe. It is important for orthodox biblical scholars and theologians to mount a bold counterattack against the idolatry and illogicality of process theism and to best the school by demonstrating the essentially social nature of the Triune God as revealed in Scripture and believed by faithful Christians down to the present day.

The second is that evangelical theology needs to pay careful attention to the teaching of Scripture regarding the social nature of God's creation. From the microworld of the atomic nucleus and its satellites to the myriad biological infrahuman families on various levels of complexity to the human family and the families of peoples and nations, God's creation is social and covenantal to the core. Only biblical faith can explain why that is so. God's creation is social because God the creator is social. God is archetypal Family who places the signature of his creative hand upon all the derivative and ectypal families of creation. Imaging the Family of God, creation itself is a vast extensive continuum of families from micro to macro, upheld by his word of power.

The implications and challenges of this fundamentally biblical approach are tremendous and beg to be worked out by evangelical scholars committed to God's self-disclosure in Scripture. What we need to offset the appeal of nonbiblical process theism are broad-ranging studies, based on the truth of Scripture and from its perspective interpreting the data of creation, that address the implications of God's plan of redemption for nature—ecology, science, technology, the whole environmental house we live in; and for the human family—marriage, sexuality, children, education, vocation, economic and political systems and responsibilities; and of course the place of the church as the most inclusive and eschatological of all the families God has been pleased to place upon the earth.

As I hinted in the preface, my next project, now underway, is to begin to address some of these issues under the rubric of the Family of God, examining first the biblical basis of belief in the social Triune God and then the exegetical data for a biblical view of the created families of earth, their fallenness, and God's eschatological plan for their redemption. It promises to be an exciting and challenging undertaking in which many scholars of evangelical persuasion will need to lend their learning and understanding of Scripture. Here, in the self-disclosure of the inexhaustible God and his will for his own creation, lies the answer to the challenge of process theism.

Author Index

Subject Index

Persuasion, divine, 165-67, 169-71, 174, 179-80. *See also* Sovereignty of God
Phenomenology, 9, 157, 168
Pluralism, 11
Polarities, 21
Possibilities, 52
Power, ratio of, 31-44
Pratitya-samutpadha. See Coorigination, dependent
Prehensions, 46, 53
Present, concepts of: apparent, 86; calculative, 86-87; causal, 83-84; influential, 84-86
Presuppositions, 163-65, 176, 194-95, 196. *See also* Hermeneutics
Primordial nature of God, 17, 46, 49-50, 52, 63

Redaction criticism, 11
Relativism, 11
Relativity, 13, 16
Resurrection, 107, 108, 176, 179, 181

Salvation, 14-15
Scripture, inspiration of, 10, 21, 30, 62, 63-64, 175, 178-79, 201
Self, enduring, 94-95
Sensa, 50 n.16, 50-51, 119, 120
Simultaneity, divine, 16, 75-99, 128-29, 132-33
Sin, 16, 179
Social nature of reality, 33, 67, 125, 200-2
Sovereignty of God, 29, 38-44, 105, 112-13, 124, 127, 130-31, 133, 151, 167-68, 174, 189-90, 192
Space, spacetime, 28, 114-16, 122, 126, 129, 131, 135

Speed of light (C), 75-76, 78, 84-85, 128-30. *See also* Time
Static, God as, 8
Subjective immortality, 192. *See also* Immortality; Objective immortality
Subordinationism, 195
Substance, 18, 20, 54, 174
Supraspacetime, 21, 91, 92, 99, 104, 130. *See also* Velocity of God
Supraspatial. *See* Supraspacetime
Supratemporal. *See* Supraspacetime
Surrelativism, 36
Symmetry, spatial, 114-16, 121. *See also* Space; Time

Tachyons, 80
Temporal extension, 89
Theodicy, 30, 33, 38, 40-44, 189
Time, timespace, 80-99; problem of, 75-99
Transspatial, 66. *See also* Supraspacetime
Transtemporal, 66. *See also* Supraspacetime
Trinity, 14, 15, 21, 54, 63, 66-67, 79, 128, 173-74, 180, 182-88, 190-91, 195, 200-2

Unconscious, God as, 46, 47, 63. *See also* God
Universalism, 16
University (vs. seminary), 141-44

Velocity of God, 75-100. *See also* Supraspacetime

World, 20, 34, 149
World religions, 153-58, 161

Zoroastrianism, 31, 171

Scripture Index

Genesis

1:3—159
1:3ff.—76
3:1—153, 167, 169
3:1-4—122
3:14-19—122
3:15—40

Exodus

3:2—63, 174
3:14—63, 67, 195
3:15—63

Psalms

139:13-16—119

Isaiah

55:6—114
57:15—76, 132

Amos

3:6b—166
5:14—166

Matthew

5:45—62
6:1-18—188

Mark

8:34-38—39
13:32—99

John

1—174
1:1—63, 64, 185
1:12—63
1:14—64
3:3—179
8:58—22, 174, 185
14—50
14:16f.—22, 183
14:26—183
17:1-5—183
17:24—22, 84

Romans

1:18-3:20—105, 110
1:19-20—183-84
1:20—66, 128
1:21ff.—184

3:9-20—40
3:23-24—73
8:18-24—136
8:18-31—40
8:18-39—192
8:21—76
8:26—188
12—192

I Corinthians

1:17-25—181
15—176, 192
15:20-57—192
15:35-50—192

II Corinthians

3:16-17—39
5:19—76

Galatians

2:20—122

Ephesians

1:3-4—84
1:4—41
2—110